W9-BSJ-460

EQUIVOCAL
COMMUNICATION

Sage's *Series in Interpersonal Communication* is designed to capture the breadth and depth of knowledge emanating from scientific examinations of face-to-face interaction. As such, the volumes in this series address the cognitive and overt behavior manifested by communicators as they pursue various conversational outcomes. The application of research findings to specific types of interpersonal relationships (e.g., marital, managerial) is also an important dimension of this series.

SAGE SERIES IN
INTERPERSONAL COMMUNICATION
Mark L. Knapp, Series Editor

1: Robert Norton
   Communicator Style: Theory, Applications, and Measures

2: Robert T. Craig and Karen Tracy (editors)
   Conversational Coherence: Form, Structure, and Strategy

3: Margaret L. McLaughlin
   Conversation: How Talk Is Organized

4: Brian H. Spitzberg and William R. Cupach
   Interpersonal Communication Competence

5: Howard E. Sypher and James L. Applegate (editors)
   Communication by Children and Adults: Social Cognitive and Strategic Processes

6: James C. McCroskey and John A. Daly (editors)
   Personality and Interpersonal Communication

7: Mary Anne Fitzpatrick
   Between Husbands and Wives: Communication in Marriage

8: William B. Gudykunst and Stella Ting-Toomey
   (with Elizabeth Chua)
   Culture and Interpersonal Communication

9: Moira Stewart and Debra Roter (editors)
   Communicating with Medical Patients

10: Carl E. Larson and Frank M. J. LaFasto
    Teamwork: What Must Go Right/What Can Go Wrong

11: Janet Beavin Bavelas, Alex Black, Nicole Chovil, and Jennifer Mullett
    Equivocal Communication

EQUIVOCAL COMMUNICATION

Janet Beavin Bavelas
Alex Black
Nicole Chovil
Jennifer Mullett

Sage Series

Interpersonal Communication 11

SAGE PUBLICATIONS
The International Professional Publishers
Newbury Park   London   New Delhi

For information address:

SAGE Publications, Inc.
2111 West Hillcrest Drive
Newbury Park, California 91320

SAGE Publications Ltd.
28 Banner Street
London EC1Y 8QE
England

SAGE Publications India Pvt. Ltd.
M-32 Market
Greater Kailash I
New Delhi 110 048 India

Printed in the United States of America

Library of Congress Cataloging-in-Publication Data

Main entry under title:

Equivocal communiction / Janet Beavin Bavelas . . . [et al.].
      p.   cm. — (Sage series in interpersonal communication ; 11)
    Includes bibliographical references.
    ISBN 0-8039-2942-0. — ISBN 0-8039-2943-9 (pbk.)
    1. Interpersonal communication. 2. Ambiguity. I. Bavelas, Janet
Beavin, 1940- . II. Series: Sage series in interpersonal
communication ; v. 11.
BF637:C45E68 1990
302.2 — dc20   90-8205
                                         CIP

FIRST PRINTING, 1990

Sage Production Editor: Astrid Virding

CONTENTS

Series Editor's Introduction   7

Acknowledgments   9

1. What Is Equivocal Communication?   11

Examples of Equivocal Communication   13

The Palo Alto Group   19

Strategic Ambiguity   21

Rule-Based Approaches to Indirect Speech Acts   22

Summary   28

2. Capturing Equivocation Quantitatively   29

Conceptual and Technical Requirements   29

Haley's Analysis of Incongruence (Disqualification)   32

Measuring the Degree of Equivocation   35

The Scaling Procedure   37

Quantification   44

Reliability   48

Isn't There a Shorter Way?   51

Summary   53

3. A Situational Theory   54

A Situational Theory of Communicative Conflict   55

Other Possible Explanations of Equivocation   61

An Experimental Strategy for Understanding Equivocation   64

Summary   66

4. The Conditions That Elicit Equivocation: First Experiments   67

Experiment 1: Evoking Equivocation   67

Experiment 2: Adding a Control Group   77

Experiment 3: Control for Unpleasantness   80

Experiment 4: Approach Versus Avoidance Conflicts   85

Experiment 5: Revised Conflict Scenarios   92

Summary   96

5. How People Equivocate: Written Messages   97

Starting with Written Messages   97

Experiment 6: Class Presentation   99

Experiment 7: Member of Parliament   106

Experiment 8: Bizarre Gift   112

Experiment 9: Car Ad   118

Possible Artifacts   124

Summary   125

6. Spoken and Face-to-Face Communication   126

Nonverbal Aspects of Communication   126

Experiment 10: Class Presentation (Spoken)   129

Experiment 11A: Bizarre Gift (Spoken)   134

Experiment 11B: Meat Market (Spoken)   139
Experiment 12: Employee Reference (Spoken)   141
Experiment 13: Car for Sale (Spoken)   150
Experiment 14A: Car for Sale (Face-to-Face)   156
Experiment 14B: Class Presentation (Face-to-Face)   162
Response Latency: Two Theoretical Alternatives   163
Summary   168

7. Truths, Lies, and Equivocations   **170**
Deception Theory and Research   170
An Alternative View   177
Evidence Distinguishing Between False and Equivocal Messages   180
Experiment 15: The Local Musical – A Direct Test of the Nonverbal Leakage
    Hypothesis   192
Summary   206

8. Children's Equivocation: Exploratory Studies   **208**
Previous Research on Children's Understanding and Use of Ambiguous
    Language   209
Experiment 16: Gift (Forced Choice)   218
Experiment 17: Class Presentation (Forced Choice)   219
Experiment 18A: New Hairdo (Spoken)   222
Experiment 18B: Gift (Spoken)   223
Discussion of Experiments 16, 17, 18A, and 18B   231
Summary   233

9. Field Studies of Political Interviews   **234**
Why Political Communication?   234
Experiment 19: A Field Study   236
Discussion   243
A Dyadic Analysis of Equivocation in Political Interviews   245
Summary   259

10. Overview and Implications   **260**
Measurement   260
Theory   261
Applications   265

Appendix A: Training Judges to Scale Messages for Equivocation   **269**
Appendix B: Statistical Data   **317**
References   325
Name Index   330
Subject Index   332
About the Authors   338

SERIES EDITOR'S
INTRODUCTION

(Series editor thinking to himself: Now, let's see, what can I say about this book? If I say it is great and my colleagues don't agree, they'll lose respect for my judgment; but if I say it is anything less than great, I'll offend my friends, the authors. Hmmm? What to do? How about something like this: "The perspective presented in this book is one that virtually any communication scholar should find extremely challenging. It is a rare tome; unique in its field. It will, no doubt, be a source of information in our field for a long time.")

The foregoing attempt to illustrate an equivocal message took me much longer to prepare than I had expected because I didn't actually feel the situational forces that the authors of *Equivocal Communication* have found to trigger equivocations. If I had truly experienced an avoidance-avoidance conflict (e.g., disliking the book and not wanting to say so, but equally opposed to saying I liked the book when I didn't), my guess is that appropriately vague and ambiguous responses would have come forth with greater ease—much like they do in our daily interactions. Whether it is thanking someone for a useless gift, writing a letter of recommendation for a person with questionable skills, or making a promise that is going to be difficult to keep, equivocal messages play a significant role in both private and public communication. When all the message alternatives seem untenable, the conditions are ripe for equivocal messages.

How do I really feel about this book? Unequivocally, it is a book that meets the highest standards of scholarly work: it is theoretically creative; methodologically sophisticated; and written in a clear and interesting style. It is an impressive contribution to the study of human interaction which:

- Grows out of the intellectual heritage of Kurt Lewin and the Palo Alto Group.
- Brings together and illumines several independent lines of contemporary communication research dealing with nonstraightforward communication: lying/deception; indirect speech acts; strategic ambiguity; devious messages; and contradictory verbal/nonverbal messages.
- Shows how equivocal communication can be effective communication.
- Challenges several widely held beliefs about the nature of deceptive messages.

7

- Places the driving force for equivocal messages in the situation rather than in the person.
- Provides a variety of experiments to document the nature of equivocal communication in face-to-face encounters, written messages, telephone conversations, children's talk, and in responses of political conventioneers.
- Integrates verbal and nonverbal components throughout.
- Illustrates how reporters and political candidates can establish a pattern of dialogue that perpetuates equivocal communication.

The subject of equivocal communication is clearly one of great practical importance. Learning how to equivocate and learning why others communicate this way is central to our understanding of effective communication.

— Mark L. Knapp

ACKNOWLEDGMENTS

A program of research spanning more than 10 years is possible only with a lot of help. Core funding was provided by research grants from the Social Sciences and Humanities Research Council of Canada, which supported us from the earliest stages and through several renewals. The University of Victoria provided supplementary financial support as well as excellent research facilities. Governmental Work-Study and Summer Employment programs funded additional research assistants.

Over the lifetime of the project, we were assisted in running experiments, working with judges, and analyzing data by Deborah Bolt, Jane Brett, Lisa Bryson, Susan Cathro, John Connors, Jennifer Evans, Mona McAllister, Diane Russell, Rhonda Sedger, and Beverly Smith. John Connors also wrote the first draft of Appendix A.

Mark Knapp suggested the book and encouraged us all along the way. Nelson Dewey did the cartoon illustrations; and Maureen Stephenson did the technical graphs. Barry Walters set up the computer to produce our tables, and Marianne MacDonald helped us get them out. Diane Rotter, Anna Butterworth, and Tod Godlien also helped with the manuscript.

We are especially grateful to the literally hundreds of judges, participants, and raters who were in the experiments described here. In our view, they are the real "communication experts," and we enjoyed meeting them.

9

1

What Is Equivocal Communication?

Mr. R and his wife, Jean, live in the same town as his parents. The interviewer inquires about this:

Interviewer: **HOW-AH does it work out for YOU, Mr. R, with your FOLKS in TOWN?**

Mr. R: [1.5 sec.] (Carefully, sounding forced; in a monotone:) **Well we— ... TRY, ah, very PERSONALLY ... I mean— ... ah ... I PREFER that JEAN takes the lead WITH them,** (Interviewer: Mhm.) **rather than MY taking the lead —** (as if hastening to add:) **oh I like to SEE them ...** (returning to a stilted monotone:) **but I DON'T-ah try too much to make it a POINT to be running OVER or have them ... they know very DEFINITELY that it's been always even BEFORE ... Jean or I ever MET-ah, and it was a THING that-ah was pretty MUCH just an accepted FACT ...** (voice drops, almost confiding:) **in our family, I was an ONLY child, and ...** (somewhat louder and faster, still with little inflection:) **they preferred that they would NEVER, to the BEST of their ability, NOT-ah, INTERFERE — I don't think there's-ah ... in any case, I think there's ALWAYS a— ... an UNDERLYING CURRENT there in ANY family, I don't care where it's OUR family or ANY family, and it is something that EVEN Jean and I feel that-when WE ... BOTH of us are—are ... rather PERFECTIONISTS.** (Interviewer: Mhm.) **And-ah ... yet AGAIN-ah, we're very c—, WE'RE-we're str— ... RIGID and, ah ... and we EXPECT that of the children, AND, but we FEEL that if you GOTTA watch out I mean ... I think THE— ...** (speeding up:)

Authors' Note: We have tried to make our transcription system as intuitively obvious as possible, for example, CAPITALS mean that the word was stressed, and a dash (—) means a word was broken off sharply. Full details can be found in Chapter 6, under the section titled "Transcription Conventions."

you can have interference with IN-LAWS, we feel, we've seen OTHERS
with it and we've just – it's been a THING that my own family've tried to
guard AGAINST but-ah . . . and-ah, (somewhat more animated:) like HERE-
why we've sst – . . . I wouldn't say we were STANDOFFISH to the folks,
but I PREFER that – . . . the lead is ALWAYS through Jean, and (Interviewer: Mhm.) it's to her END. (Transcribed from Watzlawick, 1964)

On first reading, Mr. R's answer may seem like any verbatim fragment of
spontaneous conversation. A literal transcription of what a person actually
said is quite different from tidy hypothetical or edited examples. So, although
not formally precise or correct, Mr. R's reply is natural, complex, and alive.
Read more carefully, though, it begins to appear disjointed and evasive,
almost to the point of being funny. Then, upon even more careful examination, it seems to reveal an "in-law" problem of considerable proportions,
which although denied on the surface is revealed in fragmentary details.
Alternatively, we could speculate that Mr. R has, if not a phobia about
speaking, then at least great difficulty in expressing himself to strangers.

On deeper examination, this could even be a psychiatric interview with a
marginally adjusted schizophrenic. Certainly his speech can be seen as
evidence of thought disorder, which is the primary symptom of schizophrenia. There are many abrupt breaks and pauses, which create a curious,
lurching rhythm ("Well we – . . .", "I mean – . . ."). Some of the statements
are quite illogical. For example, "BEFORE . . . Jean or I ever MET-ah"
should have been "Jean and I," because it took both of them to meet. At
another point, he says that he and his wife are perfectionists *and yet* rigid.
Other statements are enigmatic ("it's to her END") or completely empty
(e.g., when he seems to say that it was an accepted fact in his family that he
was an only child). Most of the sentences are not completed, as he continually
changes the subject. Indeed, his response covers at least 18 successive topics
without ever answering the interviewer's question: 1. We try (something).
2. I prefer that my wife takes the lead with my parents, rather than I. 3. I like
to see them, but I don't try to too much. 4. They definitely know (something),
since before my wife or I met. 5. (Something) was an accepted fact. 6. I was
an only child. 7. My parents preferred not to interfere. 8. I don't think
(something). 9. I do think there's an underlying current in any family. 10.
Even my wife and I feel (something). 11. Both of us are perfectionists and
yet rigid. 12. We expect that of the children. 13. We feel you have to watch
out for interference from in-laws. 14. We've seen others with this problem.
15. My family has tried to guard against it. 16. But, here, we've (something).
17. We're not standoffish, but I prefer that Jean takes the lead. 18. This is "to
her end."

As a matter of fact, Mr. R. is a normal, well educated, and very successful business executive, with equally normal, minor family problems. He was indeed being interviewed by a psychiatrist, but as part of a normal control group, and the psychiatrist had, unintentionally, put him on the spot with a difficult "in-law" question—almost a **"Have you stopped beating your wife?"** question. It is also true that his answer is nearly incoherent when examined closely. This example illustrates the fluctuating quality of equivocation. Like a reversible visual illusion, an equivocal message changes before one's eyes: We can see it one way, then another. It makes sense, then it doesn't. It doesn't make sense, then it does. Our goal in this book is to capture this quality, to show how such communication does and does not make sense. If we are successful, then equivocal communication will, like the reversible figure, be understood to have opposite yet reconcilable properties. With that assurance to the reader, we will next offer more examples of equivocal communication, that is, of communication:

> having two or more significations equally appropriate; capable of double interpretation; ambiguous; . . . of uncertain nature; undecided. (*Shorter Oxford English Dictionary*, 3rd ed., p. 628)

EXAMPLES OF EQUIVOCAL COMMUNICATION

This quotation was offered in an advertisement for a local play:

ABSOLUTELY HILARIOUS!
MY WIFE LOVED IT!!
(Howard Siegel, CJVI Radio)

Is it clear that Mr. Siegel loved the play? Or could he say truthfully later that he did not say that *he* loved it. It is even possible that he is commenting on the hilarity of his wife's taste in plays.

Shakespeare had a wonderful ear (and pen) for equivocal speech:

Othello: **Was not that Cassio parted from my wife?**

Iago: **Cassio, my lord! No, sure, I cannot think it,**
that he would sneak away so guilty-like,
Seeing you coming.

> (*Othello*, III, iii; suggested by Coulthard, 1977, p. 74)

Notice how Iago is able to describe in some detail what he says he cannot even think. While Mr. Siegel ostensibly offered his opinion but did not really give it, Iago ostensibly withheld his opinion but really gave it. Iago also answered a different question than the one Othello had asked: Othello had simply inquired as to the identity of the individual seen leaving. Iago answered as if Othello had asked, "Is that Cassio sneaking away guiltily because he saw me coming?" His answer introduces a dramatic, menacing change of context.

In English folklore, a harrassed Henry II is said to have cried out, in the presence of his soldiers: **Will no one rid me of this meddlesome priest?** After his men did "rid him" of his critic by assassinating the priest, Henry could say, accurately, that he only spoke rhetorically and had not asked anyone to murder for him. In modern terminology, he had perfect "deniability."

The next several replies were given by contemporary, normal subjects in the experiments to be described in this book. Some were in written form, such as this car ad:

FOR SALE   1966 VOLKSWAGEN. VERY CHEAP. PERSON WHO LIKES WORKING ON CARS WOULD BE WISE TO BUY THIS CAR.

Is the seller doing the buyer a favor to offer a car that needs work? Consider also this thank-you note, which is transcribed exactly as written:

Your gift, although much appreciatated was definately uncalled for. Can I see you to talk about it as I think my feelings were hurt by it. Thanks.

Why does this person appreciate and thank the sender for a gift that was uncalled for and hurt her feelings? And why does she only "think" her feelings were hurt by it?

Other messages were spoken on the telephone, such as this answer to a question about a product the speaker is selling. Notice the odd pitch and intonation as well as the vacuous description:

Question: **The meat that is on sale today, is it good?**

Male: [0.5 sec.] (Pitch plummeting:) **OOOhhh** (then levelling; fast, picking up some enthusiasm at the end:) **it's — it's fairly FINE yes.**

Some people were asked, also on the telephone, whether a friend of theirs was a good employee. One postponed answering by dwelling on definition:

Male: [1.3 sec.] (In a monotone at first, then rising pitch:) **Well, um, that's DEPENDS on what y'call a good EMPLOYEE.**

Another answered without answering:

Female: [1.0 sec.] (Brightly:) **Umm,** (then almost crestfallen:) **about average.**

In this message, the words themselves are completely uninformative. Because of this, the sharp change in the way the words are delivered is inexplicable: The meaningless "Umm" is said in an up-beat manner, which becomes suddenly down for the rest of the response, although neither part says anything to be up or down about. Another curious packaging of the verbal and nonverbal aspects of a message is this child's response to being asked, on the phone, how he likes the gift he received:

Male: [0.3 sec.] (Abruptly, no inflection:) **Good.**

Some people were asked, in person, about the performance of a local play:

Male: [2.5 sec.] (Initially smiles and looks away; then, pleasantly:) **AHHHM.** (Looks at the other person and smiles broadly) **it-was—** ... (rotates head and says with a slight laugh:) **INTERESTING,** (then looks down and stops smiling) **AH** ... (long pause, chews lips; then, thoughtfully:) **Well ACTUALLY, ah** ... (long pause; then looks up, winces, and says faster, while laughing:) **To tell you the TRUTH, I didn't** (smile disappears and tone becomes serious:) **EN-ENJOY it—** (nods, while smiling, and says in a very soft, gentle voice:) **completely.**

He did not enjoy the play; moreover, he seems reluctant to say so. Then why does he frequently smile and laugh?

Suppose you had given a class presentation and, a little later, you meet a fellow student (face to face) and asks how you did:

Female: [.66 sec.] (Looking at the other person, with head very tilted.) (Raises and lowers head in patronizing way while answering in a pleasant but brittle, "teacher" tone:) **Well HOW do you THINK you DID?**

That may be a very "political" way of saying that you did not do well. Indeed, political communication is a rich source of equivocation. For example, in the 1988 American presidential campaign, David Frost interviewed George Bush one week before election day:

Frost: (Pleasantly, gesturing frequently toward Bush:) **But the – OBVI-OUSLY, with seven DAYS to go in the CAMPAIGN, ah . . . it would be . . . UNREALISTIC to expect you to say ANYTHING, that was-ah announcing a new candidate** (laughing and faster:) **for vice-president or anything like that. But you WOULD have to AGREE, wouldn't you, that Lloyd BENSON has more GRAVITAS than Dan Quayle?**

Bush: [1 sec.] (Looking at Frost with little facial expression:) **I studied LATIN** (looks away and down) **for about eight years, but– refresh my MEMORY** (looks back) **as what GRAVITAS means.**

A more direct answer would have been, **"Please explain what 'gravitas' means."** To preface this with a claim to eight years of Latin creates a contradiction: A simple cognate meaning "weight" or "substance" should not be unintelligible to someone who has studied so much Latin. A few minutes later in the same interview:

Frost: (Smoothly, with one gesture toward Bush:) **Would you SAY – in terms of LABELS, since– . . . LABELS are a big FACTOR . . . ah, would you SAY that you are MORE or LESS conservative than Ronald REAGAN?**

Bush: (Looking down and rubbing his eye:) **Ah, excuse me, I've got something in my EYE. . . . It's very HUMAN.** (Smiles.)

All of the examples given so far were from psychiatrically normal people. However, it is difficult to maintain that there is any qualitative difference between these messages and that of a schizophrenic patient who sent his mother a Mother's Day card with the equivocal inscription:

For someone who has been like a mother to me.
                                        (Haley, 1959b, p. 359)

Are the following words those of a poet or a schizophrenic?

Germany is sometimes forgotten
when you learn the colours of everybody.
                                        (Bateson, unpublished manuscript; from
                                        Watzlawick, 1964, p. 36)

The next example looks more closely into the world of schizophrenia. This letter was written to a hospitalized schizophrenic woman by her mother. The parents were divorced and avoided meeting each other; they made a point of visiting separately. The patient's husband, Clem, was reported to have been sadistic to her and in any case did not visit her. The original letter was handwritten and has been transcribed with no corrections:

Dear Janet

Just a few lines again

I talked to your Dad on the phone and he said you dident answer his letter. You better write to him.

I want to have you visit me one of these days & maybe you can visit him too.

And by the way you havent written to me. (You did call me).

And you know Janet I don't like to even think of Clem it seems to remind me of trouble. Id rather just not think of him.

And dont you let the cigarette habit get stronger than you are.

Sometimes these habits have a way of doing that.

When I get a chance Ill get you a Carton.

But too much smoking is bad business.

I want so much too have you visit me as soon as possible, so be good and write to me.

Your Dad said you dident answer his letter so may be you ought to, but dont tell him I told you.

Well I better close now. Hope I can visit you soon.

Lots and lots of love.

> *Mother*
> (Weakland & Fry, 1962, p. 608)

The inconsistency of condemning smoking while offering cigarettes is the most obvious equivocation in this letter. In addition, the mother (like Iago) cannot think of Clem, while reminding the patient of him and his actions. Finally, as an exercise, the reader should try to follow carefully who says who should write or visit whom.

This section of introductory examples will conclude with two that hint at how one might make sense of equivocal communication, because they mention the speaker's situation as well as the equivocal message.

In *Sense and Sensibility*, Jane Austen described Marianne's delicate position when pressed by her sister, Elinor, for a specific opinion of Elinor's beloved but graceless Edward:

> "I hope, Marianne, . . . you do not consider him as deficient in general taste. Indeed, I think I may say that you cannot, for your behaviour to him is perfectly cordial, and if *that* were your opinion, I am sure you could never be civil to him."
>
> Marianne hardly knew what to say. She would not wound the feelings of her sister on any account, and yet to say what she did not believe was impossible. At length she replied:
>
> "Do not be offended, Elinor, if my praise of him is not in every thing equal to your sense of his merits. I have not had so many opportunities of estimating the minuter propensities of his mind, his inclinations and tastes as you have; but I have the highest opinion in the world of his goodness and sense. I think him every thing that is worthy and amiable."
>
> "I am sure," replied Elinor with a smile, "that his dearest friends could not be dissatisfied with such commendation as that. I do not perceive how you could express yourself more warmly." (1811/1982, p. 16)

Marianne did not comment on whether he was **"deficient in general taste,"** which was the issue, but rather on her lack of opportunities for judging his general taste, and then she slid smoothly over to the issue of his goodness and worthiness. Her convoluted reply might be called "tactful" or "diplomatic" rather than equivocal or evasive because, without being untrue, it permits the interaction to continue and maintains the relationship. Because we know the context, we can see that Marianne has by her reply avoided hurting her sister's feelings without actually lying.

Washburne (1969) gave amusing advice on how to avoid answering questions:

> *Managing the question.* . . . If he asks about Tuesday night, start in by saying: **"Well, Monday we had gone. . . ."** He waits, thinking you will get to Tuesday, but you never do. . . .
>
> *Limitation.* . . . **"How did you like my play"** is answered with **"I particularly noticed the shop-keeper's role; it must be extremely difficult. . . ."**
>
> *Non sequitur.* The politician, when asked about food prices, may end up talking about red-blooded Americans, motherhood, and the Fourth of July. (pp. 71-72)

You as reader may already have begun to think of explanations for these curious communications, for example, that some are simply mistakes, that some are poor communication, that the speaker may be devious, or that the reply is reasonable or even clever under the circumstances. The rest of this chapter will review the handful of scholars who have been intrigued by nonstraightforward communication and who have sought to explain rather than to dismiss it.

THE PALO ALTO GROUP

From the origins of rhetoric in classical Greece to the measurement of information in the twentieth century, communication has been studied mostly as it "should" be. For example, it should be effective, clear, persuasive, efficient, and noise-free. If it is not, then it should be improved, edited, or ignored as error. An alternative assumption was developed in Palo Alto, California, in the early 1950s, when a group of individuals from different disciplines began collaborating on a new approach to human communication. Gregory Bateson (anthropology), Don Jackson (psychiatry), Jay Haley (communication), and John Weakland (anthropology) published their first paper together in 1956 and went on to produce a series of papers (see Jackson, 1968; Watzlawick & Weakland, 1977) that are still impressive for their variety and creativity. What made their approach different was later summarized by Weakland:

> Probably the chief feature characterizing [this] approach to communication, . . . and differentiating it from others, is our concern with the study and understanding of actual communication as it really exists in naturally occurring human systems, rather than involvement with some ideal — such as "efficiency" — of what communication *should be*. . . .
>
> Such a focus may seem simple and obvious, but it has until quite recently been denied, ignored, or bypassed to an amazing extent. The study of communication involved almost everything *except* observing, recording, examining, and describing real communication and interaction in detail. (Weakland, 1967, p. 1)

One of the particular interests of these researchers was communication that "didn't make sense" — or at least appeared not to. In their classic paper on the double bind, Bateson, Jackson, Haley, and Weakland (1956) proposed that the bizarre communication of schizophrenics would make sense if considered in the family context in which it developed and that, in the same situation, any normal person might respond in the same way.

Haley (1959a) looked more closely at certain aspects of schizophrenic communication that are central to our work. He reemphasized that human communication, whether normal or abnormal, is not the simple presence or absence of a uniform signal. Rather, it consists of complex messages and their parts, all of which qualify each other to produce the total meaning. For example, in this message,

**The most senior members of the group
agree in principle with your proposal,**

the various parts of the sentence qualify each other to produce its overall meaning. When a message is spoken, the nonverbal aspects play their part as well. For example, a comment may appear sincere or sarcastic, depending on the phrasing and tone of voice. Much of the richness of human communication only becomes apparent when we consider the message as a whole and the relationships among its parts. Moreover, the qualification of parts of the message by other parts may be either congruent or incongruent; that is, the parts may work together or against each other. Examples of incongruence can be found in many of the examples given above, such as the replies of Mr. R and of the person who thanks someone for sending an uncalled-for gift. When the parts are incongruent, they were said to *disqualify* (rather than qualify) each other (Haley, 1959b), resulting in what we are calling here an *equivocal* message.

The notion of incongruently qualified or disqualified messages can be found in most of the Palo Alto Group's early writings: Haley (1958, 1959a, 1959b, 1961), Jackson (1959, 1961a, 1961b, 1962), Jackson, Riskin, and Satir (1961), Jackson and Weakland (1961), Weakland (1962), Weakland and Fry (1962), Weblin (1962), Jackson and Watzlawick (1963), Watzlawick (1963, 1964), Sluzki, Beavin, Tarnopolsky, and Verón (1967), and Walzlawick, Beavin, and Jackson (1967). Their predominant source of data was family communication, especially from the families of schizophrenics, where a pervasive and reciprocal pattern of disqualification was observed. The schizophrenic's typical communication was described as "incongruity both of gesture and manner and . . . statements which leave a lot unsaid" (Weblin, 1962, p. 7), such as **"For someone who has been like a mother to me."** These were matched by parental disqualification in which "almost no statement ever is allowed to stand, clearly and unambiguously" (Weakland & Fry, 1962, p. 622), such as in the letter to Janet. These authors also emphasized, however, that such messages occur much more widely, that is, in normal communication as well. As a result, the scope of the phenomenon expanded rapidly.

Not surprisingly, the many definitions and applications of the notion of disqualification (or incongruence) that were flourishing during this period were themselves not entirely clear or consistent. Furthermore, as the ideas of the Palo Alto Group captured the imaginations of others, these (and many other) ideas proliferated and mutated rapidly, so there has never been a single "true" or "original" definition. Still, two basic principles (which have led directly to our own work) were emphasized by Watzlawick, Beavin, and Jackson (1967) in their attempt to summarize the Palo Alto Group's work to that date: First, there exist messages that "say something without really saying it" or "say nothing while saying something," such as:

> self-contradictions, inconsistencies, subject switches, tangentializations, incomplete sentences, misunderstandings, obscure style or mannerisms of speech, the literal interpretations of metaphor and the metaphorical interpretation of literal remarks, etc. (p. 76)

The second point is that, even when such communication seems bizarre or pathological, it will make sense if seen in its situational context (p. 78). Thus, we should not only "observe, record, examine, and describe real communication," we should also examine with equal care the interpersonal situation in which a message occurs. In this view, individuals do not generate messages, situations do.

STRATEGIC AMBIGUITY[1]

To our knowledge, the term *equivocation* was first used in a study of communication by Goss and Williams (1973; Williams & Goss, 1975), who questioned Aristotle's credo that "style to be good must be clear" (Goss & Williams, 1973, p. 654). They pointed out that a politician, for example, sometimes "must address an audience which openly and perhaps vehemently disagrees with him on certain issues" (Williams & Goss, 1975, p. 166), in which case there are three possible alternatives (other than avoiding the audience altogether): to address the audience but to ignore completely the contentious issues; to address the issues clearly and openly, regardless of the hostility this engenders; or "to use deliberate vagueness, i.e., . . .to equivocate those issues with which [the audience] disagrees" (1975, p. 266). In their experimental studies of persuasive messages, Goss and Williams showed that the effect of equivocation on an audience was surprisingly positive, in that equivocal messages (written by the researchers but attributed to real public figures) were more likely than clear messages to elicit agreement and to result in better character ratings for their putative authors.

Eisenberg (1984) has also questioned clarity as a normative standard for all situations. Focusing on organizational communication in particular, he pointed out that:

> people in organizations confront multiple situational requirements, develop multiple and often conflicting goals, and respond with communicative strategies which do not always minimize ambiguity, but may nonetheless be effective. (p. 228)

Quoting Pascale and Athos (1981) that "explicit communication is a cultural assumption; it is not a linguistic imperative" (p. 102), Eisenberg went on to explore how people working in organizations may use ambiguity strategically.

RULE-BASED APPROACHES TO INDIRECT SPEECH ACTS

In realms apparently distant from those who study schizophrenia, politics, or organizations, language philosophers have also been fascinated by the "illogic" of natural communication. They too have tried to understand, rather than to dismiss, language that is not as it "should" be. Their goal has been to discover the implicit rules underlying natural communication.

Grice (1975) pointed out that natural language often diverges considerably from formal logic. That is, there is a language of "formal devices" by which ideas can be represented logically, and there is, on the other hand, language as it is actually used. Natural language often contains sequences that are not logical in the formal sense. For example:

A: **Smith doesn't seem to have a girlfriend these days.**

B: **He has been paying a lot of visits to New York lately.** (p. 51)

There is no formal logic that can connect B's reply to A's statement; it is a *non sequitur*. Grice noted that such instances would be regarded by formalists "as an imperfection of natural languages" or, worse, as "undesirable excrescences" (p. 42). Yet most of us can make the connection quite easily: B is suggesting that Smith has a girlfriend in New York. Grice proposed that, instead of ignoring such instances, we should seek to understand how it is that people use and understand them. He went so far as to suggest that these were part of a separate but valid language system:

> There are very many inferences and arguments, expressed in natural language and not in terms of [formal] devices, that are nevertheless recognizably valid. So there must be a place for an unsimplified and so more or less unsystematic, logic of the natural counterparts of these devices. . . not only do the two logics differ, but sometimes they come into conflict. . . .(p. 43)

Grice's solution was to offer what has become a classic set of "conversational maxims" aimed at making sense of natural language as it actually occurs. His was the first of what has come to be known as the "rules" or "rule-based" approach to natural communication.

Searle (1975), too, pointed out that, although there are many simple cases

> in which the speaker utters a sentence and means exactly and literally what he says. . . .notoriously, not all cases of meaning are this simple: In hints, insinuations, irony, and metaphor — to mention a few examples — the speaker's utterance meaning and the sentence meaning come apart in various ways. One important class of such cases is that in which the speaker utters a sentence, means what he says, but also means something more. (p. 59)

Searle focussed on "indirect speech acts." An example would be:

A: **Can you reach the salt?**

This statement is indirect because, in natural interaction, its interpretation is different from its literal meaning. It is ordinarily interpreted as a request to pass the salt rather than as a question about the other's reaching ability. Indeed, the question is ordinarily put this way only when there is no doubt that the other person can reach the salt. We somehow know that the speaker really means, "Pass me the salt." Therefore, a reply such as:

B1: (smile, while passing the salt)

would be appropriate, even though B does not reply directly to A's question. Whereas:

B2: **Yes, I can.** (without passing the salt)

Figure 1.1.

would be inappropriate, even though formally correct. For Searle:

> The problem posed by indirect speech acts is the problem of how it is possible
> for the speaker to say one thing and mean that but also to mean something else.
> (p. 60)

He went on to propose a theoretical apparatus for understanding these
instances. Thus, like Grice, Searle showed that a careful analysis can not only
make sense of apparently imperfect or illogical communication but can also
contribute to a wider understanding of the underlying rules of natural
communication – of how people really do talk.

Nofsinger (1976) examined certain indirect *replies* to questions:

A: **Going to be working at the office?**

B: **Is the Pope a Catholic?** (p. 177)

or

A: **Are notebooks allowed during the final exam?**

B: **Are porcupines allowed in balloon factories?** (p. 178)

Nofsinger pointed out (as Grice and Searle had) that two statements with no
"logical" relationship at all can be understood fairly readily:

> Everyday conversation is not strictly logically valid....It is, however, "rational"
> in the sense that conclusions are reached, and supporting . . . reasons are estab-
> lished. (p. 179)

He went on to propose rules by which we understand certain kinds of indirect replies.

Bowers, Elliott, and Desmond (1977) carried the rules approach one step further. They began with an analysis similar to Nofsinger's (1976), showing how a question may be answered either directly or indirectly. For example:

A: **Are you going to the pub tonight?**

Direct answers:

B1: **Yes, I am.**

B2: **No, I'm not.**

Indirect answers meaning "yes":

B3: **I always go to the pub when Leslie's waiting tables.**

B4: **It's a good night to celebrate.**

B5: **Is the Pope Catholic?**

Indirect answers meaning "no":

B6: **When my spouse is working nights, I have to stay home.**

B7: **I have to take an important test in the morning.** (Bowers et al., p. 236)

B8: **Does a submarine have screen doors?** (Nofsinger, 1974)

The indirect answers depend on unstated assumptions (e.g., the assumption that Leslie is waiting tables tonight) and on apparent rules for connecting these assumptions to the questions. Bowers, Elliott, and Desmond suggested that, because people usually do make these connections, the indirect answers are *pragmatically* satisfactory despite their semantic incompleteness or indirectness.

Bowers, Elliott, and Desmond went a step beyond previous authors by noting that such messages can be "exploited" by "devious" respondents who do not want to answer a question. They gave as an example the following exchange between a reporter (Helen Thomas) and President Nixon's Press Secretary (Ronald Ziegler) during the Watergate scandal:

Thomas: **Has the President asked for any resignations so far, and have any been submitted or on his desk?**

Ziegler: I have repeatedly stated, Helen, that there is no change in the status of the White House staff.

Thomas: But that was not the question. Has he asked for any resignations?

Ziegler: I understand the question, and I heard it the first time. Let me go through my answer. As I said, there is no change in the status of the White House staff. There have been no resignations submitted. (Adapted from Bowers et al., 1977, p. 239; original source, Walters, 1974, p. 34)

The question "**Has the President asked for any resignations?**" was not answered directly, but the respondent implied that it had been answered *indirectly*, which Bowers, Elliott, and Desmond called "exploiting pragmatic rules" (p. 235).

They went on to outline a set of circumstances in which respondents would want to create this ambiguity, that is, to "plant booby traps on the bridge linking semantics and pragmatics":

These circumstances are frequent in all of our lives. We face this exigence when we are invited to a party we would prefer not to attend, and when we are asked by parents to comment on a newborn baby's appearance. We face it when we are asked to explain our behavior to someone who would be injured by either the truth or a lie . . . Public officials constantly encounter this situation as they parry questions demanding that they account for past behavior and reveal their commitments for the future. . . . Devious messages, both sent and received, are ubiquitous in our everyday lives. (1977, p. 238)

As will be seen, their description of the situational antecedents of non-straightforward communication anticipates our own in many respects (indeed, an early nickname for our project was "the ugly baby project," because everyone could understand this communicative dilemma). However, because of our emphasis on the situation rather than the individual and on the problem-solving function of equivocal messages, we disagree with the characterization of the resulting communication as "devious," "misleading," or ordinarily "inimical to the good life" (p. 238). Nor do we agree with the assumption that the other person is necessarily a "victim" who needs to learn to "detect" such messages.

In a major application of rule analysis, Brown and Levinson (1978) proposed a universal form of linguistic "politeness" across widely differing languages and cultures. Like most rule-based theorists, they proposed a set of hypothetical cognitive "strategies." For example, people are said to act as if they should avoid disagreement (Strategy 6). Faced with the possibility of

Figure 1.2.

open disagreement, the individual may "hedge" with equivocal messages
such as:

It's really beautiful, in a way.

I don't know, like I think people have a right to their own opinion.
(Californian English)

You really should sort of try harder. (pp. 121-122)

All of the rules theorists have sought to explain rather than dismiss what
logic would tell us is "wrong" communication, and in this respect they are
broadly similar to the theories of the Palo Alto Group. However, there is a
difference that is crucial for us: The main interest of these theorists is not in
the messages themselves (and, indeed, most have used hypothetical messages
rather than systematically gathering real ones), nor is it the specific situation
in which any message occurs. Instead, rules theorists are interested in
building models of how people think and in using these models to explain
communication. They hypothesize processes in the minds of the interactants
(such as rules, inference processes, cognitions, plans, intentions, strategies,
and so forth), which are seen as the causes of messages. Hence, in this view,
the "real" nature of communication is hidden from us; the actual messages
are only the surface manifestations of mental processes that we will never
see.

We propose, in contrast, that the data of communication can be the messages themselves (Figure 1.2) and that the explanation of a message can be sought in the immediate, observable interpersonal situation in which it occurs. We need not use communicative behavior solely as a means of studying the mind; nor should it be treated as a superficial manifestation of more interesting mental processes. We can study it as systematic and fascinating behavior in its own right.

SUMMARY

Equivocation is nonstraightforward communication; it appears ambiguous, contradictory, tangential, obscure, or even evasive. Such messages were first studied (as "disqualification") by the Palo Alto Group, who sought an explanation in the speaker's communicative situation. Indirect speech acts are also forms of equivocation, and these have been pursued by other researchers, who are interested in inferring the rules that generate natural (as opposed to formal) language. We will follow the first tradition, that is, the study of messages in the situations that elicit them.

NOTE

1. This should be differentiated from ambiguity research in psycholinguistics; e.g., Kess and Hoppe (1981).

2

Capturing Equivocation Quantitatively

The previous chapter illustrated the almost bewildering variety of ways in which people can equivocate. Here we will show how to capture this elusive phenomenon — how to identify and measure the amount of equivocation in virtually any message. Our aim has been to find numbers for equivocation without losing it in the process or (worse) making it boring. Indeed, the procedure to be described here, and the numbers that ensue, have shown us new subtleties and nuances of equivocation.

Essentially, we measure equivocation by asking raters to examine a message carefully and tell us how clear it is on each of four different dimensions, which we believe are four aspects of a message affected by equivocation. We then transform these judgments into numbers that range from −2 to +2, representing low to high equivocation. More details of this procedure will be given later in this chapter, after the requirements and rationale that led to the method have been described.

CONCEPTUAL AND TECHNICAL REQUIREMENTS

To begin our research at all, it was essential to find a measure of equivocation that was both valid and reliable. That is, the measure should be compatible with our concept of equivocation and also precise and replicable in practice. When we began the project in 1977, there already were some methods for identifying or measuring characteristics similar to equivocation, but for reasons to be outlined below, none was suitable.

All of the previous methods were based on content analysis by experts. Sluzki, Beavin, Tarnopolsky, and Verón (1967) suggested several categories of what the Palo Alto Group had called *disqualification*; these categories included, for example, evasion, literality, and "sleight of hand" (answering a different question than the one asked). Another, more highly developed system was Wiener and Mehrabian's (1968) method for scoring *immediacy* and *nonimmediacy* in verbal communication. For example, when the speaker refers to "those people" instead of "these people," he or she is using less immediate language, which seems to put distance between the speaker and the people referred to. Wiener and Mehrabian (1968, Chapter 4) measured verbal indirectness (nonimmediacy) using spatio-temporal categories (distancing the topic in space or time), denotative specificity (under- or over-inclusiveness), and agent-action-object categories (separation of agent from action, or action from object, etc.).

Rule-based theories, such as those discussed in Chapter 1, have also generated principles by which apparently anomalous language can be identified. For example, Bowers, Elliot, and Desmond (1977) identified and modeled the logic of four kinds of responses to a yes-no question, such as **"Are you going to the pub tonight?"** Their four categories were explication (**"Yes, I am"**), propositional implication (**"I always go to the pub when Leslie's waiting tables."**), relational implication (**"It's a good night to celebrate."**), and transparent questions (**"Is the Pope Catholic?"**). Similarly, Nofsinger (1976) suggested several ways in which responses can be indirect, and Brown and Levinson (1978) described a large number of politeness strategies.

All of these previous methods are taxonomic, that is, they provide categories for *classifying* observed or hypothetical instances. Their advantage is that they aim to provide detailed analyses of the many ways in which people can communicate indirectly. From our point of view, however, this is also a disadvantage, because a given list might never be complete. As Bowers et al. (1977) said:

> Certain formal symptoms of devious messages may exist, but we do not pretend to have exhausted the possibilities, nor have we succeeded so far in modeling all of them. (p. 239)

Similarly, it is always possible that a researcher could find an entirely new kind of non-immediacy or a new politeness strategy. If this is so, then the taxonomy will always be incomplete; messages that were not identified as indirect at one time might later be found to be so, after a new category or technique for indirectness has been discovered or articulated. This is an intrinsic problem with any kind of taxonomy—it can always be added to or revised. We prefer to have a principle that will not change even when new instances are added. This principle should identify equivocation regardless of exactly how it manifests itself in any particular message. Ideally, the principle should also be conceptually related to our theory of equivocation as communication that *avoids* direct communication.

Traditional content analysis by experts has another disadvantage, namely, the focus is on the qualities that the expert finds in the message rather than the impact of the message on an ordinary receiver. As Wilmot (1980) has pointed out, lay participants and observers are a largely untapped source of information about communication. The linguistic means by which a message is rendered indirect are interesting and important, but measurement based on these qualities will not reveal anything about the actual effect of a message on the social situation in which it arises. It is not certain that characteristics identified by experts are even noticed by participants in the course of everyday communication. For some theories, this issue is irrelevant, but for ours it is crucial. We propose that the explanation of equivocation lies in its effect on other people in the situation, so it is essential that we assess the effects of messages on nonexpert receivers.

It is therefore not surprising that (as is usually the case in research) there was no ideal measure sitting on a shelf, waiting to be used to test our theory. However, seeing how other researchers had measured similar concepts led to several criteria for the method to be developed: As implied above, the measure should proceed from a unifying *principle* related to our theory, rather than from a taxonomy or classification scheme. Also, the method should assess the impact of the messages on nonexpert *receivers* rather than assessing characteristics identifiable only by experts.

In addition, we had a number of technical preferences for a measure of equivocation. A dichotomy of equivocal/unequivocal is far less useful than a full continuum ranging from very clear to completely equivocal; a measure of the *degree* of equivocation would detect more subtle differences among messages. The method of measurement must also accomodate messages with both *verbal* and *nonverbal* aspects, including messages that are written, spoken (as on the telephone), or delivered face-to-face. On the other hand, we would not need to analyze lengthy dialogue but only relatively short, single replies. Finally, the method must be *reliable* and *replicable*. It must produce the same numbers for the same messages even when entirely different people judge the messages. And there should be an explicit and complete set of procedures that others can follow, so that researchers anywhere can use the method. (This set of procedures is given in Appendix A.)

Figure 2.1.

HALEY'S ANALYSIS OF INCONGRUENCE (DISQUALIFICATION)

The basis of our method (originally described in Bavelas & Smith, 1982) is found in Haley's (1959a) article, which is one of the first descriptions of incongruent or disqualified communication. Haley drew attention to a basic principle of communication theory:

> The formal characteristics of any message from one person to another can be broken down into these four elements:
>
> (1) I
>
> (2) am saying something
>
> (3) to you
>
> (4) in this situation. (p. 325)

In other words, communication always involves a *sender*, some *content*, a *receiver*, and a *context*. Every message contains these elements, implicitly or explicitly; they are a basic framework of communication. These elements can be considered a fundamental aspect of communication in the sense that they are always true: There can be no communication without my saying something to you in a given situation.

Haley was interested in the possibility that the apparently bizarre communication of schizophrenics might be an attempt to negate or deny these basic elements. He proposed that a schizophrenic may deny: (1) that she is the person sending the message by, for example, claiming to be someone else or claiming that God speaks through her. It is not then "I" who says what I am saying, but someone else — although obviously "I" said it. This creates the slippery quality that is characteristic of the schizophrenic (and equivocal) communication, as does denial of the other elements; (2) Another schizophrenic may deny that he is actually saying something by, for example, speaking nonsense or by speaking in a made-up language; (3) Yet another may deny that what she says is addressed *to* the other person by "talking to herself" in the presence of the other person; or she may insist that the person being addressed is really someone else; (4) Finally, he or she may deny the situation in which the communication occurs by insisting that it is really another place or another time. Using this framework, Haley made a penetrating analysis of schizophenic communication; his article remains a classic for showing "Though this be madness, yet there is method in 't" (*Hamlet*, II ii, 211).

Although he was studying schizophrenic communication, Haley explicitly noted that these incongruencies also occur in ordinary communication as well, albeit in less extreme forms. This suggested to us the possibility that the same framework could be used for measuring equivocation. Examples of equivocating by avoiding the four elements are easy to find:

1. A person can deny, in effect, that he (personally) is saying anything by prefacing the message with **"The management requires me to inform you"** or **"They say."** In either case, he is implying that he is not the sender, although he is. Recall that Iago too denied that he was the source of his message (see Chapter 1).

2. The content of a message may be so contradictory that it cancels itself out. Take, for example, **"Well, yes and no. On the one hand I agree, but on the other hand I don't feel that I can agree,"** or the virtuoso contradictions of Mr. R (see Chapter 1). Something has been said, but nothing has been said.

3. A speaker may avoid addressing the other person — while still addressing her — by speaking to the receiver as a category rather than as an individual, for

example, **"People like you make me nervous."** Or, like Henry II (see Chapter 1), he can address **"no one"** in particular.

4. Answering a slightly different question from the one asked is a common strategy for avoiding the immediate context, namely, the question one does not wish to answer. Hence, **"How do you like my new hairdo?"** can be not-answered by **"Hey, that's a real change!"** Jane Austen portrayed evasiveness more elegantly in Marianne's reply to Elinor (see Chapter 1).

No matter which examples of equivocation we tried it on, Haley's model worked. If a message was, in our intuitive judgment, equivocal, then closer examination revealed that at least one of the four elements was unclear. Simple as these elements are, they can serve as a kind of filter, in the sense that equivocation of any kind affects them. So we decided to commit our efforts in this direction and to make the working assumption that *avoiding a direct message will inevitably avoid one or more of the four elements* (Sender, Content, Receiver, or Context). In other words, equivocation will necessarily render at least somewhat ambiguous the sender's own opinion, exactly what is being said, the fact that the message is addressed to the recipient, or the context to which the message is a response.

If this premise is true, then assessing the clarity of these four elements in a given message is a means of detecting equivocation. In a direct message, all four elements should be clear and accurate. In an indirect message, they should become relatively unclear. Put another way, we are assuming that *all messages that would (intuitively or otherwise) be called equivocal are ambiguous in at least one of the four elements*. If the clarity of these elements is assessed, then equivocation will be identified.

These are the assumptions on which our measurement is based. The reader need not initially accept them as true, only as plausible. If they turn out to be wrong, then equivocation will elude our measures, and tests of our theory will fail. Also, it is important not to overemphasize the status we are giving the four dimensions. For example, we are not proposing that individuals deliberately use these dimensions in their communication. Nor would we claim that this set of dimensions is the only conceivable basis on which equivocation could, in principle, be measured. Rather, ambiguity in these dimensions is *one* effect of equivocation and, as shall be seen, a very sensitive effect. We have found these dimensions to be an excellent prism through which to analyze communication. Just as a glass prism lets us see the colors of which light is made, these dimensions let us see the colors of equivocation. They draw attention to details and shadings that might otherwise be overlooked.

So the basis of our measurement procedure consists of asking laypersons (with no expertise in communication other than a few hours of training) the following four questions about a message:

1. To what extent is this message the *writer's* (or *speaker's*) *own opinion?* [Sender]
2. How clear is this message, in terms of just *what is being said?* [Content]
3. To what extent is the message *addressed to the other person in the situation?* [Receiver]
4. To what extent is this a *direct answer to the* (implicit or explicit) *question?* [Context]

Notice that, following Sluzki et al. (1967), we have defined *context* as the immediately preceding message and have made this message a question, actual or implied. This choice reflects our focus on the immediate, specific sequence of messages in a conversation rather than on a more global context. We assume, as did Nofsinger (1976) and Schegloff and Sacks (1973), that sequential utterances are inevitably connected, in the sense that a question requires an answer and a statement requires a reply. The other person's options are limited by what has just been said. Once addressed, he may answer or refuse to answer, but he "cannot not communicate" (Watzlawick et al., 1967).

MEASURING THE DEGREE OF EQUIVOCATION

Having decided to define equivocation by "Haley's principle," our conceptual course was set. But a conceptual definition does not, by some magic, result in numbers indicating the degree of equivocation in a given message. The usual next step would be to adopt a standard rating scale of some kind; for example, the permissible answers to the above four questions might take the form:

1 = very clear
2 = fairly clear
.
.
7 = very unclear

A scale with fixed points is very convenient for the researcher, but few researchers ever work with such a scale themselves, so they often do not appreciate how unnatural it is in practice.

The problem is that, if the rating procedure itself is arbitrary or confusing, the person making the ratings cannot do the task well or carefully. The rater must pay careful attention to the messages and the dimensions and, at the same time, use an unfamiliar and restrictive means of responding. It is as if she were taught a little bit of a foreign language and then required to respond to subtle and complex questions in this, rather than her native, language. If the primary goal is to have the person judge where a given message fits on a particular dimension, then everything else should be made as natural and unobtrusive as possible — for the person, not for the researchers. The process of communicating the judgment to the researcher should not be an additional source of work or of potential error.

To solve this problem, we adapted a method called *magnitude estimation*, which was suggested by the work of Stevens (1966) and Levine (1974) and which had proven easy for raters to use in the scaling of other complex stimuli (e.g., Beavin, 1970; Lee, 1977; MacGregor, 1975; Schaefer, 1979; Smith, 1979). It is based on the assumption that we should try to tap into the way people already make complex judgments. In other words, rather than imposing a method that people would have to learn, it is better to use one that fits naturally the way they think, so that no new learning is necessary. They are then free to devote all of their attention to the messages and the dimensions.

Mathematical psychophysicists such as Stevens (1966) and Levine (1974) have shown that people make quantitative judgments by the use of analogues, that is, by translating into a quantity that is more familiar or concrete than the stimulus being judged. Levine (1974, especially pp. 203-208) proposed that the most natural analogue is *geometric length*. Indeed, Levine argued that the very notion of a number itself is encoded as length, and his data showed that simple mental arithmetic is done by manipulating these lengths and then translating them back into numbers. Stevens (1966) had shown, earlier, that people do complex cross-modality matching (for example, adjusting a light until it is as bright as a sound is loud) by treating both, mentally, as physical length.

Because simple physical length seems to be a natural language for expressing "how much" of anything a stimulus has, we made our four dimensions into actual physical lines on a table. For example, the question "How clear is this message in terms of just what is being said?" is answered for any particular message by placing the message somewhere on a line that is only denoted as *completely clear* at one end and *completely unclear* at the other. Thus, by analogy, the abstract dimension *clarity of content* becomes the line on the table with its quantitative properties. Later, we measure exactly where the message was placed (in centimeters) and standardize these numbers. But the judges are not concerned with any of this and are free to concentrate on what we are asking them to do, namely, to tell us what they make of the messages.

THE SCALING PROCEDURE

Overview

To measure equivocation, we teach each judge about the four dimensions (Sender, Content, Receiver, Context) and then ask him or her to place each message to be scaled on a line so as to represent "how much" of each dimension the message has. We use the average of the judgments of several individuals as the value for each message. In this section, we will summarize our procedure, particularly the training phase in which the four dimensions are explained. A more detailed description, sufficient for replication, can be found in Appendix A. (If you plan to use this method, you should work from the script in Appendix A, not this chapter.)

The Judges

In the lifetime of this project, nine different experimenters have trained eight groups of 7 to 11 judges (each judge working individually) to scale the messages for our experiments. The judges were usually undergraduates recruited from English or linguistics classes at the University of Victoria. None had any background in communication research or any previous knowledge of our project. They were paid up to $5.00 per hour for each scaling session, which usually lasted an hour or so and were scheduled once every week or two over the academic year. When all the scaling sessions had been completed, the overall project, including our theory and hypotheses, was explained. Until then, they were "blind" to the purpose of the project and to any experimental conditions.

The Roles of the Experimenter and of the Judge

The twin goals of the early sessions are to train the judges to look closely and carefully at the messages and to make them aware of the differences among the dimensions. This training proceeds in slow, small steps in order to avoid overwhelming a judge by presenting too much information at once. Throughout the training sessions, the experimenter emphasizes that we want the individual's own judgment and that there is no "right" answer. Thus, we teach the judges what they should focus on but not what they should see. The goal is to produce confident, independent judges.

The relationship between the experimenter and the judge is an important aspect of the scaling procedure. Early in the training sessions, the experimenter takes an active role, almost that of an instructor, explaining the dimensions and suggesting ways that messages can differ along a dimension. After the third session, however, the experimenter becomes more of an assistant than an instructor. His or her function from this point on is to be an attentive listener and to confirm that the judge is using correct and consistent criteria for scaling each dimension. The experimenter's opinion of the message is no more valid than the judge's.

From the beginning, the judge is asked to think aloud about the reasons he or she is placing the messages on a particular spot. This is to ensure that the judge has understood each dimension and is not confusing two of them (which is a common error in the early stages). If the judge's reason for placing the message at a particular point indicates that he or she is having a problem, then the experimenter discusses the dimension and gives more examples. The focus is always on *why* the message was placed where it was, rather than on *where* it has been placed.

The benefit of this emphasis on each individual judge's own opinion is a wealth of original insights into the messages. Each judge develops a slightly different approach from the others, so that each message ends up being examined with considerable thoroughness and subtlety. Yet, in spite of this diversity, the averaged scale values (across judges) are highly reliable. (As will be seen, the intraclass correlations are consistently well above .90.)

Training the Judges

The training sessions include the first three sessions (in which the judges are given all the information needed to scale any message), then two or three practice sessions to increase their confidence in their judgments, and finally a "test" session designed to assess reliabilty.

The first session consists of introducing the judge to the scaling procedure and to the four dimensions, that is, to the characteristics of the messages he or she is going to focus on. The experimenter explains that this is a "scaling" project (i.e., we want to know where things go on a particular scale of measurement) and that we are interested in the judge's opinion of some videotaped (or spoken, or written) messages. (In this chapter, we describe the scaling of videotaped messages. The same method can be used, with appropriate changes, for written or audiotaped messages.)

1. a. How clear is this message, in terms of just <u>what is being said</u>?

   b. COMPLETELY CLEAR   COMPLETELY UNCLEAR

      Straightforward, easy to   Totally vague, impossible
      understand; there is only   to understand; no meaning
      one possible meaning.   at all.

2. a. To what extent is this message the <u>speaker's own opinion</u>?

   b. DEFINITELY   NOT AT ALL

      It is very evident that   Someone else's opinion is
      the message is his opinion;   being expressed, and you
      it is obviously his personal   have no idea what the
      opinion, not someone else's.   speaker's opinion is.

3. a. To what extent is the message <u>addressed to the other person in the
      situation</u>? (That person is, for example, Jennifer.)

   b. DEFINITELY   NOT AT ALL

      Obviously addressing the   The message is not addressed
      other person; could only   to the other person in the
      be addressing that person.   situation.

4. a. To what extent is this a <u>direct answer to the question</u>? (For example,
      "HOW are YOU?")

   b. DEFINITELY   NOT AT ALL

      This is a direct   The response is "way off" the
      answer to the   question; seems totally unrelated
      question asked.   to the question.

Figure 2.2. Introduction to the Four Dimensions

The judge sits across from the experimenter at an ordinary office desk
(60.5 × 101.5 cm) with four equally spaced strips of masking tape, one for
each dimension, running its full length. A brief phrase describing the dimension is written on each tape (e.g., "speaker's own opinion"). Each message
is represented by a 2 × 8 cm card bearing the number of the message. The
cards are to be placed somewhere along the tape, depending on where the
judge thinks the message should go. When a set of messages has been scaled
on one dimension, the experimenter records the position of each message by
writing its number on the tape, then the cards are removed to be scaled on
the next dimension.

The judge is given a written sheet (Figure 2.2) with the definition of each
dimension and some examples. The reader will notice that, in Figure 2.2 and
the following description, the order in which the judges learn and use the
dimensions is slightly different from Haley's order of presentation. The
Content dimension is always scaled first, for several reasons: We want

content to be scaled solely on the basis of the message itself, with no other information about the sender, receiver, or context. A "first impression" of the isolated message is the best assessment of its actual content. This order also sets an important precedent for scaling all of the dimensions, namely, that the judge is always to focus on the message itself and is not to make inferences about why it was said or what it "really" means.

For the *Content* dimension, the experimenter explains that the judge will be scaling *how clear* the message is. At the extreme left end of the tape go messages that are completely clear and have only one possible meaning. The experimenter plays two videotaped examples to give the judge an idea of what we mean by a perfectly clear message, one of which is a woman saying "**I have a STIFF neck**" while rubbing her neck and wincing slightly. The experimenter then explains that any messages less clear than this one would be placed away from this endpoint. Then two examples of messages are played that are, for our purposes, perfectly unclear and so belong at the extreme right end of the tape. One is "**I THINK I'm going GLOVE, impossibly**" said in a normal conversational tone. These endpoint examples serve to define the dimension concretely for the judge — what it means to be very clear or unclear. (After the endpoint examples for each dimension, the judge is given a message to scale on that dimension.)

The *Sender* dimension is defined as the extent to which the message is *the speaker's own opinion*. One of the two examples that would be scaled on the extreme left end is "**I think I have the FLU**" said in a resigned but emphatic manner — clearly, he believes what he says. At the other end of the dimension would go messages that express the opinion of someone other than the speaker and that do not reveal the speaker's own opinion at all. One example is "**ONE DOCTOR says I'm OKAY. The OTHER ONE says I need SURGERY**"; the speaker looks and sounds slightly bemused by the two opinions.

The *Receiver* dimension is defined as the extent to which the message is *addressed to the other person* in the situation. The other person is always seated across from the speaker, so the back of his or her head is visible on the screen. If relevant, the receiver's name or relationship to the speaker (e.g., friend or boss) is given. In this case, the receiver's name is given as Jennifer. For one of the messages that belongs on the extreme left end (definitely addressing the other person), the speaker looks directly at the other person, smiles, and says, "**FINE, thanks, JENNIFER.**" In one example of the extreme right end, the speaker shakes his head, points, and scowls — but all of this is directed off-screen, and he never looks at the person across from him.

The last dimension, *Context*, is defined as the extent to which the message is a *direct answer to the question asked*. For this dimension, the experimenter always gives a brief description of the situation in which the message occurred (the general context) and then the question that has just been asked (the specific context). For all of the examples given in the first session, the situation and question are as follows: Jennifer and the speaker have met in a seminar room before class, and Jennifer has asked the speaker, "**HOW are YOU?**" In one example at the extreme left, the speaker replies "**I'm FINE**" with no hesitation and the usual intonation for a "**HOW are YOU?**" — "**I'm FINE**" sequence. At the right end are messages totally unrelated to the question, for example, "**NO! I DON'T think it's going to rain!**," in an angry tone, emphasized by pounding a fist on the arm of the chair.

Having introduced the four dimensions, the experimenter goes on to point out their independence of each other. For example, a message could be scaled as being relatively clear in what is said (Content) but not necessarily a good answer to the question asked (Context). This is true of the reply "**NO! I DON'T think it's going to rain!**," given above — it is clear in itself but not responsive to "**HOW are YOU?**" To demonstrate this, the judge is asked to scale one last example on each of the four dimensions.

The next training session focuses more closely on the first two dimensions, Content and Sender. The judge is given additional information about these dimensions, including the "rules of thumb" to be used in placing the messages on these dimensions (see 1d to 4d in Figure 2.3). For the Content dimension, the stress is on the importance of focusing exclusively on the content of the message itself without inferring anything else. It does not matter who the two people are or the possible situations in which this message might be said; all that matters at this point is the clarity of the content of the message, considered strictly on its own. Besides the endpoints, a rule of thumb is given:

> *Between these two extremes [completely clear and completely unclear] would go messages that are somewhat vague, ambiguous, or hard to make out. They may have several possible meanings or be contradictory.*

The judge is asked at this point to try to make distinctions among the messages whenever possible, rather than stacking several messages in one place. Five new messages are played, which the judge scales while telling the experimenter his or her reasons for each placement.

Then the focus is shifted to the second dimension (Sender), with its endpoint examples and an expanded definition. The experimenter explains that, in some messages, there may appear to be no opinion being expressed;

1. a. How clear is this message, in terms of just <u>what is being said</u>?
   b. COMPLETELY CLEAR   COMPLETELY UNCLEAR
      Straightforward, easy to   Totally vague, impossible
      understand; there is only   to understand; no meaning
      one possible meaning.   at all.
   c. "I have a STIFF neck."   "I THINK I'm going GLOVE,impossibly."
   d. Between these two extremes would go messages that are somewhat vague,
      ambiguous, or hard to make out.   They may have several possible
      meanings or be contradictory.

2. a. To what extent is this message the <u>speaker's own opinion</u>?
   b. DEFINITELY   NOT AT ALL
      It is very evident that   Someone else's opinion is
      the message is his opinion;   being expressed, and you
      it is obviously his personal   have no idea what the
      opinion, not someone else's.   speaker's opinion is.
   c. "I think I have the FLU."   "ONE DOCTOR says I'm OKAY. The OTHER
                                         ONE says I need SURGERY."
   d. Whatever the message is, and no matter how clear or unclear it is on
      the first dimension, does the speaker state his own opinion or not?
      Or is it somewhere in between--you can't tell for sure if it's his or
      someone else's opinion.

3. a. To what extent is the message <u>addressed to the other person in the</u>
      <u>situation</u>? (That person is, for example, Jennifer.)

   b. DEFINITELY   NOT AT ALL
      Obviously addressing the   The message is not addressed
      other person; could only   to the other person in the
      be addressing that person.   situation.
   c. "FINE, thanks, JENNIFER"   "FINE, thanks, HARRY."
   d. The key issue here is whether the speaker is addressing the other
      person point-blank. If so, then the message goes on the far left.
      If not, then it goes somewhere to the right; you decide where.

4. a. To what extent is this a <u>direct answer to the question</u>? (For example,
      "HOW are YOU?")

   b. DEFINITELY   NOT AT ALL
      This is a direct   The response is "way off" the
      answer to the   question; seems totally unrelated
      question asked.   to the question.
   c. "I'm FINE."   "NO! I DON'T think it's going to
                                         RAIN!"
   d. In other words, it this a good answer to the question asked, or is
      there another question it would be a better answer to?

Figure 2.3. Summary of the Four Dimensions

in these cases, the judge would have to decide whether the speaker agreed or
disagreed with the message, using whatever information is available (tone of
voice, facial expression, etc.). The rule of thumb is:

> *Whatever the message is, and no matter how clear or unclear it is on the first*
> *dimension, does the speaker state his own opinion or not? Or is it somewhere*
> *in between—you can't tell for sure if it's his or someone else's opinion.*

Five messages, which vary in how an opinion is expressed (or not expressed),
are played, and the judge is asked to scale them and to give his or her
reasoning aloud.

After the first two dimensions have been covered separately, the judge is asked to scale three more messages, first on the Content dimension, then on the Sender dimension. This reinforces the principle that there is no correlation across dimensions, that each dimension represents a different aspect of the same message. A message can be high on one and low on another.

The third session is devoted to the last two dimensions, Receiver and Context. After reviewing the summary sheet and endpoints for the Receiver dimension, the rule of thumb is given:

> *The key issue here is whether the speaker is addressing the other person point-blank. If so, then the message goes on the far left. If not, then it goes somewhere to the right; you decide where.*

The experimenter describes various clues that can be used to decide whether or to what degree the other person in the situation is being addressed. For example, is the speaker looking at the other person? Is the message appropriate to the relationship between the two people? For the latter, the judge will be given some information about the other person in the situation (e.g., the other person is a good friend, a classmate, or anyone reading classified ads in the newspaper). The judge then scales five messages and explains the reasons, as usual.

After a brief review of the Context dimension, the rule of thumb is given:

> *In other words, is this a good answer to the question given, or is there another question it would be a better answer to?*

If the judge can think of a different question that the message fits better, then it cannot go on the far left. Some other ways in which an answer may be less than direct are also discussed; for example, the message might contain extraneous information, although it does answer the question, or it might require inferences to be made before it can be seen to answer the question. Practice messages are then played for scaling on this dimension.

This is all the instruction given to a judge for scaling messages on equivocation. The essential information is summarized in a sheet such as Figure 2.3, which is available to them in this and all subsequent sessions. Further training sessions are solely for practice and are aimed both at increasing the judge's confidence and alerting him or her to the less obvious differences among messages from "real people." In the first three sessions, the messages had been scripted and enacted by us in order to make certain teaching points and were often extreme or artificial. In the next practice sessions, the messages used are spontaneous replies by participants in previous experiments. The last step before scaling new experimental messages is the reliability session, to be explained below. After that, the judges' opinions about messages are the final word for us. We alerted them to some fine points, but they went far beyond our training. In a sense, the rest of this book contains *their* insights into messages that they have examined carefully and with a good deal of subtlety.

QUANTIFICATION

The judges are finished when the messages are placed on the tape; it is then our job to convert their judgments into numbers. Figure 2.4 gives an overview of the necessary steps, which will be described in this section.

The strips of masking tape, on which each judge's placements have been recorded, are removed and identified with a session number and the judge's initials. The distance from the extreme left (zero) to where each message number is written on the tape is measured in centimeters. These numbers are recorded on a data sheet, for example:

Content Dimension

Message	1	2	3	4	5	6	7	8	9	
Judge D.M.	71	15	79	41	97	23	74	4	34	cm
Judge J.C.	50	4	50	48	86	4	48	4	36	cm
[etc.]										

Notice that, while these two judges did not usually place the messages on exactly the same spots, they did agree on the *relative* position of each message. For example, messages 2, 6, and 8 are very clear, 5 is the least clear, and the rest are spread out in the middle. The differences in absolute value occur because we only defined the endpoints, leaving each judge to use the distance between in whatever way seemed natural. Some judges use the entire length of the tape, while others avoid the extremes and place most of their messages within the center third of the line; still others use mostly the lower (or upper) half of the line. These differences are systematic in the sense that any given judge is consistent in how he or she divides and uses the line.

Variation among judges could be a problem when it comes to averaging across judges to obtain a single value for a given message on a given dimension. If the average of these "raw" scores (in centimeters) were used to represent where a message belongs on a dimension, this raw-score average would be greatly affected by systematic, idiosyncratic differences in the

Figure 2.4.

judges' use of the line. The fact that each judge's own mean is located in a different place would lead to apparent lack of agreement among judges (see Winer, 1962, pp. 128-130). This is compounded by the fact that the judges' dispersion of messages (their variance) may also differ. We could solve the problem by insisting that all judges use the line in the same way (i.e., by imposing intervals), but this would violate our principle of minimal intrusion. Therefore, we solve the problem afterwards, statistically.

Examining the raw scores confirms that each judge has his or her own mean and standard deviation, that is, an idiosyncratic center and dispersion in the use of the line. Because statistical *standard scores* (Z scores, where

$Z = (X - M)/SD$) remove exactly such irrelevant differences, we adapted this formula to our situation: We take a given judge's raw scores for a particular set of messages on one of the dimensions and calculate the mean and standard deviation. Then this mean is subtracted from the raw score for each message $(X - M)$, and the difference is divided by the standard deviation. The result is a standard score for each message. Because the judge's raw scores are being transformed by use of his or her *own* mean and standard deviation (rather than a group mean and standard deviation, which is the usual way), we call the resulting values *ipsatized* (self-standardized) scores. For example, the data for judge D.M. given above have a mean of 48.67 cm and a standard deviation of 32.52 centimeters. J.C.'s mean is 36.67 cm, with a standard deviation of 27.95. Transformed by ipsatizing, the values for the two judges become:

Content dimension

Message	1	2	3	4	5	6	7	8	9
D.M.	.69	−1.04	.93	−.24	1.49	−.79	.78	−1.37	−.45
J.C.	.48	−1.17	.48	.41	1.77	−1.17	.41	−1.17	−.02

Both sets of new scores have a mean of zero and a standard deviation of 1, as do all standard scores. With the effect of idiosyncratic means and standard deviations removed, the similarity of the two judges' placements becomes more apparent: Both D. M. and J. C. placed message 1 about half a standard deviation above their personal means and message 2 about one standard deviation below.

Because all scores are now in comparable units, we can average the ipsatized scores across judges to get a more broadly based score for each message on a given dimension, one that takes into account all of the judges' opinions. Thus, to get a scale value for a particular message on a particular dimension, we hold the message and dimension constant and calculate the average of the ipsatized scores of all judges for that message on that dimension. If the judges' ipsatized scores agree highly (which is usually true), the resulting averages will still be standard scores, with a mean of zero and a standard deviation of 1. For example,

Content dimension

Message	1	2	3	4	5	6	7	8	9
	.59	−1.11	.71	.09	1.63	−.98	.60	−1.27	−.24

To interpret these numbers, first look at the sign: Any message below the mean is negative, while those above the mean are positive. So *negative* values indicate *clarity* (absence of equivocation), and *positive* values indicate that the message was judged more *equivocal*. Messages around zero are neither very clear nor very equivocal. (Obviously, negative and positive signs should not be associated in any way with "good" or "bad" ends of a continuum.)

Next, look at the number. A value of –2.0 would be two standard deviations below the mean and therefore very low, as standard scores go. Such a message is about as clear as it is possible to make a message. Similarly, a message with a value of 2.0 is about as equivocal as we ordinarily expect to see. Both are rare. Ordinarily, messages have values ranging from about –1.0 (fairly clear) to around +1.0 (fairly equivocal).

Because they are standard scores, these numbers are comparable across dimensions as well, so one can see at a glance exactly on which dimensions the message is equivocal and on which it is clear. Finally, we can add across dimensions to obtain a single figure, the Sum, representing the total equivocation in that message. (Summing across dimensions produces a wider range of values, with a larger standard deviation, but the mean is still zero, so the interpretation of negative and positive values as clear and equivocal, respectively, remains the same.)

For example, suppose that, after a poorly done class presentation, one student writes a note to another asking, "**How did I do?**" The other student replies, "**You were braver than I would be!**," which is a classic equivocation, with scale values as follows:

Content	Sender	Receiver	Context	Sum
–.08	–.56	–.09	1.42	.69

The Content of the message is average in clarity (effectively zero). It is a correctly formed sentence, although the judges pointed out that the use of "would" is a bit vague and it is not known what the other was braver about. On the Sender dimension, the message is clearer than average (minus sign). Both the personal pronoun and the exclamation point impressed our judges as indicating the sender's own opinion. The message is average with respect to the Receiver; we have found that messages seldom vary on this dimension. It is on the Context dimension that the message rises to one and a half standard deviations above the mean. The question was "**How did I do?**," but this message answers a different question, "**How brave was I, compared to** you?" The Sum is positive, indicating overall equivocation in this message, but the separate dimension values have shown exactly what form this took.

RELIABILITY

Before we can rely on the numbers produced by this scaling procedure, it is necessary to show that the scale values are invariant. That is, the values produced by averaging across one group of judges should be the same as those produced independently by an entirely different group of judges. (Note that, because we use the average across judges rather than the decision of any individual judge, we are interested in group reliability rather than the correlation between one individual judge and another; see Ebel, 1951).

Every group of judges has a reliability session after their initial training and before they begin scaling messages from our experiments, that is, new messages whose values we want to know and to be able to count on. In order to assess reliability, we constructed messages that varied maximally on each of the four dimensions and that also presented many subtle problems of judgment. (See Appendix A for this set.)

Statistically, there are two ways of assessing the reliability of averaged scores such as our scale values.

1. An estimate can be obtained by calculating R, the intraclass correlation coefficient (Winer, 1962, pp. 124-128). The value of R will be high when the variance due to messages is greater than the variance due to judges. That is, we expect differences among the messages but do not want much difference among the judges about those messages.
2. The direct way to assess reliability is actually to obtain a second group of judges and then to calculate the Pearson product-moment correlation, r, between the averaged scale values for the two groups on the same set of messages. That is, what did one group of judges say the values should be, compared to the other group?

We have assessed reliability both ways, and the figures agree: the reliability of the procedure is very high, often virtually perfect. Table 2.1 gives the intraclass correlations for the reliability trial of the eight separate groups of judges we have had during the project. (We have not included data on occasional overlapping groups made up of some old and some new judges.) Tables 2.2 and 2.3 give the correlation between successive groups who had the same messages in the same format on their reliability trial.

TABLE 2.1
Reliability: Intraclass Correlations

	Group	No. of Judges	Content	Sender	Receiver	Context
Written Messages						
	A	8	.94	.96	.96	.96
	B	7	.90	.94	.97	.98
	C	9	.91	.95	.96	.97
	D	11	.96	.98	.98	.98
Spoken Messages						
	E	9	.98	.95	.99	.96
	F	11	.98	.97	1.00	.97
Visual Messages						
	G	10	.96	.93	.98	.97
	H	7	.98	.90	.98	.97

TABLE 2.2
Reliability: Correlations Across Groups of Judges (Written Messages)

	Dimension											
	Content			Sender			Receiver			Context		
Group	A	B	C	A	B	C	A	B	C	A	B	C
B	.92	--		.96	--		.99	--		.97	--	
C	.88	.93	--	.94	.93	--	.97	.97	--	.95	.95	--
D	.93	.92	.91	.95	.97	.96	.99	.99	.99	.91	.94	.93

TABLE 2.3
Reliability: Correlations Across Groups of Judges (Spoken and Visual Messages)

	Dimension			
	Content	Sender	Receiver	Context
Spoken Messages (Groups E & F)	.99	.97	1.00	.99
Visual Messages (Groups G & H)	.94	.92	.99	.96

It may surprise the reader that lay people working individually in a relatively unstructured way would produce such unusually high reliabilities. Consider, though, how seldom we ever look as carefully at messages as these judges do. A few messages are their sole focus for an hour or so; they examine each one intensively, weighing its every aspect; and they are accustomed to distinguishing with equal care the differences among dimensions. We as the researchers have learned a great deal about the details of equivocation from our judges.

ISN'T THERE A SHORTER WAY?

The scaling method described here is time-consuming for judges and experimenter and, therefore, also expensive when both are being paid. For these reasons, we have tried to develop an alternative, "short-form" procedure — but unsuccessfully. The possibilites we considered or tried will be described here.

The total time required is a function of the number of judges (seen individually), the number of training sessions, and the number of dimensions. It can be shown statistically that reducing the number of judges must decrease reliability; six is the minimum we would feel comfortable with. Another way of reducing the amount of judge time would be to have group instead of individual sessions. However, our scaling method requires that judges work individually, in order that the experimenter can monitor the judge's scaling and, even more important, so that each judge provides independent information.

If the number of training sessions were decreased, judges would have less practice and would have to move from experimenter-generated messages to "real" messages too quickly. We have found, through experience, that judges need practice time to learn to focus precisely on the more complex and subtle characteristics of messages from experiments.

Finally, the number of dimensions might be reduced. We considered and rejected the possibility of asking for a single, global scaling of unclarity (rather than the four separate dimensions), because there would be no assurance (a) that all four kinds of equivocation would be included or (b) that judges would even be defining the dimension similarly.

However, we did try reducing the number of dimensions in another way. As will be seen in subsequent chapters, the Context dimension was the most sensitive (or most used) in the sense that this dimension always detected a significant difference between experimental conditions, even when the other dimensions did not. We reasoned that perhaps, if we had scaled *only* this dimension in our experiments, we still would have detected differences between experimental conditions and therefore would have reached the same general conclusions. It could even be that most of the training time was attributable to the necessity to make distinctions between dimensions; one dimension would eliminate this requirement.

So we developed a procedure in which (new) judges were individually taught only the Context dimension, in one session. Then they scaled several sets of experimental messages, and these results were correlated with the values from the full scaling procedure. Unfortunately, the results were not consistent enough for us to recommend the shorter procedure. Over two separate sets of short-form judges, the correlations between the short and full procedures ranged from .44 to .99. When the distinctions among messages were subtle (as in Experiment 15, Chapter 7), the short-form values were actually somewhat misleading. Our interpretation of these results is that the additional training and practice (including making distinctions among dimensions) are necessary. It is the time-consuming concentration and cumulative experience of the full procedure that produce the high reliabilities. Adding more practice sessions to the shorter procedure would simply bring the time involved close to the present procedure, yielding much less information for very little savings.

It may be that other researchers will be able to develop a reliable short form for scaling equivocation. In the meantime, we can only assure users of our present method that the time and expense are repaid by the precision and thoroughness of the numbers obtained. Perhaps it is amazing that such an ephemeral quality as equivocation can be measured at all.

SUMMARY

We assume that equivocation affects one or more of four essential aspects of a message: Sender, Content, Receiver, or Context. In other words, equivocation renders ambiguous the sender's own opinion, the content of the message, the fact that the message is addressed to its particular recipient, or the context to which it is a response. Lay judges can be trained to scale the clarity of a message on each of these four dimensions (Sender, Content, Receiver, and Context). The resulting standard scores are both reliable and subtle indicators of the amount and kind of equivocation in a message. The procedures outlined in this chapter (and given fully in Appendix A) were used to measure equivocation for all of the experiments to be described in this book.

3

A Situational Theory

We propose that, although an individual equivocates, he or she is not the cause of equivocation. Rather, equivocation is the result of the individual's communicative situation. Equivocation is avoidance; it is the response chosen when all other communicative choices in the situation would lead to negative consequences.

This idea was first proposed by Watzlawick, Beavin, and Jackson (1967, pp. 72-80) following their analysis of Mr. R's monologue (see Chapter 1). Recall that Mr. R was a volunteer being interviewed by Don Jackson, a psychiatrist who specialized in the family. Jackson and his colleagues in the Palo Alto Group wanted to compare families that included a psychiatric patient (such as a schizophrenic) to those without one, in order to see whether there were differences that would suggest a familial origin of psychopathology. However, this put an unintended pressure on interviewees, such as Mr. R, who were in the normal control group. Living up to the label *normal* is not easy or comfortable. What if he said something that revealed to the psychiatrist that all was not perfect, that he and his family were not always idyllically happy?

In this context, the question, **"How does it work out for you, Mr. R, with your folks in town?"** became a veritable mine field. If Mr. R said there were sometimes in-law problems, the psychiatrist might interpret this as pathology; if Mr. R said there were no problems, the psychiatrist might not find this credible. Both paths (**"There are some problems"** and **"There are no problems"**) could lead to negative consequences, so both had to be avoided. In this light, Mr. R's reply can be read as a successful attempt to avoid both negative options. He never says directly either that there are problems or that there are none. His incomplete sentences can be seen as constant "zig-zagging" away from one or the other of the negative options. The communicative dilemma set up by the question caused his apparently incoherent discourse:

From the communicational point of view there is, therefore, no essential difference between the behavior of a so-called normal individual who has fallen into the hands of an experienced interviewer and of a so-called mentally disturbed person who finds himself in the identical dilemma: neither can leave the field, neither can *not* communicate but presumably for reasons of their own [both] are afraid or unwilling to do so. In either case the outcome is likely to be gibberish, except that in the case of the mental patient the interviewer . . . will tend to see it only in terms of unconscious manifestations, while for the patient these communications may be a good way of keeping his interviewer happy by means of the gentle art of saying nothing by saying something. Similarly, an analysis in terms of "cognitive impairment" or "irrationality" ignores the necessary consideration of *context* in the evaluation of such communications. . . . [What may appear to be] "crazy" communication (behavior) is not necessarily the manifestation of a sick mind, but may be the only possible reaction to an absurd or untenable communication context. (Watzlawick et al., 1967, p. 78)

A SITUATIONAL THEORY OF COMMUNICATIVE CONFLICT

We have formalized the explanation just given by adapting Kurt Lewin's conflict theory (Lewin, 1938; Barker, 1942; Bavelas, 1978, Chapter 17) to communicative behavior. (We have also made substantial changes whenever our view differed from either the Palo Alto Group or Lewin. For example, the Palo Alto Group treated conflict as less interesting than paradox, because it was easier to resolve; we do not. Lewin's was a theory of the individual; he included the situation only through the individual's phenomenological view of his or her situation; we treat the situation as a distinct reality, separate from the individual.)

To begin, visualize any communicative situation as a metaphorical *field*, where we can map the circumstances bearing on communication at that moment. Physical and spatial metaphors are very useful for describing many communicative situations, as long as we remember that the important aspects of the field are seldom physical or literal; usually, they will be social. For example, what determines communication with another is likely to be how "close" or "distant" that person is socially, not physically. It is the social "closeness" of two people—not their physical proximity—that determines whether or not one of them will initiate interaction; a person may shout a greeting to a close friend walking across the campus but is unlikely to address a stranger even when they are crowded together in an elevator. The social psychological characteristics of the field determine a person's behavior.

The communicative field in a given situation is determined by the social factors that shape communication – other people and the context in which the interaction takes place. Abstracted from all other aspects of the situation, what we mean by the *communicative field* can be thought of as a set of options, or paths. These options are simply the possible messages in the situation. Having been addressed, a person may say one thing, or another, or smile, or say nothing. Some of these paths are more direct and obvious (**"How are you?"** – **"Fine, thanks."**) whereas others are more indirect or unusual (**"How are you?"** – **"How would you feel if you just flunked an exam?"**). The choice of one message over another is what we aim to predict.

Each of the paths or options that make up the field has a consequence for the individual. It changes the field irreversibly. Having been addressed, if a person says one thing, it will lead to one outcome; another message would lead to another outcome; silence would lead to still another. For our purposes here, these consequences or outcomes can be seen simply as positive or negative. A message that leads to something pleasant (e.g., an appreciated compliment to a friend) is a path with a positive effect on their relationship, whereas a course of action that leads to something unpleasant (e.g., insulting a friend) is a path with a negative outcome. Communication, perhaps even more than other behaviors, affects the field in which it occurs.

In many situations, there may be only one positive (and one or more negative) alternatives, so the choice is easy. However, there are many other situations in which a choice must be made among several positive alternatives or among only negative alternatives. These are situations of *conflict*, and in order to predict what will happen, it is necessary to add one more assumption about the consequences of a path: The intensity of the consequence (whether positive or negative) is stronger the closer the person comes to that option – a positive outcome becomes more positive as the person moves toward it, and a negative one becomes more negative. This principle is also known as the *goal gradient* and can be seen in everyday situations: The bearer of good news can hardly wait to tell, becoming more and more impatient for the moment to arrive. The bearer of bad news, in contrast, becomes more and more reluctant, with increasing dread as the moment draws nearer.

These simple principles lead to interesting predictions regarding different kinds of communicative conflict, when a choice must be made. Suppose the conflict is between equally appealing positive options – which Lewin called an *approach-approach conflict*. In this case, the person will do whichever he or she started to do first (even by chance). Because of the goal gradient, the attraction of the approached alternative will increase just because it is now

Figure 3.1.

closer, while by the same principle the attraction of the other alternative will decrease. Figure 3.1 is a schematic illustration of this effect.

When the alternatives are negative — an *avoidance-avoidance conflict* — the same theory predicts a different result. As illustrated in Figure 3.2, the person will begin by avoiding one negative option, thereby moving toward the other. However, the very fact of coming closer to this one will make it worse, while the one previously avoided will now be less negative because it is farther away. However, turning back to the first alternative will set off the same cycle, trapping the person in vacillation unless it is possible to "leave the field," that is, not to choose at all. The best solution is to avoid both alternatives, if this is possible. An avoidance-avoidance conflict is therefore much more difficult to resolve (and more interesting to study) than an approach-approach conflict, which is resolved fairly easily.

A *communicative* avoidance-avoidance conflict exists when the only available direct messages are negative, yet a reply must be made. (Recall that this was Mr. R's predicament.) We propose that a person in this situation will avoid a direct or clear reply of any kind, because all of them are negative. He or she will, if possible, leave the field — "saying nothing while saying something" — which avoids the negative consequences of the direct replies. Less direct communication is equivocal communication, and it is characterized by what it *avoids saying* as much as by what it does say. Thus, equivocation will occur in a communicative avoidance-avoidance conflict.

Figure 3.2.

Many everyday situations create a communicative avoidance-avoidance conflict. Perhaps the most common involves a choice between saying something false but kind and something true but hurtful. For example, a person who has to comment on an unsuitable gift from a well-liked friend has two negative choices of message: saying, falsely, that she likes the gift or saying, hurtfully, that she does not. We propose that, if possible, the person will avoid both of these — especially when a hurtful truth serves no purpose. As Turner, Edgley, and Olmstead (1975) pointed out, telling a truth when it only hurts someone we care about is itself a relationship lie:

> Is it honest to tell someone a truth that would sever or greatly jeopardize your relationship with a person if that is honestly not what you want to do? . . . In other words, being truthful and honest at all times may have consequences which are neither truthful nor honest. . . . (p. 83)

Notice that these authors refer to *a* truth rather than *the* truth, a practice we will continue because we agree that in many situations there is more than one truth. (And, for reasons that will be elaborated in Chapter 7, we will avoid the term *lie* as well.)

So, in the "unwelcome gift" conflict, a truth about the gift will be false in terms of the relationship. However, a false message about the gift is also a poor option, whether because of personal values, social disapproval, or the risk of being caught. Besides, there is still another, better alternative: *equiv-*

ocation, such as "**My wife loves it!**," "**It's amazing!**," "**I appreciate your thoughtfulness**" (with no mention of the actual gift), or "**Where did you ever find it?**"

Our method of measuring equivocation fits the theoretical framework given here and permits us to test it. When the person is asked how he likes the unwelcome gift, the direct path would be a message that takes the form "*I am saying this to you, in this situation.*" For example, "**I really love the birthday gift you sent me!**" However, when this is not true, it has a negative valence. The equally clear and direct alternative, "**I don't like the birthday gift you sent me**," is also negative. An alternative to both is equivocation. Avoiding Sender, Content, Receiver, or Context (as in the examples in the previous paragraph) avoids the negative consequences of a direct reply. Giving the wife's opinion obviously avoids giving his own (Sender). "**It's amazing!**" has several possible meanings and therefore none (Content). Commenting on the friend's thoughtfulness or asking where she got the gift avoids answering the question about the gift (Context). Thus we predict that, when we scale messages chosen in avoidance-avoidance conflicts, these messages will be higher in equivocation than those not chosen. Also, messages elicited in such conflicts should be higher in equivocation than those elicited in nonconflict conditions.

A variation on the "hurtful truth" conflict in human relationships is the case where a truth may be against one's own self-interest. This problem can arise, for example, when someone writes an ad for a used car that is not in good condition; when a job applicant describes her qualifications for a job that she is not really suited for; or when a person is asked for a promise he cannot keep.

Another common dilemma is being caught between offending either of two people (or groups) who want opposite replies. Two friends of the individual may disagree with each other and ask the individual which one he agrees with. Opposing constituencies often demand that a political candidate take a stand for one and against the other. A professor who must write a letter of reference for a poor student is caught between doing a disservice to the student or to the recipient of the letter.

The reader may be harboring the belief that in such situations, there must exist a better alternative than those we have described — some direct alternative that would not have negative consequences or perhaps some "softened" truth. Or, the reader may feel that, in many situations, one should be prepared to take a stand and accept the negative consequences (writing a candid car ad, saying the student was terrible, etc.). Imagining oneself in the situation is a good way to test these options, to explore the negative outcomes of each alternative, as well as to see that "softened" truths are equivocations. In the end, however, it is an empirical question. The purpose of the experiments to be described in this book is to find out what people do in just such situations.

Stated more generally, we propose that whenever two equally negative direct alternatives face the communicator, he or she will avoid both and equivocate instead. According to our theory, equivocation is a good solution to a bad situation. It is better than the other communicative alternatives and may even succeed in solving the dilemma entirely. Seen out of its eliciting situation, equivocation appears to be "poor" communication, but seen in context, it is the only good (or the least bad) alternative. Thus, the communicative situation is the crucial variable that accounts for the reversible illusion of an equivocal message: On its own, the message may be ambiguous; indeed, ambiguity is a necessary property of a message that must avoid saying anything. But when the eliciting situation is known, an ambiguous message becomes perfectly understandable.

Ducking, Dodging, Hedging, and Other Evasive Actions

Parenthetically, we find it intriguing that colloquial language for equivocation (and for the conflict that evokes it) includes many terms that are also metaphors of spatial position and physical movement, just as in Lewin's theory and ours. Such instances do not, of course, have any value as "proof" for our theory. They are simply fun, and they do suggest that there is an intuitive basis for a communicative field theory — *field* itself being a physical metaphor — as are the following:

A person *caught* in an avoidance-avoidance conflict is *on the spot* or in a tight (or tricky) *spot*. He is *in a bind* or *squeeze* or *pinch* or *crunch* — all metaphors for being constricted by something negative. In other words, he is *in a corner*, a *box*, a *hole*, or at an *impasse*, *at the end of his rope* (or *tether*), with *nowhere to turn,* so he is at a *standstill*.

Sometimes the two sides of the conflict are named: He is caught between *a rock and a hard place, the frying pan and the fire, the devil and the deep blue sea,* or in classical mythology, between *Scylla and Charybdis.*

In this conflict, he will try to avoid going one way or the other, that is, he may *shrink, recoil, hang back,* or *pull back* from the choice. He sees *both sides* of the question and would prefer to *come down squarely in the middle,* to *sit on* or *straddle the fence.* Or, he may *escape* by *circumventing* or *getting around* the issue. If he is (verbally) agile, he may *dodge* or *duck* the question, *sidestep* the issue, or *shy away from* or *shift* the topic to get *off the spot.* He may *sidetrack* or *shunt off* the issue, as if communication were a railway. In sporting terms, he may *fence* or *parry* the unwanted question. He may even *tergiversate*, which means "to turn one's back on straightforward action or statement."

If escape is not possible and he must respond, he may *pussyfoot* or *weasel*, that is, move as those animals do, or he may use *weasel words*. In other words, he may *prevaricate* ("to walk crookedly") or *vacillate*. To *leave the field*, he may *hedge* ("to go aside from the straight way") or *skirt* the issue. He may *beat around the bush* or give the other person the *runaround*. By *evasive* or *elusive* phrasing, he may *shift his position, back and fill, waffle* (from "waff," to move to and fro). In any case, his reply is likely to be *tangential* rather than *direct, straightforward*, and *forthright*. He may even *deviate* from the truth or not say the truth *straight-out*. . . .

OTHER POSSIBLE EXPLANATIONS OF EQUIVOCATION

There are several plausible alternatives to our theory, some of which may have already occurred to the reader. First, the cause of some or most equivocation could be, simply, *error*. What we are calling *equivocation* could be occasional random deviation from normal communication, which would otherwise be straightforward and clear. In other words, sometimes people make mistakes and speak (or write) inaccurately; this can happen to anyone, so such errors would reveal nothing. If this is so, then (recalling the examples in Chapter 1) we should not make too much of Mr. R's reply, the letter from a schizophrenic patient's mother, or the messages given by subjects in our experiments, despite their obvious syntactic and semantic oddness. If this explanation is applied, many of our examples can be dismissed as nit-picking, not worth following up or even dwelling upon. Also, two empirical predictions should hold: the incidence of equivocation should not be high (because it is error rather than the norm), nor should the frequency of equivocation vary with the characteristics of the situation.

A more substantial and traditional class of explanations would place the cause in the *equivocator*, that is, the person who generated the message. In this view, equivocation is attributable to the individual, hence not random (as error would be). A common intrapsychic approach is to invoke *individual differences*, that is, consistent traits or attributes that make individuals behave differently from each other. The equivocator is seen as different from other people, for reasons that might include the following: Some individuals are incompetent communicators, so that what they say does not usually make sense; some people are inarticulate and have difficulty making themselves understood; others are unscrupulous and avoid the truth; still others are very skillful at handling delicate issues diplomatically; politicians always waffle, never answering directly; people (such as Mr. R) who try to hide problems will inevitably reveal themselves unconsciously by their stammering, mistakes, and especially by nonverbal behaviors; schizophrenics (and their families) have cognitive or communicative deficits; and so forth. This approach, too, leads to empirical predictions: Again, the incidence of equivocation should not be high (because not all individuals have the characteristics that lead to it), and certain individuals should equivocate consistently, that is, there should be consistency across individuals rather than across situations.

Finally, there is another kind of explanation focused on the individual, although on general processes rather than individual differences. These processes might be, for example, the rules inferred by theorists such as Bowers, Elliott, and Desmond (1977), Brown and Levinson (1978), and others (described in Chapter 1) who explain direct and indirect communication by cognitive processes "inside" the communicator. We would point out that such theories focus on *how* equivocation might be generated, when it occurs, rather than on *why* it happens (or why it does not happen all the time). When the speaker is described as being polite (or devious), the nature of the eliciting situation is left implicit. The focus of the theory is on the internal processing that generates the message rather than on the situation that causes it. Without a statement about the situations that evoke it, such a theory cannot predict when equivocation will occur and when it will not.

Whether they propose general processes or individual differences, explanations focused on the person are easy to think of and quite plausible when applied to equivocal messages. Indeed, an explanation that is not focused on the person may seem strange: Virtually all traditional theories of human behavior assume that the cause of behavior is inside the individual. As noted at the end of Chapter 1, the inevitable result of this theoretical position is to relegate both the communicative situation and the communication itself to secondary status. Messages are studied only in order to understand the person, while situations are usually ignored.

We find none of the above alternative explanations of equivocation satisfactory and will rely for our explanation solely on our theory of the characteristics of the communicative situation in which equivocation occurs. Rather than portraying communication as a process that emanates from the individual and reflects primarily the individual's mental state, we use a wider focus that includes the impact of the individual's immediate social situation. Isolated individuals do not engage in communication. Communication only occurs when two or more people interact, and this interaction directly affects the messages that are chosen. Nor does an individual's message cease being important once it has been uttered or written. It will affect the receiver(s) and, therefore, the social situation of the sender. In order to find the causes of equivocation, we need to look at the immediate communicative situation.

It is, of course, tempting to reject any single explanation and to take instead an eclectic approach that accepts all three explanations—treating some instances as error, some as traits of individuals, and some as a reaction to the situation. This kind of explanation, if applied after the fact, would never be wrong. But it is the business of science to be wrong some of the time. A good theory makes a statement before the fact that can be shown by the data to be right or wrong. If we can always explain anything, then we will also never eliminate plausible but false ideas and move on to explore those that have a more promising empirical basis. It may well be that the phenomenon of equivocation is more complicated than our initial explanation proposes, but the phenomenon—and not timidity—should lead us to that conclusion.

If it is better to choose among theories, as we have done, it is equally important to clarify the metatheoretical assumptions behind our choice. Emphasizing the communicative and situational aspects of behavior is not to deny that people have minds, feelings, or reasons for what they do. We only propose to study another, equally interesting aspect of human existence, namely, the messages that people exchange. A situational theory of communication should not be confused with a *behaviorist* theory in psychology, wherein all intrapersonal processes are either denied or relabeled as overt behavior (e.g., motivation becomes "number of hours since last feeding," and expectations become "anticipatory goal responses"). We have no doubt that people think and feel; we simply believe that these private processes should be studied for their own sake and not as the necessary explanation of overt behavior such as communication. People do not usually say exactly what they think or feel, because overt behaviors are shaped by different parameters than are intrapsychic processes. Indeed, it is difficult to imagine what social interaction would be like if each individual interacted with others only on the basis of his or her own mental processes, without being affected by or affecting the other person. Social situations have their own rules, and the discovery of these rules is the goal of our approach to communication, including the specific case of equivocal communication.

AN EXPERIMENTAL STRATEGY FOR
UNDERSTANDING EQUIVOCATION

One advantage of a situational theory is that it permits truly experimental research, a method we prefer for reasons outlined below. This section will describe the overall strategy used to test our theory experimentally. Because laboratory experiments are not the usual or first choice of many communication and linguistic researchers, we will first look at the other alternatives.

There are a number of possible methods for studying equivocation (or any other communicative phenomenon). The method used by earlier theorists (both the Palo Alto Group and the rules theorists) was to offer a wide variety of examples. These might be clinical case studies, public events (such as news conferences), excerpts from fiction or film, or even examples created by the theorist to make a particular point. In many cases, the situation leading to the equivocation can be inferred from the example (e.g., in Chapter 1, Mr. R's "no-win" situation, or Ron Zeigler's reasons for not answering Helen Thomas's question). We call this method *exemplification*, in that the researcher either looks for or generates examples of the phenomenon. Although examples are invaluable for initial understanding, they can never be *proof* of a theory, because counter-examples can always be offered.

A more formal alternative is what is often called a *correlational* or a *field* study, in which the researcher would deliberately find circumstances where equivocation could be expected to arise and then examine whether it does. For example, the dialogues of marital couples who have serious conflicts could be compared to the dialogues of happily married couples. Strangers who are known to have different opinions on an important issue could be put together to discuss the issue, and their discourse could be compared to that of strangers who hold compatible opinions. However, even if the results show that the messages of such groups differ as predicted, the cause of the difference will not have been identified precisely: It could be attributable to any difference, known or unknown, between the two groups (e. g., differences in background, education, and so on). In other words, there would virtually always be alternative explanations for the results. This method, which we call *selection*, has advantages over exemplification, but it cannot convincingly settle theoretical issues of cause and effect because the researcher cannot have a firm grasp on the causal variables.

Finally, the researcher can arrange for certain important aspects of the situation to occur (or not occur) and then examine the consequences. If the basic logic of experimentation has been followed so that the groups are completely comparable except for the crucial variable, then the researcher can make causal inferences from the results: Some aspect of the situation can be identified as leading to equivocation because equivocation occurred only when this aspect of the situation was present. The true experiment, then, requires the direct *creation* of the conditions in which responses will be made.

So researchers have the choice of exemplification, selection, or creation. In simpler terms, the researcher may *notice* an example, *seek* contrasting groups, or *arrange* for groups to differ in predetermined ways. A great deal has been written about the characteristics of research conducted by these different methods, but there are only two true differences.

First, and most important, the phenomenon itself can limit the method. Any extremely rare or little understood phenomenon can only be studied initially by exemplification. Or, when the researcher cannot, for practical or ethical reasons, arrange for the causal process to happen (e.g., a long-standing family conflict), then this process can only be studied by the selection of contrasting groups. This is why situational theories can usually be tested by experimentation, but theories emphasizing personal characteristics of individuals (i. e., individual differences) usually cannot.

Second, the experimental method, when it can be used, is the most powerful way of studying a phenomenon. It delivers information more quickly and less ambiguously than the other two methods can, because alternative explanations can be systematically eliminated. True experiments are particularly good at establishing the probable cause of a phenomenon; indeed, this was the purpose for which the method was developed. Therefore, although we could study equivocation by the other two methods, we chose initially to do experiments.

We had another choice to make as well, namely, how to achieve some generalizability of our results. At best, the results of any successful experiment mean only that the same conditions should lead to the same result in the future. Such results can lead us to hope that the same principle would hold in other conditions as well, but the other conditions must themselves actually be studied to confirm this hope.

This is also the case for the methods of exemplification and selection, although many researchers wrongly believe that these methods are intrinsically more "naturalistic" and generalizable (e.g., Bavelas, 1984). What is true is that experimental control is a double-edged sword: It works best in simple situations. That is, it permits clear inference by removing alternative explanations, but (some would say, though we disagree) it thereby limits the richness and complexity of the phenomenon studied — the very richness and complexity that might make clear inference impossible.

In the case of equivocation and its situational causes, the problem comes down to the complexities of the situations and messages included in a particular experiment. An experiment eliciting equivocation in written messages will not tell us anything about face-to-face messages, where nonverbal aspects would also be available. Yet our research group respected the complexity of face-to-face messages far too much to tackle them first. Similarly, we wanted to use clear and controlled situations to evoke equivocation and yet to show that the effect generalized to many different situations.

Our solution has been to take a longer-term, programmatic view, planning a series of experiments over a considerable period of time, with the goal of increasing generalizability as we went along. That is, we began with experiments in which virtually every aspect was highly controlled; then we systematically broadened the scope of our experiments as we understood the phenomenon better. In this way, if at some point the results changed, we would be able to identify the problem. We entered the labyrinth of equivocation like Theseus, with a string tied securely at the entrance.

We have also used the principle of *varied replication*, in which we explored a deliberately varied class of carefully controlled situations at one level before moving on to the next. At the next level, we repeated some of the same situations and added some new ones. By this means, we hoped to pick up or "snowball" considerable generalizability.

SUMMARY

We propose that equivocation is caused by situations that present an avoidance-avoidance conflict, in which all direct messages would lead to negative consequences. The only way to avoid these consequences is to avoid direct communication, that is, to equivocate. Equivocation, then, is the communicative equivalent of "leaving the field." We do not accept explanations that would treat equivocation as error, as a function of individual differences, or solely as the product of cognitive processes such as internal rules. In order to test our theory, we have chosen a long-term experimental strategy of increasing complexity and varied replication.

4

The Conditions That Elicit Equivocation: First Experiments

The theory just described predicts that people frequently use equivocal communication, that when they equivocate depends upon their communicative situation, and that the specific element of the situation that causes equivocation is an avoidance-avoidance conflict.

To test these hypotheses, we initially conducted a series of five experiments (Bavelas, 1983), using a variety of hypothetical situations in which participants could chose among several written replies, including at least one equivocal reply. We used this "forced choice" among replies written by us (rather than obtaining the participants' own spontaneous replies) because our purpose was to understand the characteristics of the communicative *situation*, which we propose is the cause of equivocation, rather than to study equivocation itself. Of course, this format would tell us nothing about naturally occurring equivocation, but we could (and did) go on to study people's own equivocations in subsequent experiments. First, though, we needed a clear test of whether our theory was viable at all. As will be seen, this restricted format had the desirable quality of being able to falsify our theory quickly. If a theory is wrong, it is better to know quickly from simple experiments than to be prevented from knowing because of the complexity of the data gathered.

EXPERIMENT 1: EVOKING EQUIVOCATION

The Situations

Participants in this experiment read the following instructions on a sheet of paper:

Try to imagine the situation described below, as vividly as possible. Then read all the choices and indicate which you would write in this situation.

Remember, (1) try to really put yourself in the situation, and also (2) limit yourself to just the choices given. (3) We are not interested in what you think you should say, but in what you think you actually would say.

They went on to read one of three different scenarios, each with a different set of messages. A random third of the participants was presented with this scenario:

Another student in a small class, which meets three times a week for the entire year, has just given a class presentation. It was very badly done—poorly prepared and poorly delivered. After he sits down again, he passes you a note: "How did I do?" You have to jot something down and pass it back to him. Which of the following would you write down?

You did very well. I really liked it.

You were terrible; bad job.

Not well, but don't feel bad about it.

You were braver than I would be!

The conflict in this situation is that telling the other person he did badly (which was true) would be hurtful, while telling him he did well would be kind but false. As can be seen, the replies we wrote offered four different options: A false message ("**You did very well. I really like it**"), a hurtful truth ("**You were terrible; bad job**"), an attempt to be truthful about the presentation without hurting the person ("**Not well, but don't feel bad about it**"), and not answering the question ("**You were braver than I would be!**"). As will be explained later, the order of these alternatives was randomly varied.

Another third of the participants read a different scenario:

You have received a gift from someone you really like a lot, but the gift is awful, and you don't like it at all. Now you have to write a thank you note to that person (who lives in another province). Which of the following conveys the gist of what you would say?

The gift is perfect; I really love it.

I don't like the gift and am going to exchange or return it.

I like you, but I don't like the gift.

I appreciate your thoughtfulness.

Again, the conflict is between telling a hurtful truth or a kind falsehood, and the four possible replies fit the same four tactics: A pleasant but false message ("**The gift is perfect; I really love it.**"), a brutal truth ("**I don't like the gift and am going to exchange or return it.**"), an attempt to handle the conflict by telling the truth about both the gift and the relationship ("**I like you, but I don't like the gift.**"), and avoiding saying anything about the gift ("**I appreciate your thoughtfulness.**").

Finally, one third of the participants were given still another scenario:

> *You are caught in a bind between two people you know and like equally well. "A" is someone who worked for you some time ago; "B" is another person, who is thinking of hiring "A." The trouble is "A" was not a good employee— nice but incompetent. You must write a letter of reference about "A" to "B". Which tack would you take, that is, which of the following corresponds to the gist of the message you would write?*

"A" was an excellent employee; I recommend him.

Don't hire "A"; he was not a good employee.

"A" is a nice person but not a good employee.

It's been years since I employed "A," so I can't answer specifically.

This is a conflict between loyalties—telling a truth to "B" (which would hurt "A") or misleading "B" on an important matter. The four replies represent the same four options as in the other scenarios: a falsehood ("**A was an excellent employee; I recommend him.**"), a truth ("**Don't hire A; he was not a good employee.**"), an attempt to handle the conflict by telling both truths ("**A is a nice person but not a good employee.**"), and not answering ("**It's been years since I employed A, so I can't answer specifically.**").

Scale Values of the Messages

We had written the messages intending them to vary from clear to equivocal. To verify this, our judges scaled the four alternatives for each scenario according to the procedures described in Chapter 2. These values are given in Tables 4.1, 4.2, and 4.3. Browsing through the scale values for these messages is a good way to get a feeling for the four different dimensions and what our judges saw that makes a message high or low on each.

Consider the "Class" set in Table 4.1 (of which the fourth message was analyzed in Chapter 2). Recall that the Content dimension (first column)

TABLE 4.1
Experiment 1: Class Presentation (Forced Choice) — Message Values

Message	Content	Sender	Receiver	Context	Sum
You did very well. I really liked it.	-.54	-.78	-.38	-.63	-2.33
You were terrible; bad job.	-.35	.10	-.32	-.58	-1.15
Not well, but don't feel bad about it.	.97	1.24	.79	-.21	2.79
You were braver than I would be!	.08	-.56	-.09	1.42	.69

TABLE 4.2

Experiment 1: Employee Reference (Forced Choice)—Message Values

Message	Content	Sender	Receiver	Context	Sum
"A" was an excellent employee; I recommend him.	-.24	-.74	-.25	-.63	-1.86
Don't hire "A"; he was not a good employee.	-.26	.62	-.32	-.51	-.47
"A" is a nice person but not a good employee.	.14	.57	.34	.77	1.82
It's been years since I employed "A," so I can't answer specifically.	.35	-.45	.24	.36	.50

TABLE 4.3
Experiment 1: Gift (Forced Choice)—Message Values

Message	Content	Sender	Receiver	Context	Sum
The gift is perfect; I really love it.	.05	.11	-.02	-.70	-.56
I don't like the gift and am going to exchange or return it.	-.17	-.11	.46	-.64	-.46
I like you, but I don't like the gift.	.08	-.11	-.34	-.03	-.40
I appreciate your thoughtfulness.	.05	.11	-.11	1.36	1.41

refers to how clear or unclear the message is, in terms of what is being said. The first two messages have the lowest values on this dimension (–.54 and –.35), which means that they are relatively clear in content. The message with a value of –.08 is at the average (which is always zero) for this set: saying that "**You were braver than I would be!**" introduces a hypothetical comparison and is somewhat less clear than saying, plainly, either "**you were terrible**" or "**you did very well**". The more laconic and cryptic third message ("**Not well, but don't feel bad about it.**") is one standard deviation (.97) above the mean of zero, that is, its content is relatively unclear compared to the three other messages in this set.

Moving over one column to the Sender dimension, we can see the extent to which the message is the writer's own opinion. The two messages with the lowest (negative) values both contain a first-person pronoun ("**You did very well. I really liked it.**" and "**You were braver than I would be!**"). The second message ("**You were terrible; bad job.**") does not contain "**I**" but gives a firm opinion and was scaled around zero (.10) on this dimension. The third message has the highest value (1.24). It avoids using "**I**" and does not say or even imply clearly *who* thinks he did "**not well**" — perhaps the class, perhaps the writer, perhaps both. To understand its vagueness on this dimension, imagine rewriting this message to make the sender clear; for example, "**I don't think you did well, but don't feel bad about it**" is much more direct — and more painful.

The third message is also the highest on the Receiver dimension (.79); it is not as clearly addressed to the other person in the situation as are the other three messages, all of which contain "**you**".

The Context dimension indicates how well the message answers the question asked ("**How did I do?**"). The first three messages answer this question directly and have low values (–.63, –.58, and –.21). The fourth message answers an entirely different question ("**How brave was I, compared to you?**") and, at 1.42, is almost one and a half standard deviations above the mean.

The last column is the Sum over all four dimensions. The first two messages (one true, one false) are clear, with overall negative values, while the two other alternatives are equivocal, with positive Sums.

The same principles can be seen in the other two sets of messages as well. For example, in the Context column of Table 4.2 (the Employee scenario), the first message answers the question ("**What kind of an employee was A?**"), but the third message answers a different, unasked question first ("**Is A a nice person?**"). Their respective values are –.63 and .77. In the Gift scenario (Table 4.3), "**I appreciate your thoughtfulness**" is even more equivocal, as it does not at all answer the implicit question, **"How do you like the gift I sent you?"** Its scale value on this dimension is 1.36. However, this message is about average on the other three dimensions; it is a good answer to the wrong question.

The values of these messages on the Sender and Receiver dimensions tended to be determined by the presence of **"I"** or **"you,"** respectively. Another clue was the appropriateness of the message for the receiver. For example, messages that focus solely on the person's qualifications as an employee and make a hiring recommendation (i.e., the first two messages in that set) were judged relatively more likely to be addressed to "a fellow employer who is asking for a reference" than was a message that begins by saying that a potential employee is a "nice person."

In all three scenarios, we had intended the first two alternatives to be the most direct and unequivocal; this was confirmed by their scale values. The Sum (last column) for these messages was always negative. In contrast, the Sum for the patently evasive fourth message in each set was always above zero. We did not know, in advance, whether messages that addressed the conflict (the third message in each set) would be seen as clear or not. To our initial surprise, the judges scaled them as the *most* equivocal messages in the Class and Employee scenarios. A message that describes a contradictory situation is likely to be contradictory itself. It is apparently difficult or impossible to be straightforward within the constraints of some situations. Put another way, softening the blow means being less clear.

Design Considerations

Each of the three different scenarios was an avoidance-avoidance conflict, and the replies that were offered represented the possible communicative options. We predicted that people would avoid the direct replies (whether true or false) in favor of the more indirect ones. If, as outlined in Chapter 3, equivocation is merely error, then the equivocal options would be chosen infrequently. Similarly, if equivocation is a function of individual differences (such as deviousness, an inability to communicate well, or a more serious pathology), then some people would choose the equivocal replies, but most would not.

In order to be able to interpret the results unambiguously, possible defects in our experimental format had to be considered beforehand. First, it could be argued that hypothetical situations offering messages written and provided by the researchers would create a completely artificial situation, unlike anything in ordinary life. The important question to ask about such a criticism is: If this were so, what would be the effect on people's choices? Presumably, if the situations were meaningless to the participants, their choices would be made randomly. Conversely, a nonrandom pattern of choices would suggest that participants were responding to the situation.

A second, related possibility is that the participants would not put themselves fully into situations that they were only reading about, so there would be no real conflict. However, in our pilot studies, people reading the situations groaned, winced, or smiled wryly—reactions indicating to us that they readily recognized or identified with the conflict. In any case, the data again would tell: If there were no conflict, the participants would choose one of the two direct replies, because it would not matter that these were (hypothetically) hurtful or false.

Third, it could be argued that, although the participants might project themselves into the situation as requested, they would simply role-play and choose stereotyped, "proper" answers, rather than what they would actually say if they were in the situation. In that case, they would probably choose one of the direct answers (especially a true one) rather than the patently evasive and temporizing replies.

We were also curious about whether there exists a kind of "double standard" in such situations: one *should* tell a truth but one *would* (really) equivocate. We tested this by having two different instructions. Recall that the introduction (given at the beginning of this chapter) asked for what they actually *would* say; a second version, given to half of the participants, asked for what they felt they *should* say:

Try to imagine the situation described below as vividly as possible. Then read all the choices and indicate which you should write *in this situation.*

Remember, (1) try to really put yourself in the situation, and also (2) limit yourself to just the choices given. (3) We are not interested in what you think you actually would *say, but in what you think you* should *say.*

That is, we deliberately sought the stereotyped or role-playing choices. If the two different instructions produced different choices, this would mean that there is a discrepancy between principle and practice in such situations. Communicative avoidance-avoidance conflicts would be more complicated than our theory proposes, in which case our theory would have to be amended.

A fifth problem could be that people might simply tend to choose the first (or last) message they read. To ascertain this, the order of the choices was systematically varied across respondents. There are 24 possible orders in which four replies can be offered, and all of these were used.

Finally, it is possible to think of specific aspects of any one of the scenarios (e.g., lack of familiarity with writing a letter of reference or the particular way one of the replies was phrased) that would affect an individual's choice for a given scenario. So we used three different scenarios, each with entirely different messages to choose from. If the same results obtained in all scenarios, then it must be that minor specific aspects do not matter.

For the reasons just given, we crossed three different scenarios (Class, Gift, and Employee) with two different instructions ("would" versus "should") and 24 different orders of messages. Each of the resulting 144 unique stimuli was typed on a single sheet by a programmable typewriter. Two of each stimulus were produced, and these 288 sheets were put in random order, using permutation blocks of the six scenario/instruction combinations. In addition, several dozen extras were added, because more than 288 participants were available and in case some of the 288 could not be used for any reason.

Experimental Procedure

The participants were students in two large introductory psychology classes. The experimenter came at the beginning or end of the class period and asked them to volunteer by completing one of the sheets (which were being handed out in their random order). She summarized the general instructions, emphasizing that they should imagine they were actually in the situation and also that they should limit themselves initially to the replies given on the sheet. If they felt that another response would be more suitable, they could write that response on the back of the sheet afterwards. When everyone was done, the purpose of the study was explained and questions were answered.

It is important to emphasize that these procedures gave the participants complete anonymity. The response sheets contained no identifying information, and because there were 144 different versions, it was virtually impossible for either the researchers or neighboring students to know which choice was being made.

We analyzed 287 of the completed sheets. Some of the extras that had been filled in were used to replace any of the original 288 that were not usable (e.g., because the choice was not clearly indicated). In this way, only 1 stimulus sheet was still missing (we had only one, not two, of a particular order of messages for a "Class/would" version).

Results

The frequencies of people's choices, along with the Sum of scale values, are given in Table 4.4. As the chi-square values clearly indicate, people did not choose randomly. The most equivocal messages were the most frequently chosen. Indeed, the frequency with which participants chose a message in each scenario was almost perfectly correlated with the Sum for that message. There was no significant difference between the choices people said they *would* make and those they said they *should* make. Nor was there any effect of the order in which a message appeared among the choices.

These results eliminated two theoretical alternatives described in Chapter 3: Equivocation was chosen far too frequently to be considered either mere error or attributable to some characteristic of particular individuals. Errors and individual differences could not account for the 80% to 98% of participants who chose messages with the highest mean scale values.

The results also eliminated potential problems specific to the format we used. If the situation had been entirely artificial to the participants, they would have chosen randomly — but their choices were distinctly nonrandom. If the situation had created no conflict between hurtful truths and kind falsehoods, then they should have chosen these direct replies — but they did not. Nor was there any evidence that participants avoided the evasive messages in favor of stereotyped "proper" replies (the direct messages). The results also indicated that what one *should* say in this situation is the same as what one *would* say. We interpret this as confirming our assumption that most people feel that they would not, by their personal choice, be either untruthful or tell a hurtful truth and also that they should not, as judged by others, do so either.

Finally, the results were the same regardless of the particular scenario or set of messages each participant saw. We can therefore conclude that, in any conflict similar to these three, people would choose an equivocal message, that is, one with high scale values. The scaling and the experiment were two entirely independent procedures, yet the values from the former predicted choices in the latter.

EXPERIMENT 2: ADDING A CONTROL GROUP

The success of Experiment 1 led to an ironic problem, which was the possibility that the messages we call equivocal are not rare but are in fact the

TABLE 4.4

Experiment 1: Frequencies of Choice in Class, Employee, and Gift Situations

Situation	Message	Sum	Frequency[a]
Class	You did very well. I really liked it.	-2.33	3
	You were terrible; bad job.	-1.15	5
	Not well, but don't feel bad about it.	2.79	48
	You were braver than I would be!	.79	39
Employee	"A" was an excellent employee; I recommend him.	-1.86	0
	Don't hire "A"; he was not a good employee.	-.47	2
	"A" is a nice person but not a good employee.	1.82	66
	It's been years since I employed "A," so I can't answer specifically.	.50	28
Gift	The gift is perfect; I really love it.	-.56	11
	I don't like the gift and am going to exchange or return it.	-.46	4
	I like you, but I don't like the gift.	-.40	5
	I appreciate your thoughtfulness.	1.41	76

a. Chi-square for first two versus second two messages (as listed above): Class = 67.48, $df = 3$, $p < .001$; Employee = 118.34, $df = 3$, $p < .001$; Gift = 151.42, $df = 3$, $p < .001$

usual replies in these situations. It may be that, for some reason unrelated to conflict, people simply prefer to choose indirect or ambiguous replies rather than direct ones. Alternative explanations of this kind would predict high levels of equivocation regardless of whether conflict is present in the situation and so could be tested by the use of a control group in which no conflict existed. We had not included a control group in Experiment 1, which was already a large and complicated experiment, so this was our next priority.

Control group designs are also the closest we can come to testing any of the "rules" approaches to equivocation (described in Chapter 1). As noted in Chapter 3, current rules theories do not offer the possibility of direct tests because they consist of descriptive analyses or cognitive models of how indirect communication might have been generated, rather than specifying the conditions under which it will and will not occur. If we can show that equivocation occurs in certain situations and not in others, then we can at least show the limitations of a rules approach, which cannot make such predictions.

The Gift and Class scenarios were modified to produce an alternative version in which no avoidance-avoidance conflict existed, for example:

> *You have received a gift from someone you really like a lot. The gift is great, and you like it very much. The friend, who lives in another province, expects a thank-you note telling how you like the gift. So you are going to write a short note. Which of the following conveys the gist of what you would say?*

The gift is perfect; I really love it.

I don't like the gift and am going to exchange or return it.

I appreciate your thoughtfulness.

While the second choice does not make much sense in the control condition, the first and third messages are both reasonable choices, so participants would be choosing between a straightforward truth and a pleasant equivocation.

There were two minor changes (from Experiment 1) made in both the conflict and control versions of this scenario. First, there was an explicit requirement to comment on the gift (the friend "expects a thank-you note telling how you like the gift"), because this was the implicit question that had been used for scaling the messages on the Context dimension. Also, the third alternative ("**I like you, but I don't like the gift.**") was not included, because it was seldom chosen in Experiment 1 and was a highly implausible choice in the control condition. Except for these changes, the conflict version was just like the Gift scenario in Experiment 1.

The control version of the Class scenario read as follows:

> *Another student in a small class, which meets three times a week for the entire year, has just given a class presentation. It was very good—well prepared and well delivered. After he sits down again, he passes you a note: "**How did I do?**" You have to jot something down and pass it back to him. Which of the following would you write?*

The conflict version was exactly as in Experiment 1, and the same four messages were offered as choices. Of these four, two were also plausible alternatives in the control condition (the truth and the equivocation).

The same general introduction and instructions were used. Because there had been no difference between the "would" and "should" instructions, only "would" was used in this and all future experiments. Again, all possible orders of the messages for each scenario (6 orders of the three Gift alternatives and 24 orders of the four Class alternatives) were used and randomly assigned.

Because the frequencies of choice in Experiment 1 had been so overwhelming, we did not need to use such a large number of participants in this experiment. A different introductory psychology class was approached with the same oral instructions and 96 randomly permuted sheets. There were 48 each of the Class and Gift scenarios, half in the conflict version and half in the control version. Each of these subsets of 24 contained equal numbers of all possible orders of messages.

The results are summarized in Table 4.5. The conflict versions replicated (proportionately) the results of Experiment 1. In the control versions, equivocal messages were seldom chosen, indicating that they are not invariably preferred. When there was no communicative conflict, direct messages were chosen. Only when conflict existed were equivocal messages the predominant choice. Thus, the situation determined the choice of message.

EXPERIMENT 3: CONTROL FOR UNPLEASANTNESS

One of the precepts of experimental work is to keep saying, "Yes, but . . ." Odd as it sometimes seems, trying to attack a theory is the best way to strengthen it. So we considered another possible explanation for the results of these two experiments.

TABLE 4.5

Experiment 2: Frequencies of Choice in Conflict and Nonconflict Conditions (Class and Gift)

Situation	Message	Sum	Condition[a]	
			Conflict	Nonconflict
Class	You did very well. I really liked it.	-2.33	0	23
	You were terrible; bad job.	-1.15	1	0
	Not well, but don't feel bad about it.	2.79	13	0
	You were braver than I would be!	.69	10	1
Gift	The gift is perfect; I really love it.	-.56	4	21
	I don't like the gift and am going exchange or return it.	-.46	0	0
	I appreciate your thoughtfulness.	1.41	20	3

a. Chi-square for first two vs. second two messages in conflict vs. nonconflict Class conditions = 40.33, $df = 3$, $p < .001$.
Chi-square for first two versus third message in conflict vs. nonconflict Gift conditions = 24.13, $df = 2$, $p < .001$.

All of the conflict situations we had created were unpleasant to imagine oneself in. Perhaps this global unpleasantness, rather than the specific presence of a communicative conflict, caused people to choose equivocation. There are two plausible reasons why this might be so. First, our theory may be correct in casting equivocal communication as avoidance communication but incorrect about what is being avoided; it may be the general unpleasantness rather than the communicative conflict that people are avoiding. The other possibility is that, when faced with such an unpleasant situation, people simply communicate poorly. They may lose their focus or make errors at a much higher rate than would normally be expected. Because the control conditions had been pleasant, this alternative explanation could easily account for the results of both Experiments 1 and 2.

The issue can be resolved by creating a control condition that is also unpleasant, but for reasons other than a communicative conflict. The "unpleasantness" hypothesis would have to predict that equivocal messages would then be chosen in both the conflict and control versions. We predict that only the conflict condition will elicit equivocation.

Therefore, we rewrote the Class and Gift scenarios one last time, creating unpleasant but nonconflictual control versions, for example:

You are in a class which meets three times a week for the entire year. Each student has to make an individual presentation to the class. Today you and another student gave your presentations, separately—first you, then him. You were both very scared. Yours went terribly. You were not ready yet, too nervous, and generally did a very bad job.

The other student, after you, did very well—his presentation was well prepared and well delivered. After he sits down again, he passes you a note: "**How did I do?**" *You have to jot something down and pass it back to him. Which of the following would you write?*

I think you did fine.

I think you did a bad job.

Not bad.

We assumed that personally failing in a presentation would be very unpleasant but would not present a communicative conflict with regard to the question asked by the other person. One might wish to have done better, but it is too late and in any case irrelevant to the other person's question. Thus, while unpleasant, a personal failure does not make the communicative options in this control situation into bad ones.

(The only conceivable effect of personal failure on the communicative options was the possibility that, especially because the choice was anonymous, a respondent might admit to wanting to "sting" the successful other by choosing the second or third message. This possibility would be revealed by different results in this versus the other scenario.)

In the conflict version, the participant was to imagine that he or she had done well on the presentation but that the other person did badly. Only the specific words necessary to create this difference were changed; the two versions were otherwise identical, and the same three messages were offered in both versions. (The written suggestions of several participants in Experiment 1 had given us "**Not bad**" as a new equivocation.) The scale values of these messages are given in Table 4.6. Notice that our increased familiarity with the factors affecting scale values (that is, what we were learning from the judges about the details of messages) permitted us to write alternatives that were distinctly different on all four dimensions.

The Gift scenario was changed to include an unpleasant control condition by having the person thoughtlessly forget a friend's birthday:

You have received a birthday gift from someone you really like a lot. This person's birthday is on the same day as yours, but you completely forgot it this year, and you sent nothing. The gift you received is great, and you like it very much.

The friend, who lives in another province, expects a thank-you note telling how you like the gift. So you are going to write a short note about the gift you received (without mentioning the one you didn't send). Which of the following conveys the gist of what you would say?

I really like the gift you sent. Thank you very much.

I don't like the gift you sent.

Thank you very much for the gift, it was very kind of you.

Again, the control version was designed to produce unpleasantness but not conflict. It is unpleasant to have forgotten a good friend's birthday (especially when it is on the same day as one's own!), but this does not produce any conflict over what to say to the friend about the gift he or she sent. In the conflict version, the person had remembered to send a gift, but the one received was awful. The two versions were otherwise identical, with the same three alternatives offered as messages. The scale values of these messages are also given in Table 4.6.

TABLE 4.6
Experiment 3: Class Presentation and Gift (Forced Choice) — Message Values

Situation	Message	Content	Sender	Receiver	Context	Sum
Class	I think you did fine.	-.38	-.58	-.58	-.52	-2.06
	I think you did a bad job.	-.73	-.58	-.36	-.62	-2.29
	Not bad.	1.11	1.16	.94	1.15	4.36
Gift	I really like the gift you sent. Thank you very much.	-.22	-.50	-.25	-.60	-1.57
	I don't like the gift you sent.	-.32	-.51	-.20	-.55	-1.58
	Thank you very much for the gift, it was very kind of you.	.53	1.01	.44	1.15	3.13

Both versions of the two scenarios (with equal numbers of all possible orders of the three alternatives) were prepared in the same format as before and randomly ordered. We also attached a second sheet, a questionnaire that included a request to rate how uncomfortable the situation was. Seventy-two students in several different classes participated.

The first result of interest is the check on our manipulation of unpleasantness; these ratings would indicate whether the conflict and control conditions were matched as we had intended. The mean rating of uncomfortableness was actually higher for the control version of both scenarios than for the conflict version. For the Gift scenario, this difference was statistically significant ($t = 2.32$, $df = 34$, $p < .05$, two-tailed). Thus, if unpleasantness were the causal factor, the control condition should elicit, if anything, more equivocation than the conflict condition.

The choices of messages (given in Table 4.7) confirmed that it is conflict, and not just unpleasantness, that leads to the choice of equivocal messages. In both scenarios, few people chose the ambiguous messages unless there was a communicative conflict. Without a conflict, unpleasantness alone did not deflect the directness of communication, even when the unpleasantness was greater than that produced by the conflict. Thus, unpleasantness that is apart from the immediate communicative situation is not sufficient to elicit equivocation. The essential antecedent of equivocation is that direct messages lead to negative consequences.

EXPERIMENT 4: APPROACH VERSUS AVOIDANCE CONFLICTS

Experiments 2 and 3 had narrowed the antecedents of equivocation to a communicative conflict. Equivocal communication is much preferred when, and only when, such a conflict exists. The purpose of the last two experiments to be conducted in forced-choice format was to refine the causal evidence even further, to show that it is specifically an *avoidance-avoidance* conflict that leads to equivocation.

Recall (from Chapter 3) that an *approach-approach* conflict should lead to direct communication. Although there is a conflict (because once one option has been chosen, the other must be foregone), nothing in the situation opposes clear communication. When the direct alternatives lead to positive outcomes, no avoidance is required. Thus, if these two different kinds of conflict existed in essentially the same situation, we would predict that only

TABLE 4.7

Experiment 3: Frequencies of Choice in Conflict and Unpleasant Nonconflict Conditions (Class and Gift)

Situation	Message	Sum	Condition[a]	
			Conflict	Nonconflict
Class	I think you did fine.	-2.06	4	17
	I think you did a bad job.	-2.29	1	0
	Not bad.	4.36	13	1
Gift	I really like the gift you sent. Thank you very much.	-1.57	1	11
	I don't like the gift you sent.	-1.58	0	0
	Thank you very much for the gift, it was very kind of you.	3.13	17	7

a. Chi-square for first two versus third message (as listed above) in conflict and nonconflict conditions: Class = 16.8, $df = 2$, $p < .001$; Gift = 12.5, $df = 2$, $p. < .001$.

the avoidance conflict would lead to equivocation. The approach conflict should be resolved by choosing one or the other of the direct messages.

We created two new scenarios in which there could be either two negative, direct messages plus an equivocation *or* two positive, direct messages and the same equivocation. The first was the Report scenario. The approach-approach version was as follows:

> *Someone you work with arrives at a staff meeting, where she is going to present a report. She is wearing a new dress and also has a new hair style. Both are great — she really looks good. She sits down next to you and passes you a note:* "How do I look?"

> *You are going to write a note and pass it back to her. Of the choices below, which would you write?*

> **Your dress is really nice.**

> **Your hair looks great that way.**

> **Don't worry — you'll do fine.**

Notice that, because of the forced choice, one and only one message can be chosen; it is not possible to say that both the dress and hair look good. The person has to opt for one and leave the other unsaid. This is the essence of an approach-approach conflict.

The reader can probably guess by now the avoidance-avoidance version of the Report scenario:

> *Someone you work with arrives at a staff meeting, where she is going to present a report. She is wearing a new dress and also has a new hair style. Both are awful — she really looks bad. She sits down next to you and passes you a note:* "How do I look?"

> *You are going to write a note and pass it back to her. Of the choices below, which would you write?*

> **Your dress doesn't suit you.**

> **Your hair doesn't look good that way.**

> **Don't worry — you'll do fine.**

The conflict in this case was between two unkind truths (just as the approach conflict was between two kind truths). When both of the direct messages would be hurtful, both should "repel" the individual.

Each set of three messages was scaled separately. As one would expect, though, the positive and negative versions of the same message (e.g., "**Your dress is really nice**" and "**Your dress doesn't suit you**") received virtually identical equivocation values. In Table 4.8, the average of the positive and negative versions is given as the value for both members of the pair.

The other new scenario was the Application, which also had two versions:

Someone you know quite well is filling out a job application. He is both bright and a really nice person—easy to get along with and intelligent as well.

*He asks for your advice about filling out the application. In particular, one of the questions is, "**What is your most important good quality?**" and he wonders what to say. You are interrupted by a phone call, so he says to leave him a note with what you think is his most important good quality.*

If you had to choose from the following three replies, which would you write?

You are very intelligent.

You are exceptionally easy to get along with.

What do you think?

The avoidance version had the same structure but read as follows:

Someone you know quite well is filling out a job application. He is not very bright and also not a particularly nice person—neither easy to get along with nor intelligent.

*He asks for your advice about filling out the application. In particular, one of the questions is, "**What is your most important fault?**" and he wonders what to say. You are interrupted by a phone call, so he says to leave him a note with what you think is his most important fault.*

If you had to choose from the following three replies, which would you write?

You are not very intelligent.

You are quite difficult to get along with.

What do you think?

This is a particularly fiendish avoidance conflict, offering a choice of two insults and a way to avoid choosing. The scale values for these messages are in Table 4.8.

Notice that, as in all of the experiments in this format, we have provided reasons why the response must be in written form (here, because of the interrupting phone call). If we had asked respondents what they would say

TABLE 4.8

Experiment 4: Report and Application (Forced Choice) — Message Values

Situation	Message[a]	Content	Sender	Receiver	Context	Sum
Report	Your hair looks great that way. Your hair doesn't look good that way.	-.41	-.09	.16	-.70	-1.04
	Your dress is really nice. Your dress doesn't suit you.	-.45	-.12	-.90	-.35	-1.82
	Don't worry—you'll do fine.	.86	.21	.74	1.05	2.86
Application	You are exceptionally easy to get along with. You are quite difficult to get along with.	-.44	-.53	-.33	-.48	-1.78
	You are very intelligent. You are not very intelligent.	-.40	-.12	.02	-.53	-1.03
	What do you think?	.84	.65	.31	1.01	2.81

a. Both approach and avoidance versions of the first two messages are given; their scale values, which are virtually identical, were averaged.

(in person), there would be no way of knowing *how* each was thinking of saying it—enthusiastically, hesitantly, or whatever.

In both scenarios, the messages themselves help induce the conflict. The two direct choices, which create the conflict, were always the first two messages, and the equivocation was always the last. It was important that the two options (hair versus dress, intelligence versus getting along) were emphasized equally, so their order in the text and their order in the messages were varied in random permutations. The two scenarios (Report and Application), two kinds of conflict (approach or avoidance), two orders of option in text, and two orders of option in messages produced 16 unique combinations. We also attached a questionnaire that asked a question about the reasons behind the choice.

Ninety-six students in a number of different classes participated, with the usual instructions and random assignment. Their choices are given in Table 4.9. There was a significant difference as predicted for the Report scenario: Participants chose the equivocal message more in the avoidance than in the approach conflict. However, many chose the equivocation in the approach conflict as well. We concluded, based on the respondents' written comments, that the question **"How do I look?"** was often interpreted as a request for reassurance about presenting the report. The equivocal alternative happened also to be reassuring, and this may be why it was chosen so frequently in the approach conflict. However, if we accept this interpretation, then we must also accept it for the avoidance conflict—the third message may have been chosen because it was reassuring, not because it was equivocal.

In any case, the results for the Application scenario did not support our theory at all; the choices for the approach version were statistically indistinguishable from those for the avoidance version. The participants' questionnaire responses made it clear that we had not analyzed this situation accurately. To the participants in the approach version, the two direct alternatives (**"You are very intelligent."** and **"You are exceptionally easy to get along with."**) carried a risk of negative consequences. The participants were not sure which would impress the employer more, intelligence or sociability. If the employer wanted someone easy to get along with and the participant had said to emphasize intelligence instead, then the applicant might not get the job. The participant, in giving the advice, would have said the wrong thing. It may be better not to give advice at all when it could be wrong, especially if the wrong advice would have practical consequences. Therefore, equivocation would be preferable. This plausible interpretation illustrates how difficult it is to create pure instances of particular kinds of conflicts. The

TABLE 4.9

Experiment 4: Frequencies of Choice in Approach-Approach and Avoidance-Avoidance Conditions (Report and Condition)

Situation	Message	Sum	Condition[a] (Approach-Approach) +/+	(Avoidance-Avoidance) -/-
Report	Your hair looks great that way. Your hair doesn't look good that way.	-1.04	11	1
	Your dress is really nice. Your dress doesn't suit you.	-1.82	2	0
	Don't worry—you'll do fine.	2.86	11	23
Application	You are exceptionally easy to get along with. You are quite difficult to get along with.	-1.78	4	2
	You are very intelligent. You are not very intelligent.	-1.03	7	6
	What do you think?	2.81	13	16

a. Chi-square for first two versus third message in approach versus avoidance conflict: Report = 14.5, $df = 2$, $p < .001$; Application = .78, $df = 2$, p = n.s.

immediate communicative situation may have other, unintended aspects, not immediately apparent to us, some of which affect the respondents' choices. Fortunately, we had asked participants to explain their choices, and their comments told us where we had gone wrong.

However convincing this explanation is (after the fact), the reader will have noticed that it remains a rationalization. What we are saying, essentially, is: Although we had intended to create an approach conflict, on second thought (and after having seen the results), it was really an avoidance conflict, in which case the frequent choice of equivocation makes sense. But a plausible after-the-fact interpretation does not, by alchemy, transform an empirical failure into a success. The interpretation must become an hypothesis that can be tested, like any other hypothesis, by predicting new results *before* the fact. This was the purpose of the next experiment.

EXPERIMENT 5: REVISED CONFLICT SCENARIOS

The results of Experiment 4 taught us a good deal about the subtlety of writing conflict situations and choices of messages. Putting that into practice, we rewrote the Application scenario by removing any practical consequences with a potential employer. It became the Quiz scenario:

> *Someone you know quite well is filling out a "personality quiz" in a magazine. He is both bright and a really nice person—easy to get along with and intelligent as well.*
>
> *He asks you for your advice about filling out the "quiz." In particular, one of the questions is, "What is your most important good quality?" and he wonders what to say. You are interrupted by a phone call, so he says to leave him a note with what you think is his most important good quality.*

The avoidance version was produced by changes similar to those in Experiment 4, that is, a person who was both hard to get along with and not intelligent was filling out the magazine quiz. In both versions, the choice of messages offered was the same as in Experiment 4. The Application scenario from Experiment 4 was also included, unchanged, so that we could compare results within the same experiment. We predicted that the Application scenario would replicate the results of Experiment 4, but that the Quiz scenario would show the predicted difference between approach and avoidance versions, with equivocation chosen in the avoidance but not in the approach version.

Figure 4.1.

Recall that the Report scenario had some problems as well, which we examined in this experiment by deleting the report. This became the New Look scenario, in which the other person arrives with a new dress and new hair style to attend a regular staff meeting; there is no mention of a report. The original scenario, with the Report, was also used. Both scenarios, however, had a new equivocal alternative, which was evasive without being reassuring: **"You've changed!"** We predicted that, with these changes, the results should follow our theory even more strongly. Both avoidance versions (and not the approach versions) should elicit equivocation, which would eliminate the alternative interpretation that the equivocal message was merely reassuring.

To summarize, there were four scenarios (Application and Quiz, Report and New Look), each of which had an approach and an avoidance version. We predicted that the equivocal reply would be chosen in the avoidance version of all four scenarios and also in the erstwhile approach version of the

TABLE 4.10

Experiment 5: Revised Approach and Avoidance Conflicts(Forced Choice) — Message Values

Situation	Message[a]	Content	Sender	Receiver	Context	Sum
Report and New Look	I think your hair looks great that way. I don't think your hair looks good that way.	-.56	-.47	.03	-.61	-1.61
	I think your dress is really nice. I don't think your dress suits you.	-.53	-.47	-.94	-.36	-2.30
	You've changed!	1.09	.92	.91	.97	3.89
Application and Quiz	You are exceptionally easy to get along with. You are quite difficult to get along with.	-.30	-.72	-.48	-.55	-2.05
	You are very intelligent. You are not very intelligent.	-.52	-.40	-.50	-.60	-2.02
	What do you think?	.82	1.11	.98	1.15	4.06

a. Scale values for approach and avoidance versions of the same message are virtually identical and were averaged here.

TABLE 4.11

Experiment 5: Frequencies of Choice in Revised Approach and Avoidance Conflicts

Situation	Message	Sum	Report [+/+]	Report [-/-]	New Look [+/+]	New Look [-/-]
Report or New Look	I think your hair looks great that way. I don't think your hair looks good that way.	-1.61	11	3	15	2
	I think your dress is really nice. I don't think your dress suits you.	-2.30	6	2	0	2
	You've changed!	3.89	3	15	5	16

Situation	Message	Sum	Application [+/+]	Application [-/-]	Quiz [+/+]	Quiz [-/-]
Application or Quiz	You are exceptionally easy to get along with. You are quite difficult to get along with.	-2.05	8	9	12	5
	You are very intelligent. You are not very intelligent.	-2.02	6	1	3	0
	What do you think?	4.06	6	10	5	15

a. Chi-square for first two versus third message in approach versus avoidance conflicts: Report = 14.55, $df = 2$, $p < .001$; New Look = 12.13, $df = 2$, $p < .001$; Application = 1.67, $df = 2$, $p = $ n.s.; Quiz = 10.00, $df = 2$, $p < .01$.

95

Application scenario. The messages and their scale values are given in Table 4.10.

Because there had been no effect of the order in which options appeared in the text and among the messages, we did not include all possible combinations this time. The order in the text was simply reversed in the messages. This meant only eight unique stimuli, in the usual format and with a questionnaire attached. These stimuli were randomly assigned to 160 volunteers in classes, following the same procedure as in previous experiments.

Our predictions were confirmed in all cases (see Table 4.11). In the Report, New Look, and Quiz scenarios, avoidance conflicts led to equivocation, while approach conflicts led to direct messages. The new situations acted exactly as we had predicted and also confirmed our post hoc interpretations of Experiment 4: A different equivocal message was still chosen in the Report scenario, which eliminated any possible "reassurance" interpretation. And, as predicted, there was no significant difference between the two versions of the old Application scenario. This result, contrasted with the Quiz choices, confirmed that advice-giving situations with practical consequences are inevitably avoidance-avoidance conflicts.

SUMMARY

These experiments were aimed to test a situational explanation of equivocation, using forced-choice among experimenter-written alternatives. The results confirmed that equivocation is chosen overwhelmingly in situations where a communicative avoidance-avoidance conflict exists. The high rate at which equivocation is chosen argues against its being due to communication errors or to individual differences. Nor is an equivocal response chosen when the situation is merely unpleasant or when an approach-approach conflict is presented. The essential condition for equivocation is a situation where direct (unequivocal) responses are negative and must be avoided.

5

How People Equivocate: Written Messages

The experiments described in the previous chapter strongly supported our predictions regarding the situations that lead to equivocation: Equivocal messages are chosen in avoidance-avoidance conflicts and not in otherwise similar situations. Our next step was to move on to spontaneous written messages (Bavelas & Chovil, 1986). Recall that our overall strategy in this project was to begin with a secure base of highly controlled experiments and to move toward experiments that included more typical kinds of communication. The results of the forced-choice experiments had been encouraging, but it would have been quite unsatisfactory to stop at that point, principally because (except for greeting cards) people do not usually communicate by choosing among messages written by another person. Several important questions remained: Would respondents spontaneously generate equivocal messages when faced with an avoidance-avoidance conflict? What would these messages be like? In other words, *how* do people equivocate?

In the experiments to be presented in this chapter, the participants wrote their own messages in response to hypothetical scenarios. As in Experiment 2, there were two versions of each scenario: a conflict condition in which all direct responses led to negative consequences and a nonconflict (control) condition in which direct responses had positive outcomes.

The scenarios were ones in which a brief written message was the natural and appropriate means of replying. There were two major reasons for asking participants to write replies rather than having them speak their replies and using the transcriptions. First, we were interested in seeing how (and whether) people equivocate in written, purely verbal messages before moving on to spoken messages. Second, it is important, in our view, to retain all of the information contained in an original message, in order to preserve the integrity of the message. When the message is to be written, people adapt to the limits of this medium of communication; for example, they use punctuation (such as exclamation points) to denote information that might otherwise be conveyed paralinguistically. Asking participants to give spoken replies and then transcribing their responses (as is often done) effectively discards the information provided by tone of voice, pauses, and so forth. Transcription could even affect experimental results; for example, if equivocation consisted of an incongruency between the words said and the tone of voice used, the latter would be lost when the message was transcribed, and the message would be scaled as clear. For all of these reasons, we chose to focus first on written messages.

There are a number of scenarios, including those used in Chapter 4, in which a brief written reply is the obvious way of communicating: People pass notes in a class or meeting (when talking out loud would be disruptive) or they write social notes to friends and relatives thanking them for gifts or hospitality. Other examples of messages that are usually written are memos, letters of reference, telegrams, politicians' campaign statements or press releases, written directions or instructions, and ads or notices.

Because of our overall strategy of varied replication, some of the scenarios used in the present experiments were ones we had used in the forced-choice experiments. That is, we wanted to show that our theory extends into the new format, in this case, to spontaneously written messages. If anything went wrong at this point, the problem could only be the new format. We also added some nonoverlapping, new scenarios in order to gain generalizability for our theory.

The basic procedure was the same for the four experiments. All participants were volunteers from University of Victoria classes, usually from the psychology department "subject pool." Each was seen individually by an experimenter, who gave the following instructions:

Try to imagine the situation I'm about to describe as vividly as possible. Try to really put yourself in the situation and write down what you actually would say.

The experimenter then gave the (randomly assigned) conflict or nonconflict version of the scenario to the participant, and the participant wrote his or her reply. Afterwards, the experimenter explained the purpose of the study and answered all of the participant's questions.

These messages were later typed, without correction of grammatical or spelling errors, onto cards with no identifying information as to who the writers were or which experimental condition they were in. All of the typed messages for a given scenario were arranged in random order and scaled as a set by the judges, who did not know there were two different experimental conditions (or anything else about our theory). After each set of messages was scaled, the judges' raw scores were ipsatized and averaged as usual to arrive at a value for each message on each dimension.

The number of participants in each experiment was, in contrast to the earlier experiments, fairly small, for several reasons: First, there is a limit to the number of unique messages that can be scaled at one time by our judges. Twenty brief written messages are very taxing, and sets larger than this would have to be divided and scaled in more than one session. Second, we felt that it was possible, as a result of our earlier work, to create situations and conditions precise enough to produce effects even with small N's. Third, although many researchers rely on a single large N to establish the generalizability of their results, we prefer the replication strategy recommended, for example, by Winer (1962, pp. 213-216). In our view, several independent replications with experiments that differ in all irrelevant particulars are the best way to establish a general principle. So we created situations that had virtually nothing in common except the presence and absence of a communicative avoidance-avoidance conflict. Intuition alone suggests that different experiments — conducted at different times with different scenarios and different subjects who wrote unique messages — could not repeatedly yield the same results merely by chance.

The rest of this chapter will describe the scenarios, the messages written by participants, and our analysis of the scale values of these messages. The reader is encouraged to think about how he or she would respond in each situation and then compare his or her response with those written by the participants in our experiments. (Experiments are numbered sequentially throughout the book.)

EXPERIMENT 6: CLASS PRESENTATION (WRITTEN)

In the first experiment of this series, the Class Presentation scenario from the forced-choice experiments was used to elicit brief written replies. The experimenter asked 20 participants to imagine the following:

Another student in a small class, which meets three times a week for the entire year, has just given a class presentation. It was very badly done — poorly prepared and poorly delivered. After he sits down again, he passes you a note,

"**How did I do?**" *You have to jot something down and pass it back to him. What would you write as an answer?*

As noted in Chapter 4, the problem faced by the writer in this scenario was to avoid hurting the other student's feelings by telling a truth about the presentation, yet to avoid being dishonest about it as well. In the nonconflict version, the situation was the same except for the key sentence about the presentation, which read:

It was very well done—well prepared and well delivered.

Table 5.1 contains the messages written by our 20 participants. The messages are divided by condition, beginning with those written in the nonconflict condition. All of the messages presented in the tables (and text) have been reproduced as faithfully as possible, without correction of spelling, grammar, or punctuation. Overall, the messages suggest that the participants took the scenario seriously and wrote credible, original responses. We were impressed with the variety of responses in both the conflict and nonconflict conditions. Each individual wrote a unique and often elaborated response to the question "**How did I do?**"

Table 5.1 also gives the scale values for each message on the four dimensions and the Sum. The messages are ordered, within condition, by their Sum values (lowest to highest, i.e., clearest to most equivocal). At the bottom are the reliabilities, means for the two conditions, and *t*-tests. The reader will notice in this and subsequent tables that the conflict and nonconflict means often seem to mirror each other, that is, they are usually identical except for the sign. To understand this apparent coincidence, recall that ipsatized scores have the properties of standard scores, which includes adding to zero. When the judges agree highly, their averaged ipsatized scores remain standard scores, and any division into two halves produces means that, within rounding errors along the way, add to zero.

The mean scale value of the conflict condition differed in the predicted direction from the mean scale value of the nonconflict condition for each dimension and the Sum; the difference for the Context dimension was statistically significant. In other words, the messages written to a fellow student who gave a poor presentation are significantly less responsive to the question "**How did I do?**" than are the messages written to a student who gave a good presentation.

Qualitative analysis of the messages supplements these quantitative results. Examination of the messages in Table 5.1, dimension by dimension, reveals a number of differences between messages high and low in equivocation. First of all, on the Content dimension, our judges noticed that some messages (written in the nonconflict condition) are very explicit about how the person did on the presentation:

> **Your presentation was really good. The whole class seemed interested and they all listened. You didn't even seem nervous, I'm sure you'll get a good mark.**

and

> **You did very well.**

On the other hand, some messages (written in the conflict condition) use vague or noncommittal phrases, which left the judges wondering how the person did on the presentation:

> **Better than I probably would have done.**

or

> **It was okay.**

Some of the longer nonconflict messages with low scale values consist of parts that are separately clear and also consistent with each other:

> **You did just great! Your ideas came across and I understood everything. I didn't even fall asleep.**

In contrast, many of the messages written in the conflict condition are internally contradictory. These messages often begin with a positive phrase, followed by a criticism of the presentation. As can be seen in Table 5.1, three of the four messages containing "but" have high scale values:

> **It was okay, but sometimes I wasn't quite sure what you were getting at!!**
>
> **Not to bad — but you could have done more work on it!**
>
> **it was o.k. but there were things that could be improved.**

TABLE 5.1
Experiment 6: Class Presentation (written)

Condition	Content	Sender	Receiver	Context	Sum
Nonconflict Condition					
You did just great! Your ideas came across and I understood everything. I didn't even fall asleep.	-.91	-.80	-.86	-1.21	-3.78
Your presentation was really good. The whole class seemed interested and they all listened. You didn't even seem nervous, I'm sure you'll get a good mark.	-1.27	-.11	-2.05	.29	-3.14
I think your presentation was well thought-up & well delivered.	-1.20	-.96	-.82	.54	-2.44
I thought you did very good. It was well persented.	-.10	-.87	.01	-.81	-1.77
You did very well because I didn't fall a sleep.	-.12	-.48	.00	-.97	-1.57
You did very well.	-.21	.67	.48	-1.10	-.16
"I'm impressed"	-.13	-1.08	.54	.79	.12
You did alright	.14	.68	.54	-.63	.73
Well done	.40	.64	.60	.59	2.23
Very well	1.64	1.53	.82	-.99	3.00
Conflict Condition					
You should've spent more time preparing. It wasn't really clear as to what you were getting across. I'll explain more during our lunch break.	-.68	-.45	-.94	.13	-1.94

Statement					
I wasn't quite sure what it was you were driving at sometimes. but the idea behind it was good Why don't we have coffee after class so we can talk more easily.	-.33	-.62	-1.38	.67	-1.66
You should have spent a little more time preparing for the presentation. All it needed as just a little more work and it would have been a really good presentation.	-1.17	.13	-.65	.37	-1.32
It was okay, but sometimes I wasn't quite sure what you were getting at !!	.29	-.35	.08	.62	.64
Better than I probably would have done.	.31	-.30	.64	.03	.68
Not to bad – but you could have done more more work on it!	.23	.32	.39	-.27	.67
I thought it sounded alright	.26	-.68	.47	.77	.82
it was o.k. but there were things that could be improved.	.38	.49	.61	.90	2.38
Not so hot	1.55	1.15	.76	-.68	2.78
It was okay	.90	1.08	.76	.97	3.71
Summary Statistics					
Reliability (intraclass R) =	.93	.91	.94	.90	
Nonconflict mean =	-.18	-.08	-.07	-.35	-.68
Conflict mean =	.17	.08	.07	.35	.68
t =	.97	.44	.39	2.29	1.45
p (one-tailed) =	n.s.	n.s.	n.s.	<.03	n.s.

Such answers seem to reflect directly the conflict in the situation faced by the respondents. On one hand, the writers tried to tell the person that the presentation was badly done, and on the other hand, they tried to avoid hurting him as well. Their messages are like the "third option" in the Experiment 1 scenarios and were, like those, scaled by our judges as unclear because the result is an apparent contradiction.

Although the difference between the means was not statistically significant on the Sender dimension, the judges picked up some qualitative differences between messages written in the nonconflict and conflict conditions. The messages with the lowest scale values on the Sender dimension are ones containing the first-person pronoun ("**I**"):

  "**I'm impressed.**"

Messages with high scale values are just the opposite; they avoid the use of "**I**," leaving it unstated whose opinion is being given:

  Not to bad – but you could have done more work on it!

or

  it was o.k. but there were things that could be improved.

Two of the nonconflict condition messages containing "**I**" have the words "think" or "thought" as well and were scaled as even more definitely the sender's opinion:

  I think your presentation was well thought-up & well delivered.

  I thought you did very good. It was well persented.

Only one of the messages obtained in the conflict condition uses the words "**I thought**," and it was scaled as clear on the Sender dimension.

We found that messages differed little on the Receiver dimension in this scenario. This anticipated most later experiments as well – it is rare for messages produced by our participants to differ on this dimension.

As already noted, there was a statistically significant difference between the two groups of messages on the Context dimension. Replies written in the nonconflict condition are usually a "tight fit" to the question, "**How did I do?**":

> You did just great! Your ideas came across and I understood everything. I didn't even fall asleep.

or

> You did very well.

In contrast, the conflict condition messages avoid answering the question asked. There seem to be three kinds of nonresponsive answers: First, equivocal messages often make the slight but distinct change from **"You did"** to **"It was."** This subtly changes the referent from the person to the presentation:

> it was o.k. but there were things that could be improved.

and

> It was okay.

A second group of messages scaled high on this dimension postpone the unpleasant answer. The writer answers obliquely then changes the topic by suggesting a meeting later to talk more about the presentation – rather than answering the question fully and directly in the present message:

> You should've spent more time preparing. It wasn't really clear as to what you were getting across. I'll explain more during our lunch break.

and

> I wasn't quite sure what it was you were driving at sometimes. But the idea behind it was good. Why don't we have coffee after class so we can talk more easily.

The third kind of equivocal response is one that hints at an answer without coming out and answering the question directly. Faced with this **"Don't make me actually say it"** tactic, the receiver would have to infer from the response what the other person actually thought of the presentation:

> You should have spent a little more time preparing for the presentation. All it needed as just a little more work and it would have been a really good presentation.

EXPERIMENT 7: MEMBER OF PARLIAMENT (WRITTEN)

In the next experiment, the experimenter asked 16 participants to imagine:

You are a Member of Parliament in Ottawa. A highway route is being planned in your home riding [electoral district]. There are two routes being considered — route A and route B. Both routes have advantages and disadvantages. Half your voters favour route A. The other half favour route B. You receive a telegram from a local newspaper reporter that says: "**Which route do you prefer, route A or route B?**" *What would you reply in a telegram?*

In this scenario, the writer of the telegram must avoid offending either side (voters in favor of route A and voters in favor of route B). In the nonconflict condition, the key sentence about the voters' being split was replaced by:

Route A is clearly the best route and is favored by your voters.

The messages of two of our 16 participants were not included because these individuals did not understand the situation. The remaining 14 messages are given, along with their scale values, reliabilities, and *t*-tests, in Table 5.2. The differences for Content, Context, and the Sum were statistically significant. In other words, the telegrams written in the conflict condition were significantly less clear in content and less responsive to the question "**Which route do you prefer, route A or route B?**" and were more equivocal overall than were the telegrams written in the nonconflict condition.

Qualitatively, even though the format of a telegram dictated the use of incomplete sentences and limited the number of words that could be used, writers in the nonconflict condition usually wrote messages that are clear on the Content dimension:

> **Route A is clearly preferable
> am available for interview on my
> return.**

and

> **I'd prefer to choose route A.**

In contrast, the message that received the highest scale value on the Content dimension was from the conflict condition and is awkward and ungrammatical:

Figure 5.1.

Undecides as of yet.

In other telegrams, also written in the conflict condition, the writers were more articulate in their vagueness:

I don't think that my personal preference can enter into this matter — I'm here simply to represent my constituent's wishes.

or

I will have to look into this further considering that I seem to have the deciding vote.

TABLE 5.2

Experiment 7: Member of Parliament (written)

Condition	Content	Sender	Receiver	Context	Sum
Nonconflict Condition					
Route A is clearly preferable am available for interview on my return.	-.50	-.12	-1.94	-.76	-3.32
Dear Sir I would prefer Route A due to its obvious favorable aspects.	-.40	-1.18	-.12	-.98	-2.68
Signed					
I'd prefer to choose route A.	-.72	-1.21	.68	-1.23	-2.48
In depth study is being done into the question right now stop all the results aren't back yet stop but I feel optimistic towards Route A. stop.	-.15	-.25	-.09	-.34	-.83
I intend to present the advantages and favourability of the proposed Route A as felt by my constituents. My support will be behind the passage of the Route A plan.	-.36	1.04	-.16	-.52	0.00
Rt. A.	.77	.66	.96	-1.28	1.11
Studies show that route A is more feasible.	-.78	1.30	.73	-.08	1.17
Conflict Condition					
In the event of a final decision I feel that the best plan would be plan B. I am not going to say what influenced my decision, except that I do feel it is for the better.	-.01	-.57	.04	-.51	-1.05

I would vote for the Route that would be the least expensive, & the route that would not have to tear as much property down in order for it to be built.	-.20	-.77	-.36	.78	-.55
I don't think that my personal preference can enter into this matter— I'm simply here to represent my constituent's wishes.	.08	.02	-.54	.93	.49

Dear Sir
    Since both routes have their inherent advantages and disadvantages I plan to seek the route which will benefit our community the most.
 	
        Sincerely
	.34	.25	-.73	.75	.61

I will send the facts to a committee for further consideration.	-.26	.28	.44	1.20	1.66
I will have to look into this further considering that I seem to have the deciding vote.	.55	-.18	.22	1.12	1.71
Undecides as of yet.	1.66	.73	.87	.92	4.18

Summary Statistics

Reliability (intraclass R) =	.89	.94	.94	.98	
Nonconflict mean =	-.31	.03	.01	-.74	-1.00
Conflict mean =	.31	-.03	-.01	.74	1.01
t =	1.93	.16	.04	5.35	2.10
p (one-tailed) =	<.05	n.s.	n.s.	<.001	<.05

As in the Class scenario, the writer was asked to give his or her opinion on an issue. Messages with low scale values on the Sender dimension usually state the writer's opinion directly:

Dear Sir,
   I would Prefer Route A due to its
obvious favourable aspects.
   Signed

_____

or

I intend to present the advantages
and favorability of the proposed
Route A as felt by my constituents.
My support will be behind the passage
of the Route A plan.

The judges noticed that two writers (one in each condition) avoided giving their opinion by "passing the buck" to another source, such as a committee or "studies":

Studies show that route A is more
Feasible.

I will send the facts to a committee
for further consideration

(Recall that there were no studies or committees mentioned in the instructions; even in this hypothetical situation, the participants drew on their imaginations.)

The two groups of messages did not differ significantly on the Receiver dimension either. The judges did, however, notice that some messages (both conflict and nonconflict) contain elements that were more clearly related to the scenario (a reporter questioning a Member of Parliament). References to interviews or the use of terms such as "constituents" were seen as more likely to be addressed to a reporter than to just anyone and thus were scaled by our judges as less equivocal on this dimension.

On the Context dimension, messages that were scaled as more responsive to the question, "**Which route do you prefer, route A or route B?**" actually contain the words "**prefer**" and/or "**route.**" In other words, there is a tight fit between the question and the answer:

> **Dear Sir,**
>   **I would prefer Route A due to its**
> **obvious favorable aspects.**
>   **Signed**
>
> ———————

or

> **I'd prefer to choose route A.**

As in the Class scenario, one way of getting out of the conflict is to answer a slightly different question. For example, some messages seem to be answering the question "**What do you plan to do?**" rather than "**Which route do you favor, route A or route B?**"

> **I would vote for the Route that would**
> **be the least expensive, & the route**
> **that would not have to tear as much**
> **property down in order for it to be built.**

or

> **Dear Sir**
>   **Since both routes have their inherent advantages and disadvantages I**
> **plan to seek the route which will benefit our community the most.**
>   **Sincerely**

It is interesting to note that these messages also avoid saying which route was favored by writing about a (hypothetical) best route.

In other telegrams, the writers postponed the answer by stating that the matter would have to be looked at in further detail before a decision could be made:

> **I will send the facts to a committee**
> **for further consideration**

and

> **I will have to look into this further**
> **considering that I seem to have the**
> **deciding vote.**

EXPERIMENT 8: BIZARRE GIFT (WRITTEN)

In the next two written experiments, we used a "double blind" procedure in order to eliminate even the remotest possibility that the experimenters might be influencing the writers (e.g., by their facial expressions when they described the conflict version). Instead of reading the instructions and the scenario to the participant, the experimenter gave each of the participants a sheet to read. These sheets were randomly arranged by condition, and the experimenter did not see the sheet until after the participant had finished the experiment.

We created a new variation on the Gift scenario, different from the one used in the forced-choice experiments:

Imagine that a good friend has sent you a gift. You are not sure if it is meant as a joke or if it is to be taken seriously as it is quite bizarre. You receive a letter from him/her asking, "How did you like the gift I sent you?" Write your reply.

The dilemma in this situation is that the writer does not know what to make of the gift. Treating it as a joke runs the risk of offending the friend if it was serious. On the other hand, if the gift is taken seriously, the writer may look foolish (or offend the friend) because it was really a joke. In the nonconflict condition, the key sentence about the gift was replaced with:

You can tell that it was carefully selected with your tastes and interests in mind.

The messages written by our 18 participants, their scale values, reliabilities, and *t*-tests are given in Table 5.3. All means differed in the predicted direction, and the differences between conditions were significant for the Content, Sender, and Context dimensions, and the Sum. Thus, the messages obtained in the conflict condition were not only significantly less clear in content and less responsive to the question asked (as was true in one or both of the first two experiments) but they were also less clearly the writer's opinion than were their nonconflict counterparts.

Qualitatively, on the Content dimension, messages written in the non-conflict condition are straightforward and clear:

I have received your gift. It must have taken a lot of thought and time to have selected it. Thank you very much I really like it a lot.

or

> I received your letter this a.m. Thanks for the book, it's one I've wanted for
> quite a while. How'd you find it? It's quite rare. Well, write again to
>   Tom

Recall that in the conflict condition, the writer is faced with not knowing whether the gift was serious or a joke. A solution some of our writers hit upon was to use words or phrases with double meanings. This in effect allowed them to "cover both bases"; their replies could be about the gift *or* about their friend's sense of humor. The judges noticed this equivocality and scaled these messages as less clear on the Content dimension:

> **Fantastic! Thank you *very* much!**

and

> **I got a kick out of your gift. It was what I would have expected from you.**

In music, an "equivocal chord" is one that can be resolved into different keys. These messages, too, can be resolved in either direction.

As in the Class scenario, some of our participants wrote contradictory messages in the conflict condition. For example, the gift is described as "**bizarre but wonderful**":

> **I received the gift you sent. As you know I myself can be quite bizarre at
> times, so when I am in that type of mood I will always think of your
> wonderful gift. Thank-you for the gift.**

Or, as "**great but strange**":

> **Thanks for the lovely and unusual gift. Are you serious? It's great but a
> little strange.**

The message with the highest scale value on the Content dimension is full of contradictions:

> **Your gift, although much appreciatated was definately uncalled for. Can I
> see you to talk about it as I think my feelings were hurt by it. Thanks.**

The writer begins by stating his or her appreciation of the gift, then goes on to say the gift was uncalled for and he was hurt by it, yet finishes by thanking the person.

TABLE 5.3

Experiment 8: Bizarre Gift (written)

Condition	Content	Sender	Receiver	Context	Sum
Nonconflict Condition					
Thank you so much for the terrific gift. It is something I have always wanted. Whenever I use it I will always think of you. Thanks again.	-.77	-.88	-.14	-.71	-2.50
Love					
I can't tell you how thrilled I was to receive the present you sent me. Obviously you spent some time selecting it, and I appreciate it.	-.60	-.68	-.34	-.16	-1.78
Thank you so much for your letter— Your gift was just lovely so very much to my liking. I should have answered immediately but was delayed from doing so. I hope you weren't thinking that it had not arrived.	.21	-.43	-.44	-1.00	-1.66
I have received your gift. It must have taken a lot of thought and time to have selected it. Thank you very much I really like it a lot.	-.81	-.11	.07	-.78	-1.63
I loved it! How did you know it was exactly what I wanted? You are always so thoughful. How do you find the time?	.60	-.67	-.32	-1.05	-1.44
You asked how I liked the gift you sent. Well, it could hardly have been more perfect! You have a real knack for knowing just what would appeal to me. I've already used it several times, with great success. And several other people have loved it as well.	-.69	.44	-.26	-.91	-1.42
The gift you sent proved to be very useful, in fact I had contemplated buying the exact thing for myself. I do like it and I want to thank-you very much.	-.83	-.53	.55	-.56	-1.37
I received your letter this a.m. Thanks for the book, it's one I've wanted for quite a while. How'd you find it? It's quite rare. Well, write again to Tom	-.89	.15	.07	.13	-.54

Conflict Condition

Thank you so much for the picture. She is lovely. She reminds me of you so much. I am so eager to meet her and to hold her. So precious. Congratulations.	.36	.36	-.19	-.42	.61	.36
I got a kick out of your gift. It was what I would have expected from you.	.19	.19	-.47	-.24	-.32	-.84
Thank-you for your letter and for the gift. Im really not quite sure how I will use it- but it was nice to know that you were thinking of me! - much love (signed)	-.20	-.20	.05	-.91	.98	-.08
I recieved the gift you sent. As you know I myself can be quite bizarre at times, so when I am in that type of mood I will always think of your wonderful gift. Thank-you for the gift.	.26	.26	.05	-.68	.41	.04
In reply to your recent letter, I would like to thank you for your gift. Presently, the gift is being put to good use. Hope to hear from you soon. Take care in the meantime.	-.68	-.68	.64	-.04	.99	.91
Thanks for the lovely and unusual gift. Are you serious? It's great but a little strange.	.65	.65	.48	.12	-.07	1.18
I have to be honest with you, I'm not sure what you mean by it, please let me know how I can best use your unique gift.	.51	.51	-.10	.61	.98	2.00
Fantastic! Thank you very much!	.99	.99	.99	.99	.98	2.21
Your gift, although much appreciatated was definately uncalled for. Can I see you to talk about it as I think my feelings were hurt by it. Thanks.	1.40	1.40	.23	.83	.68	3.14
Yes I received your gift. They say a person gives what he would like to receive. Hopefully one day, Ill be able to return the favor some way or another. Have a nice day.	.29	.29	1.02	.55	1.53	3.39

Summary Statistics

Reliability (intraclass R) =	.86	.86	.71	.65	.93	
Nonconflict mean =	-.38	-.38	-.32	-.14	-.49	-1.33
Conflict mean =	.38	.38	.32	.14	.49	1.33
t =	2.67	2.92	1.11	3.16	4.75	
p (one-tailed) =	<.01	<.005	<.005	n.s.	<.005	<.001

On the Sender dimension, messages scaled as more clearly the writer's opinion are often devoted to the sender's feelings about the gift:

> **I loved it! How did you know it was exactly what I wanted? You are always so thoughtful. How do you find the time?**

or

> **The gift you sent proved to be very useful, in fact I had contemplated buying the exact thing for myself. I do like it and I want to thank-you very much.**

Receiving a gift that one does not like is probably a situation that most people have had experience with or can at least imagine. A familiar way of getting out of the conflict is simply to thank the person for the gift without mentioning whether you like it. This was a solution used by some of our writers in the conflict condition; the judges noticed that in these messages the writer's opinion of the gift is not there:

> **In reply to your recent letter, I would like to thank you for your gift. Presently, the gift is being put to good use. Hope to hear from you soon. Take care in the meantime.**

and

> **Thank-you for your letter and for the gift. Im really not quite sure how I will use it — but it was nice to know that you were thinking of me! — much love (signed)**

In another message the writer avoids giving his or her opinion by using the classic, anonymous "**They**":

> **Yes I received your gift. They say a person gives what he would like to receive. Hopefully one day, Ill be able to return the favor some way or another. Have a nice day.**

As in the two previous scenarios (Class and Member of Parliament), we found there was no appreciable difference between conflict and nonconflict messages on the Receiver dimension. However, messages containing phrases such as "**much love**" or "**as you know**" were seen by the judges as more likely to be addressed to a friend than to just anyone.

Figure 5.2.

On the Context dimension, messages scaled as more direct answers to the question refer directly to liking or loving the gift:

I loved it! How did you know it was exactly what I wanted? You are always so thoughful. How do you find the time?

and

Thank you so much for your letter — Your gift was just lovely so very much to my liking. I should have answered immediately but was delayed from doing so, I hope you weren't thinking that it had not arrived.

Equivocal messages, on the other hand, sometimes effect subtle changes of topic. Rather than answering the question asked ("**How did you like the gift I sent you?**"), some writers began by answering a different question, such as "**Did you receive my gift?**" and then went on to quite different topics:

> **I recieved the gift you sent. As you know I myself can be quite bizarre at times, so when I am in that type of mood I will always think of your wonderful gift. thank-you for the gift.**

or

> **Yes I received your gift. They say a person gives what he would like to receive. Hopefully one day, Ill be able to return the favor some way or another. Have a nice day.**

Postponement of the answer appeared again; some participants asked to talk to the person about the gift, rather than saying whether they liked it:

> **Your gift, although much appreciatated was definately uncalled for. Can I see you to talk about it as I think my feelings were hurt by it. Thanks.**

and

> **I have to be honest with you, I'm not sure what you mean by it, please let me know how I can best use your unique gift.**

EXPERIMENT 9: CAR AD (WRITTEN)

The final scenario used to elicit written messages was the Car Ad:

> *Your car (a 1966 Volkswagen Bug) is in bad condition but you need to sell it because you are really short of money. Write the ad for the newspaper describing the general running condition of the car.*

Here the writer is caught between "the devil and the deep blue sea." He or she should avoid deceiving a prospective buyer about the car's running condition but should also avoid hurting his or her own self-interest by being blunt about the car's condition. In the nonconflict condition, the key sentence about the car read:

Your car (a 1966 Volkswagen Bug) is in good condition but you need to sell it because you are really short of money.

Eighteen participants wrote ads for us. These ads, their scale values, reliabilities, and *t*-tests are presented in Table 5.4. The mean scale values were significantly different for all four dimensions and the Sum. Messages written in the conflict condition were significantly less clear in content, avoided giving the writer's opinion, were less clearly addressed to the appropriate receiver, and answered the question less directly than those written in the nonconflict condition.

As in the Member of Parliament scenario, the format restricted the writer to short phrases. Yet, even within this constraint, messages written in the nonconflict condition are clear on the Content dimension:

> **For sale — '66 VW Bug, good condition,**
> **lady driven, must be sold quickly,**
> **asking about $800 cash, good mileage**
> **on highways**

and

> **FOR SALE 66, VOLKSWAGON BEETLE GOOD**
> **RUNNING CONDITION EASY ON GAS IDEAL**
> **SECOND CAR**

Some of the ads with higher scale values are even more laconic, to the point of being enigmatic. These ads, written in the conflict condition, give very little information about the car:

> **VW Beetle, 1966. Needs work. $500.**
> **592-1626 after 5:30 p.m.**

or

> **1966 VOLKSWAGEN BUG AS IS QUICK**
> **SALE FOR CASH**
> **PHONE_____**

Another ad that received a high value on this dimension borders on double-entendre. The last half of this ad could be taken either literally or as a warning to potential buyers:

> **FOR SALE   1966 VOLKSWAGEN.   VERY CHEAP.**
> **PERSON WHO LIKES WORKING ON CARS WOULD**
> **BE WISE TO BUY THIS CAR.**

Again we found contradictory messages, containing "but" or "however." Some writers began with positive comments about the car (such as "**in running order**" or "**best year of the bug**") and then went on to mention problems with the car such as "**would need some minor repairs**" or "**needs some bugs removed.**"

> **For sale: 1966 Volkswagen Bug, in**
> **running order, but would need some**
> **minor repairs**

or

> **MECHANIC'S DREAM – 1966 Volkswagon –**
> **best year of the bug – however needs**
> **some bugs removed by caring mechanic.**
> **Sacrifice at $2500.xx.**

Messages that received low scale values on the Sender dimension mention the word "student" or contain a personal reference to the car.

> **have to sell my good old buddy '66 VW**
> **Bug. Excellent runner, good milage**
> **and good bargain!!**

and

> **Bargain! Student needs to sell much**
> **loved VW. This 1966 Bug is a great**
> **old car. Perfect for a mechanical**
> **tinkerer.**

Messages with high scale values omit any reference to the seller of the car. In these ads, it is as if the writer is "standing back" from the ad and dissociating him- or herself from the car. Looking at Table 5.4, it can be seen that these ads could have been written by anyone, not necessarily by the owner.

The Receiver dimension redeemed itself in the Car Ad scenario. The judges noticed (although we had not) that some messages in the conflict condition redefine the receiver from a general audience (anyone reading the classified ads) to a more specialized audience (someone who works on cars):

> **MECHANIC'S DREAM – 1966 Volkswagon –**
> **best year of the bug – however needs**
> **some bugs removed by caring mechanic.**
> **Sacrifice at $2500.xx.**

or

> **FOR SALE 1966 VOLKSWAGEN. VERY CHEAP.**
> **PERSON WHO LIKES WORKING ON CARS WOULD**
> **BE WISE TO BUY THIS CAR.**

Notice that only one message in the nonconflict condition qualifies who the buyer should be.

On the Context dimension, the ads scaled as more responsive give the requested information (recall that all participants were asked to describe the running condition of the car):

> **1966 VW – good running condition, new**
> **brakes, new tires OFFERS – PHONE 321-1234 after 5 p.m.**

and

> **FOR SALE 66, VOLKSWAGON BEETLE GOOD**
> **RUNNING CONDITION EASY ON GAS IDEAL**
> **SECOND CAR**

In contrast, some of the messages scaled high on equivocation avoid specifying the car's running condition, although they often hint at problems. For example, the ads mention a need for some repairs or work to be done on the car:

> **For sale: 1966 Volkswagen Bug, in**
> **running order, but would need some**
> **minor repairs**

TABLE 5.4

Experiment 9: Car Ad (written)

Condition	Content	Sender	Receiver	Context	Sum
Nonconflict Condition					
MUST SELL: 1966 V.W. BUG. EXCELLENT CONDITION RUNS GREAT. ONLY 5000 MILES ON IT. BEST DEAL IN THE CITY! PLEASE PHONE SOON — THIS DREAM WILL GO FAST!	-.60	-.48	-.59	-.62	-2.29
For Sale! 1966 Volkswagon Bug in good operating condition. Any reasonable offer. Please phone xxx-xxxx	-.67	.03	-.85	-.77	-2.26
1966 VW – good running condition, new brakes, new tires OFFERS – PHONE 321-1234 after 5 p.m.	-.67	.51	-1.00	-1.03	-2.19
have to sell my good old buddy '66 VW Bug. Excellent runner, good milage and good bargain!	.19	-1.26	-.60	-.48	-2.15
Must sell 1966 VW Bug, good running condition. very good on gas. No reasonable offer will be refused.	-.20	-.04	-.50	-.90	-1.64
VOLKSWAGON FOR SALE BODY AND ENGINE IN GOOD CONDITION. ONE OWNER, MUST SELL BEFORE DEC 15 PHONE _____ ASK FOR MARK	-.16	-.35	-.64	-.39	-1.54
For Sale - '66 VW Bug, good condition, lady driven, must be sold quickly, asking about $800 cash, good mileage on highways	-.73	-.17	-.02	-.24	-1.16
FOR SALE 66, VOLKSWAGON BEETLE GOOD RUNNING CONDITION EASY ON GAS IDEAL SECOND CAR	-.65	.08	.63	-1.02	-.96
Bargain! Student needs to sell much loved VW. This 1966 Bug is a great old car. Perfect for a mechanical tinkerer.	.60	-.96	.75	1.17	1.56
Conflict Condition					
For sale a 1966 V-W bug in excellent running condition. Price is right for an egar buyer in need of transportation.	.22	.16	-.37	-.84	-.83

Advertisement					
For sale: 1966 Volkswagen Bug, in running order, but would need some minor repairs.	.05	.69	.09	-.15	.68
For sale a 1966 Volkswagen bug, it is in poor running condition, but just needs some tender loving care and a mechanic mind.	.46	.19	.92	-.72	.85
1966 Volks Bug - student must sell to survive summer, needs some body work, but mechanically o.k.	.55	-.39	.35	.50	1.01
Want to sell 1966 Bug, good body but some engine trouble - needs work.	.06	.40	.36	.28	1.10
VW Beetle, 1966. Needs work. $500. 592-1626 after 5:30 p.m.	-.58	.67	-.01	1.33	1.41
1966 VOLKSWAGEN BUG AS IS QUICK SALE FOR CASH PHONE	.92	.76	-.87	1.87	2.68
MECHANIC'S DREAM - 1966 Volkswagen - best year of the bug - however needs some bugs removed by caring mechanic. Sacrifice at $2500.xx.	.47	.13	1.41	.73	2.74
FOR SALE 1966 VOLKSWAGEN. VERY CHEAP. PERSON WHO LIKES WORKING ON CARS WOULD BE WISE TO BUY THIS CAR.	.74	.03	.95	1.28	3.00

Summary Statistics

Reliability (intraclass R) =	.76	.75	.91	.98	
Nonconflict mean =	-.32	-.29	-.31	-.48	-1.40
Conflict mean =	.32	.29	.31	.48	1.40
t =	2.98	2.66	1.99	2.47	4.88
p (one-tailed) =	<.005	<.01	<.05	<.03	<.001

and

**Want to sell 1966 Bug, good body but
some engine trouble — needs work.**

It may be stretching a point, but the following message seems to us an example of the "postponement" tactic found in the previous experiments. The minimal information given postpones the discovery of the car's condition, as the potential buyer must actually phone or go see the car in order to find out about the running condition:

**1966 VOLKSWAGEN BUG AS IS QUICK
SALE FOR CASH
      PHONE_____**

POSSIBLE ARTIFACTS

In addition to the above quantitative and qualitative analyses of the messages from each experiment, we looked at two other characteristics: the length of each message and the completeness of sentences within each message.

It would be reasonable to propose that the scale values obtained for our dimensions could possibly be an artifact of the length of the messages, with shorter messages receiving higher scale values. To determine whether this was the case, we correlated the number of words in each message with the scale values for each dimension. Although in some cases shorter messages had higher scale values on the Content, Sender, and Receiver dimensions, this was not consistent across scenarios and dimensions. Of the 16 possible correlations, only 4 were significant. (See Appendix B, where these correlations are reported for all experiments in this book.) The lack of consistency across scenarios and the fact that the correlations were never significant for the Context dimension, which consistently differentiated between conditions, strongly suggest that our results were not an artifact of message length.

Another possible artifact could be the completeness of sentences. There are five messages in the Class scenario that have incomplete sentences and one message in the Gift scenario. These all have above-average scale values, but they are also shorter messages. *None* of the car ads has complete sentences, so this factor could not influence scale values for these messages. Of the four Member of Parliament messages with incomplete sentences, the two longer messages were scaled as clearer than the two shorter ones. Apparently, length of message is more important than completeness of sentences, but neither can consistently differentiate between conditions, as our dimensions do.

Finally, for each experiment, we correlated the four dimensions with each other across both conditions, in order to examine their degree of redundancy. As can be seen in Appendix B (which contains these correlations for all subsequent experiments as well), there was no clear pattern of overlap. In the Class Presentation scenario, Content, Sender, and Receiver intercorrelated significantly, whereas in the Car Ad scenario, only Content and Context did so. In the other two scenarios, there were no significant intercorrelations. The four dimensions of equivocation are not redundant in written messages.

SUMMARY

Participants in four experiments were presented with hypothetical scenarios to which they had to respond with a written reply. In each experiment, half of the participants were in a communicative avoidance-avoidance conflict, and the other half were in a control (nonconflict) condition. The resulting messages were all unique, yet scaling revealed that those written in the conflict conditions were significantly more equivocal on at least one dimension than were those written in the nonconflict conditions. This quantitative analysis was supplemented by a qualitative examination of the particular techniques by which people spontaneously equivocate.

6

Spoken and Face-to-Face Communication

As proposed in Chapter 3, our plan has been to move from highly restricted to increasingly complex situations and from purely verbal, written messages to those with nonverbal aspects as well. The six experiments to be described here (Bavelas, Black, Chovil, & Mullett, in press) took us much further along this continuum. First, we added the audible (vocal) nonverbal aspects of speech — such as tone of voice, emphasis, rhythm, rate of speech, and hesitations — so that the messages included all of the verbal and nonverbal information available, say, on the telephone. Then we added the visual (bodily) aspects of nonverbal communication — including facial expressions, gestures, body movements, and direction of gaze — all of the information available when people interact face to face. As well, the scenarios went from rather schematic and scripted to somewhat richer and more open to the participants' own interpretations.

Including the nonverbal aspects of communication would permit us to generalize our findings beyond written notes. In addition, messages with both verbal and nonverbal aspects are of particular theoretical interest. The previous literature on incongruency and disqualification (e.g., Bateson, Jackson, Haley, & Weakland, 1956; Bugenthal, Kaswan, & Love, 1970; Haley, 1959a; Mehrabian & Ferris, 1967) has emphasized discrepancies between the verbal and nonverbal aspects of a message — for example, saying "I love you" in a cold tone of voice. The experiments described in Chapters 4 and 5 have shown that people can equivocate using words only, so equivocation does not *require* a verbal-nonverbal incongruency. What changes, if any, would the availability of nonverbal information introduce?

For example, would speakers shift to verbal-nonverbal discrepancies, producing messages that are verbally clear but rendered equivocal by the way in which they are said?

We predict that such discrepancies will *not* be found. Our view of communication is that a message is delivered as a unified whole and not in separate "channels" that might vie with each other. The speaker skillfully uses all of the possibilities available in a given situation. In written communication, everything must be conveyed verbally, but when nonverbal communication is also possible, words can be assisted or even replaced by other means of expression. For example, an enthusiastic tone of voice might be "synonymous" with exclamation points and underlining in a handwritten note. Similarly, gestures often illustrate speech to such an extent that they can be considered part of language (McNeill, 1985). In our "integrated message" model, the verbal and nonverbal aspects of a message are highly interwoven and, to a substantial extent, interchangeable. Therefore, we expect to see equivocation, when it occurs, in the whole message — in both its verbal and nonverbal aspects.

We began by adding only the audible nonverbal concomitants of speech — often called the *paralinguistic* aspects — so the next series of experiments was conducted on the telephone. The participant talked to another person (played by an experimenter) over a telephone hook-up between two rooms in our lab; these conversations were tape recorded at the same time. This procedure (rather than using only the audiotape of a conversation that actually occurred face to face) follows our principle that the message should be obtained in exactly the same form as it will be studied. We assumed that people talking on the telephone would naturally limit themselves to verbal and paralinguistic information. Speaking into the microphone of a tape recorder would impose the same limitation, but pilot work quickly revealed that this was much less comfortable for the speaker than was the telephone. The telephone format turned out to be so natural for participants and experimenters that both became engrossed in their roles and continued the conversation until its natural conclusion, which was often several exchanges after the initial reply to the question (which was all we needed).

The four "spoken" experiments were similar in many respects: The participants were undergraduate volunteers. There were two experimenter roles, which were taken by several different individuals (male or female). Each participant met Experimenter 1 in our usual room, which now had a telephone on the desk, and was told the following:

What you will be doing is having a telephone conversation with another person. The other person is next door in the other room. This conversation will be recorded.

Experimenter 1 then gave the scenario (which, as will be seen, was either an old, new, or modified one), mentioned that the other person would ask a question (without saying what the question would be), and concluded by saying,

Your response should be really brief. Try to limit it to one or two short statements. When I leave the room, imagine that the phone has just rung, pick up the receiver, and say "Hello." The other person will be on the line.

When the participant had said "Hello," Experimenter 2 (who had not met the participant and did not know the experimental condition) made an introductory remark or two, asked the question, and waited for the reply. Then Experimenter 2 and the participant continued the conversation until a mutual conclusion, after which Experimenter 1 returned, explained the experiment, and answered any questions. Later, the participants' initial replies (along with Experimenter 2's question) were transferred to a master tape, in random order, and scaled by the judges.

Notice that, in contrast to the written format, the participant had to respond "in real time," because he or she did not know the exact question until it was asked. This made the situation even more realistic, as did the absence of Experimenter 1, who had been an irrelevant third party in the written experiments. The spoken format also permitted us to measure latency (how long the respondent took from the end of the question until the beginning of the reply); this aspect of the messages will be discussed at the end of the · chapter.

Transcription Conventions

In presenting the messages obtained in these experiments, we have included not only the words but our description of how these messages sound, using conventions that we hope are self-explanatory:

- The gender of the speaker gives an idea of voice quality.
- Latency [in seconds] is the time between the end of the question and the beginning of the first utterance (whether a word or just a vocalization such as "**Ah**").

- A subjective description of the manner in which the phrases following are spoken, as well as indications of unusual volume, pace, or fluency, are given in parentheses followed by a colon.
- The words spoken are in **boldface.**
- Words stressed by the speaker are in CAPITALS.
- A dash (−) means the speaker breaks off sharply.
- Two (or more) words or sounds run together as if they were one word are hyphenated.
- A comma indicates a slight pause, usually associated with a phrase within a sentence.
- A period denotes the kind of pause and intonation ordinarily heard at the end of a sentence.
- Three unspaced, boldface dots (. . .) indicate a longer pause.

While a written transcript cannot truly convey the paralinguistic aspects of the messages, you can get a feeling for the messages by reading them aloud to yourself, using the above conventions as a guide.

EXPERIMENT 10: CLASS PRESENTATION (SPOKEN)

This familiar scenario was adapted to require a telephone conversation instead of a written note:

Imagine that the person on the telephone is a fellow student. The two of you have a class that meets three times a week for the entire year. Each student has to make an individual presentation to the class. Today this other student (the one on the telephone) gave his/her presentation. You had helped him/her by supplying reference material. Unfortunately, his/her presentation was poorly organized and badly delivered. The class ended late, and you didn't get a chance to talk, so the other student calls you on the telephone to discuss the presentation.

In a few minutes, you will have a telephone conversation with this student. Let the other person start the conversation. He/she will ask you a question that we would like you to respond to. Your response should be really brief. Try to limit it to one or two short statements.

*So when I leave the room, imagine that the phone has just rung, pick up the receiver, and say "*Hello.*" The other person will be on the line.*

Any questions? When you're finished, hang up the phone and remain in the room. I'll return.

In the nonconflict version, the key sentence was changed to

His/her presentation was well organized and well delivered.

When the participant had picked up the phone, Experimenter 2 said:

HI! This is [FIRST NAME]. I DIDN'T get a chance to TALK to you after class, and I just wanted to ASK, HOW did I DO on my PRESENTATION?

This experiment started out as a pilot study, so the two conditions were not randomly assigned. They were instead alternated; due to experimenter error, the last participant was in the conflict rather than nonconflict version, so the *n*'s were 7 and 5 rather than 6 in each condition.

As we had hoped, the format and scenario appeared to be quite realistic for the participants. Their initial replies (the first utterance after the experimenter's question) are transcribed in Table 6.1, along with the scale values, reliabilities, and *t*-tests.

The differences between conditions on both the Sender and Context dimensions were statistically significant. The speakers in the conflict condition were less likely to give their own opinions and to answer the question directly than were those in the nonconflict condition. The means for Content and Sum also differed in the predicted direction, while the means for the Receiver dimension differed (nonsignificantly) in the opposite direction. Inspection of the scale values on this dimension suggests that this occurred because of one message in the conflict condition, which was scaled over two and a half standard deviations below the mean, principally because the speaker used the receiver's first name.

Qualitative analysis shows that, on the Content dimension, the nonconflict messages were usually well formed, fluent, and to the point:

Male: [0.8 sec.] (very warmly:) **Well, it just went over GRR-REAT!**

Female: [0.4 sec.] (softly, warmly:) **Really WELL. I thought you did a really GOOD job.**

In contrast, praise in the conflict condition was tempered both by stammering and by covert verbal signals that all is not well:

Female: [1.2 sec.] (Brightly:) **WELL, ah! . . .** (Quickly, then becoming hesitant:) **You seemed to 've, you know, covered — used a lot of the REFERENCES I — I lent you, anyway.**

Similarly, in the following message, the effect of the hesistant tone and the question at the end is to leave the praise hanging precariously in the air. The judges found this message almost contradictory:

> *Female:* [1.0 sec.] (Hesitantly, sounding somewhat surprised:) **Oh, um . . . WELL, it was-um,** (then faster, but still unsure:) **it was very GOOD. W-why do you ask?**

On the Sender dimension, the use of "**I**" did not differentiate sharply between conditions, as it had done for the written messages. ("**I**" or "**me**" appeared in four of the five nonconflict messages and five of the seven conflict messages.) Additional cues such as phrasing and tone of voice indicated to the judges that the nonconflict messages were unequivocally the sender's own opinion:

> *Female:* [1.0 sec.] (Fast, almost breathlessly; pitch rising on emphasized words:) **I thought it was just GREAT! I was really IMPRESSED!**

> *Male:* [1.0 sec.] (Matter-of-factly:) **Well, it looked pretty good to ME. Ah . . . as far as I could tell,** (then more warmly:) **you were well PREPARED —** (ends abruptly).

In contrast, the conflict messages were both hesitant in tone and evasive as to whose opinion is being given; for example,

> *Female:* [1.3 sec.] Tsk. (Carefully, almost hesitantly:) **WELL, ah, I think the FEELING was that it WAS, ah . . . tsk,** (then businesslike and faster:) **a DIFFICULT thing to DO under the CIRCUMSTANCES, but maybe it could be a BIT better ORGANIZED in the FUTURE.**

Although this message starts with "**I think,**" it switches quickly to an impersonal source ("**the feeling was**"), so the speaker herself is not responsible for the evaluation given.

As noted earlier, the major difference on the Receiver dimension was the use of the receiver's first name by one speaker. Otherwise, messages that mentioned or implied a class presentation were scaled below the mean.

On the Context dimension, the fit between question and answer was noticeably looser here, even for the nonconflict messages, than had been the case in written messages. The message with the lowest scale value kept the same phrasing as the question (which was "**HOW did I DO on my PRESENTATION?**"):

TABLE 6.1

Experiment 10: Class Presentation (spoken)

Condition	Content	Sender	Receiver	Context	Sum
Nonconflict Condition					
Female: <0.4 sec.> (Softly, warmly:) Really WELL. I thought you did a really GOOD job.	-.64	-.71	.38	-1.10	-2.07
Male: <1.0 sec.> (Matter-of-factly:) Well, it looked pretty good to ME. Ah ... as far as I could tell, (then more warmly:) you were well PREPARED-- (ends abruptly).	-.53	-.55	-.19	-.61	-1.88
Female: <1.0 sec.> (Fast, almost breathlessly; pitch rising on emphasized words:) I thought it was just GREAT! I was really IMPRESSED!	-.35	-.77	.34	-.91	-1.69
Male: <0.8 sec.> (Very warmly:) Well, it just went over GRR-REAT!	-.37	-.24	.44	-.74	-.91
Male: <1.0 sec.> (Off-handedly:) FINE, as far as I'M concerned.	.43	-.47	.62	-.54	.04
Conflict Condition					
Male: <1.4 sec.> (Assertively and fast:) Ah, to tell you the TRUTH, I think you could of .. ah, spent a (then more firmly, almost as if scolding:) little more time ORGANIZING it, Jennifer.	-.56	-.73	-2.67	.04	-3.92
Female: <0.8 sec.> (Very softly, with resignation:) How did ya' do. ...: (Thoughtfully, and still very softly:) Hm. (Then slightly louder, at first regretfully and then brightening:) Well, I'm afraid it wasn't--as ORGANIZED as it could have been, but I know you got your POINTS across.	-.63	-.55	.11	-.12	-1.19

Female:	<1.3 sec.> (Voice has a "school-marmish," prissy quality throughout:) Ah ... perhaps you were not THOROUGH enough. Ah, you could have covered, ah, FAMILY LIFE better ... ahhm ... been more specific on your IDEAS, on where you wanted people to, to sort of, ah, QUIZ you on. Um ... I think it's very IMPORTANT that we're always ... very CLEAR and specific on what we do, ah—want to STRESS (then more slowly and even more distinctly:) as our aim of RESEARCH. Is there anything else that you ... (finishes hesitantly:) can—? (ends abruptly.)	-.08	.53	-.10	1.06	1.41
Female:	<0.6 sec.> (Brightly:) Ah ... WELL, it-ah didn't go too BADLY, but-um there could be some (slight suggestion of a laugh) improvements here and THERE!	.54	.50	.30	.20	1.54
Female:	<1.2 sec.> (Brightly:) WELL, ah! ... (Quickly, then becoming hesitant:) You seemed to 've, you know, covered— used a lot of the REFERENCES I— I lent you, anyway.	.61	.32	-.29	1.15	1.79
Female:	<1.3 sec.> Tsk. (Carefully, almost hesitantly:) WELL, ah, I think the FEELING was that it WAS, ah ... tsk. (then business-like and faster:) a DIFFICULT thing to DO under the CIRCUMSTANCES, but maybe it could be a BIT better ORGANIZED in the FUTURE.	.44	1.71	.48	.54	3.17
Female:	<1.0 sec.> (Hesitantly, sounding somewhat surprised:) Oh, um ... WELL, it was-um. (then faster, but still unsure:) it was very GOOD. W-why do you ask?	1.14	.95	.57	1.02	3.68

Summary Statistics

Reliability (intraclass R) =	.84	.95	.99	.95	
Nonconflict mean =	-.29	-.55	.32	-.78	-1.30
Conflict mean =	.21	.39	-.23	.56	.92
t =	1.49	2.41	.53	5.26	2.09
p (one-tailed) =	n.s.	<.05	n.s.	<.001	n.s.

Female: [0.4 sec.] (softly, warmly:) **Really WELL. I thought you did a really GOOD job.**

But another message shifted to **"it was"** and was still scaled as a responsive answer:

Female: [1.0 sec.] (Fast, almost breathlessly; pitch rising on emphasized words:) **I thought it was just GREAT! I was really IMPRESSED!**

Responses scaled above the mean were answering completely different questions. In each case, the reader can easily infer the other question (or questions) actually being answered:

Female: [1.2 sec.] (Brightly:) **WELL, ah!** ... (Quickly, then becoming hesitant:) **You seemed to 've, you know, covered— used a lot of the REFERENCES I— I lent you, anyway.**

Female: [1.3 sec.] (Voice has a "school-marmish," prissy quality throughout:) **Ah ... perhaps you were not THOROUGH enough. Ah, you could have covered, ah, FAMILY LIFE better ... ahhm ... been more specific on your IDEAS, on where you wanted people to, to sort of, ah, QUIZ you on. Um ... I think it's very IMPORTANT that we're always ... very CLEAR and specific on what we do, ah-want to STRESS** (then more slowly and even more distinctly:) **as our aim of RESEARCH. Is there anything else that you ...** (finishes hesitantly:) **can— ?** (ends abruptly)

EXPERIMENT 11A: BIZARRE GIFT (SPOKEN)

Experiments 11A and 11B were conducted together, one immediately after the other, with the same 12 participants. Conflict and nonconflict versions of the Gift scenario were randomly assigned to participants in 11A, then the opposite version was given for the new scenario in 11B. This was a strong test of our situational theory, because a given participant would be in a conflict in one scenario and not in the other. We expected the individual's use of equivocation to change with the experimental condition.

The general instructions were the same as those used for Experiment 10, with the following description of the scenario:

Imagine the person on the telephone is a friend who has sent you a gift for your birthday. You received the gift a few days ago, but you are not sure if it is meant as a joke or if it is to be taken seriously, as it is quite bizarre.

In the nonconflict version, the last sentence read:

You can tell that it was carefully selected with your tastes and interests in mind.

Experimenter 1 then gave the instructions about answering the phone and left the room. When the participant picked up the phone and said "**Hello,**" Experimenter 2 (playing the role of the friend) said:

HI, this is [FIRST NAME]. SORRY I didn't get a chance to SEE you on your birthday. I was just wondering, HOW did you LIKE the GIFT I sent you?

The transcribed messages, their scale values, reliabilities, and *t*-tests are given in Table 6.2. The conflict messages were substantially more equivocal than the nonconflict messages: The scale values differed significantly on all four dimensions and their Sum.

The qualitative differences are similar to those found in the Class Presentation messages. On the Content dimension, the nonconflict messages are fluent, articulate, and precise about why the gift was welcome:

Female: [0.3 sec.] (Warmly and enthusiastically:) **Oh, it was REAL-LY nice; you obviously went to a lot of trouble to pick out something that I'd like.**

Female: [0.7 sec.] (Warmly yet formally:) **I thought it was really LOVELY, and I-I could tell that it was — CAREFULLY picked out.**

In contrast, the conflict responses are delivered awkwardly and use ambiguous terms such as "**not bad**" and "**intriguing**":

Female: [0.8 sec.] **Umh** (with slight laugh). (Starts hesitantly, then brightening:) **It was-ah, not BAD** (ends with very slight laugh).

Female: [0 sec.] (Sounding puzzled:) **Ah?** . . . (Slight laugh, which slurs into first word:) **It's quite INTRIGUING.**

The same four messages also illustrate the qualitative differences on the Sender dimension. The first two messages state an opinion in a firm, unhesitant manner, whereas the second two are in hesitant or uncertain tones of voice, along with an uneasy laugh. Overall, these paralinguistic aspects, as well as the use of "**I**," determined the Sender value in the spoken messages.

In most of our experiments, the two conditions did not differ on the Receiver dimension, but this scenario was an exception. The difference was

TABLE 6.2
Experiment 11A: Bizarre Gift (spoken)

Condition	Content	Sender	Receiver	Context	Sum
Nonconflict Condition					
Female: <0.3 sec.> (Warmly and enthusiastically:) Oh, it was REAL-LY nice; you obviously went to a lot of trouble to pick out something that I'd like.	-1.07	-.75	-1.52	-1.15	-4.49
Female: <0.7 sec.> (Warmly yet formally:) I thought it was really LOVELY, and I-I could tell that it was-- CAREFULLY picked out.	-.73	-.78	-.87	-.73	-3.11
Female: <0.2 sec.> (Warmly, forcefully: pitch rising on stressed words:) Just BEAUTIFUL, BEAUTIFUL! It's exactly what I would have wanted.	-.58	-.72	-.84	-.88	-3.02
Male: <0.5 sec.> (Matter-of-factly, pleasantly:) It was very NICE. It was just what I was LOOKING for, actually.	-.46	-.52	-.16	-.60	-1.74
Male: <0.3 sec.> (In a warm tone:) OHH ... it was really V-VERY good. (Then more neutral:) Showed-- quite a bit of taste.	-.13	.10	-.12	-.30	-.45
Male: <0.3 sec.> (With mild enthusiasm:) Oh, it was GREAT. (then much softer:) terrific.	.72	-.09	.89	-.34	1.18
Conflict Condition					
Female: <0.5 sec.> (In a warm but restrained tone:) I think it's GREAT.	.68	-.75	.73	-.66	0.00
Male: <0.7 sec.> (Sounding surprised at first:) Oh! It's-ah (then recovering and becoming formal:) very INTERESTING. I'm sure I can put it to good USE.	-.39	.29	.35	.28	.53

Female: <1.9 sec.> (Softly, seriously; sounding almost hurt:) A-ah, well Jennifer I'm NOT SURE how to, how to TAKE— ah, the gift. I wasn't sure if it was a JOKE, or-or if you're trying to send me a MESSAGE, give me a messy.

-.58	.52	-.25	1.26	.95

Female: <0.6 sec.> (Sounding puzzled but not hesitant:) Ahhmm, I APPRECIATE it, but I'm NOT exactly how-how to take it. I'm not sure how you ... how you MEANT it.

.38	.17	.13	.90	1.58

Female: <0 sec.> (Sounding puzzled:) Ah? ... (Slight laugh, which slurs into the first word:) It's quite INTRIGUING.

.94	1.00	.89	1.11	3.94

Female: <0.8 sec.> Umh (with slight laugh). (Starts hesitantly, then brightening:) It was—ah, not BAD (ends with very slight laugh).

1.20	1.51	.78	1.10	4.59

Summary Statistics

Reliability (intraclass R) =	.92	.92	.94	.97	
Nonconflict mean =	-.38	-.46	-.44	-.67	-1.93
Conflict mean =	.37	.46	.44	.67	1.93
t =	1.93	2.62	2.27	4.06	3.40
p (one-tailed) =	<.05	<.02	<.03	<.001	<.005

based partly on tone of voice and partly on what was said. The first five messages in Table 6.2 are warm and appropriate to a friendship, both in tone and words; for example:

> *Female:* [0.3 sec.] (Warmly and enthusiastically:) **Oh, it was REAL-LY nice; you obviously went to a lot of trouble to pick out something that I'd like.**

A noncommittal message in a restrained, somewhat impersonal tone did not seem to our judges to be addressed to a friend:

> *Female:* [0.5 sec.] (In a warm but restrained tone:) **I think it's GREAT.**

It is interesting that, although one message uses the receiver's first name, its overall awkwardness—both verbally and nonverbally—almost cancels out this obvious clue. Its stiffness, mainly due to hesitant starting and stopping, does not sound like an exchange with a good friend:

> *Female:* [1.9 sec.] (Softly, seriously; sounding almost hurt:) **A-ah, well Jennifer I'm NOT SURE how to, how to TAKE— ah, the gift. I wasn't sure if it was a JOKE, or-or if you're . . . if you're trying to send me a MESSAGE, give me a messy.**

All of the messages in the nonconflict condition (and the first message in the conflict condition) have negative values on the Context dimension because they directly answer the question, **"HOW did you LIKE the GIFT I sent you?"** Both the **"messy"** message (just given above) and the following one answer a different question, namely, **"Do you know how to TAKE the gift I sent you?"**

> *Female:* [0.6 sec.] (Sounding puzzled but not hesitant:) **Ahhmm, I APPRECI-ATE it, but I'm NOT exactly how-how to take it. I'm not sure how you . . . how you MEANT it.**

Two replies are so vague that they were not considered good answers to *any* question:

> *Female:* [0 sec.] (Sounding puzzled:) **Ah? . . .** (Slight laugh, which slurs into first word:) **It's quite INTRIGUING.**
>
> *Female:* [0.8 sec.] **Umh** (with slight laugh). (Starts hesitantly, then brightening:) **It was-ah, not BAD** (ends with very slight laugh).

EXPERIMENT 11B: MEAT MARKET (SPOKEN)

After the participants had replied to the question about the gift, Experimenter 1 returned and explained that the procedure would be the same except that the situation had changed. The second half of this experiment used what was to become (because of the replies) one of our favorite scenarios. It was suggested by a previous participant who, when discussing our theory after an experiment, told the experimenter about a communicative conflict he had been in, which we adapted as follows:

You work in a grocery store, and you know that Tuesday is the day they sell off all the old meat at a reduced price. Some of it is very old and poor quality.

On this particular Tuesday, the telephone rings. You answer it, and it is someone who saw the sale of the meat at a reduced price advertised in the newspaper. They have never shopped at your store, so they have called to get some information before coming to the store.

When the participant picked up the phone, a different Experimenter 2 than in 11A said:

HELLO, I've NEVER been to your STORE before, and I was wondering, the MEAT that is on SALE today, Is it GOOD?

Telling the customer that the meat is not good would be true but would have negative consequences (turning away business, being disloyal to one's employer, or perhaps losing a job). Saying that the meat is good would be false and would engender some responsibility for the deceived customer's subsequent actions. In the other version, no such conflict existed:

. . . Tuesday is the day that they sell the meat at a reduced price, just to make sure it doesn't accumulate. It is all fresh and good quality meat. . . .

If the participant had been assigned to the conflict condition in 11A, he or she was given the nonconflict version of this scenario, and vice versa. Thus, experimental condition was still random with respect to individuals, based on the first assignment. We predicted that the messages would "flip" with the experimental condition, so that the same individuals who had equivocated in 11A would be clear and straightforward in the present situation, and vice versa.

The messages and the quantitative data are in Table 6.3. The means for all dimensions differed in the predicted direction, and this difference was significant for Content, Context, and Sum. This is strong evidence for the importance of the situation over individual differences, because all participants changed their communicative style with the situation. The same people who had responded clearly and articulately in the Gift scenario now gave highly equivocal replies to the Meat Market question, and the group who equivocated about the gift became direct and straightforward a few minutes later. (In Table 6.3, the speaker's position in Table 6.2 is given in the last column, so the reader can compare messages in the two parts of the experiment.)

Qualitatively, the messages with low scale values on the Content dimension are easy to understand:

Female: [0.8 sec.] (Briskly:) **It's good quality MEAT, YES.**

Female: [1.4 sec.] (As if stating the obvious; possible "smile" in her voice:) **Well, we wouldn't be selling BAD meat, you'd only bring it BACK.**

Our growing stock of vague phrases was enriched by two new descriptions, **"fairly fine"** and **"the usual,"** both high on the Content dimension:

Male: [0.5 sec.] (Pitch plummeting:) **OOOhhh** (then leveling; fast, picking up some enthusiasm at the end:) **it's— it's fairly FINE yes.**

Female: [0.8 sec.] (Sing-song:) **IT'S— the USUAL.**

Because **"I"** was seldom used, tone of voice determined the position of messages on the Sender dimension. Most of the nonconflict messages, and the first of the conflict messages, convey unequivocally by their tone that the message is the sender's own opinion. The other messages, with high values on this dimension, are spoken in startled, sometimes odd voices, with long pauses and stammering. The message with the highest value also shifts obliquely to **"they,"** as if reporting the opinion of others:

Female: [1.0 sec.] (Sounding rattled:) **UMM ... AH-no— the REASON why they're selling it is because it's, um ... it's a l-little bit OLD.**

Values on the Receiver dimension were determined by whether the message was appropriate to the roles of the two people. For example, the message with the lowest value refers to the sale of meat and also to **"we"** who are selling and **"you"** who is buying:

Female: [1.2 sec.] (As if stating the obvious; possible "smile" in her voice:) **Well, we wouldn't be selling BAD meat, you'd only bring it BACK.**

All of these clues are noticeable by their absence from the message with the highest Receiver value, which also struck some judges as sounding almost flippant, not deferential or respectful enough to be a salesclerk talking to a customer:

Male: [0.5 sec.] (Pitch plummeting:) **OOOhhh** (then leveling; fast, picking up some enthusiasm at the end:) **it's— it's fairly FINE yes.**

The judges also noticed that one person speaks more as if she were another customer, rather than the salesclerk:

I haven't had any FAULT with-WITH the meat there BEFORE.

The nonconflict messages with low values on the Context dimension respond to the question about the meat, **"Is it GOOD?"** by saying, simply, that it is good and perhaps adding relevant details. After the first conflict message, the others can be seen to use a variety of now-familiar techniques to avoid answering the question. The second and fifth conflict messages answer different questions (**"WHY is the meat on SALE?"** or **"WHAT is the REASON they are SELLING the meat?"**). The third message answers that the meat is good but then adds several qualifications and long digressions. The fourth and sixth messages are too vague to answer any question well.

Because these equivocal replies were made by the same people who spoke clearly when in the nonconflict condition in 11A, we have further evidence that individuals do not cause equivocation — situations do.

EXPERIMENT 12: EMPLOYEE REFERENCE (SPOKEN)

We had used the employee reference scenario early in the forced-choice experiments (Chapter 4). The present version was not nearly so restricted as that earlier version, which had provided "ready-made" information in two senses: The messages themselves were provided, and the fact that the employee was incompetent was simply given in the instructions. Here we not only let people respond spontaneously with their own replies, we also let them reach their own conclusions about the employee's competence.

TABLE 6.3
Experiment 11B: Meat Market (spoken) a. Speaker's position in

Condition	Content	Sender	Receiver	Context	Sum	Order[a]
Nonconflict Condition						
Female: <0.8 sec.> (Briskly:) It's good quality MEAT, YES.	-1.35	-.47	-.37	-1.09	-3.28	11
Female: <0.4 sec.> (Confidently:) It SURE is, it's top grade A MEAT.	-1.02	-.64	-.47	-1.15	-3.28	10
Female: <0.2 sec.> (With enthusiasm:) YES, it is VERY good QUALITY.	-.20	-.68	.29	-1.15	-1.74	12
Female: <1.2 sec.> (As if stating the obvious; possible "smile" in her voice:) Well, we wouldn't be selling BAD meat, you'd only bring it BACK.	-.92	.68	-1.26	.02	-1.48	7
Male: <0.2 sec.> (Smoothly, sounding very professional:) OH, YES. It's ALL very fresh. Ah— we just PUT it on sale to reduce INVENTORY.	-.11	.31	-.53	-.52	-.85	8
Female: <1.8 sec.> (Breathlessly, timidly:) U-u—umm, I can be— BE reasonably— ASSURED THAT it's good, it—I haven't had any FAULT with—WITH the meat there BEFORE. ... If you—if you FIND something, um, has gone BAD— like the CHICKEN, ah, it can be exchanged.	-.65	-.57	.71	-.03	-.54	9
Conflict Condition						
Male: <0.6 sec.> (Fast, confidently:) I think it's quite good, YES, (then, almost a question:) for the price.	.66	-1.09	.59	-.11	.05	4
Male: <1.7 sec.> (As if conceding a point:) WE-LLL it—it is on SALE because it—ah (then speeding up and more matter-of-fact in tone:) HAS been in the store for a WHILE but that doesn't mean that it's BAD.	.09	.15	-.42	.31	.13	6

Female:	<0.5 sec.> (Fast, sounding startled at first:) Ah, y-- WELL ... yes it IS good meat. It-the-ahh, I'd like you to REALIZE though that it IS-ah, day OLD meat. or older. (Then more business-like, still fast:) So that it-it may not have some of the COLOR that, ah the meat that you would find cut FRESHLY today... . (More slowly:) SO and it's-ah ... NOT-ah TOP quality meat, y' know. It's-- (then fast and slow in bursts:) there's nothing WRONG with the meat, but-ah, it's not your, ahm, CROSS r†-- your ... STANDING rib roast, or your-ah SIRLOIN steaks that are on sale. But it's ALL, um ... there's nothing at all WRONG with it that, but the COLOR may be gone on-- out of it.	.36	.49	-.71	.77	.91	1
Male:	<0.5 sec.> (Pitch plummeting:) OOOhhh (then levelling; fast, picking up some enthusiasm at the end:) it's-- it's fairly FINE yes.	1.07	.10	1.02	.41	2.60	5
Female:	<1.0 sec.> (Sounding rattled:) UMM ... AH-no-- the REASON why they're selling it is because it's, um ... it's a l-little bit OLD.	.65	1.43	.15	1.29	3.52	3
Female:	<0.8 sec.> (Sing-song:) IT'S-- the USUAL.	1.43	.27	.99	1.25	3.94	2

Summary Statistics

Reliability (intraclass R) =	.97	.90	.91	.97	
Nonconflict mean =	-.71	-.23	-.27	-.65	-1.86
Conflict mean =	.71	.23	.27	.65	1.86
t =	5.08	1.12	1.23	4.08	4.37
p (one-tailed) =	<.001	n.s.	n.s.	<.001	<.001

143

It could be argued that, because we had told our participants that the employee (or car, class presentation, meat, etc.) were good or bad, we had effectively encoded their messages for them. In other words, they might simply have been repeating back what they were told. It is our reading of their messages that people were considerably more imaginative than that, because they added many rich details purely of their own invention (e.g., **"it's not your, ahm, CROSS ri – your … STANDING rib roast"** or **"you could have covered, ah, FAMILY LIFE better"**). Still, we wanted to give participants uncoded data, in order that they would have to *form* their own opinions as well as to express them.

So, in this experiment, participants were given an "Employee Appraisal Form" containing evaluations of performance in six general areas. In the conflict condition (see Figure 6.1), the employee's performance was rated as borderline or poor in almost every area. In the nonconflict condition, performance was rated as excellent or good in every category. After the usual general directions about a telephone conversation, Experimenter 1 gave these specifics:

> *You work for the [Provincial] government as a personnel officer, and every three months you receive employee evaluations. This month, an evaluation on Pat Green (a friend of yours) was sent over to you.*
>
> *Pat has applied for another position in the government. In a few minutes, you will receive a phone call from another friend regarding this application. So in this situation, both Pat and the person calling you are good friends of yours. Any questions?*

He or she was then given the Employee Appraisal Form, with conflict and nonconflict versions randomly assigned. Experimenter 1 waited while it was read, told the participant that he or she was to answer the phone (which would now "buzz" when Experimenter 1 left), gave the usual remaining instructions, and left the room. On the phone, Experimenter 2 said:

> **HI, is this** [participant's FIRST NAME]? **This is** [own FIRST NAME]. **I'm CALLING because PAT GREEN has applied for a JOB here and used your name as a REFERENCE. Is PAT a GOOD employee?**

The planned *N* was 12; because one person misunderstood the instructions, a thirteenth was added as a replacement. The 12 messages, given in Table 6.4 along with all of the quantitative data, confirm that the participants had read the information, formed an impression from it, and had come up with their

EMPLOYEE APPRAISAL FORM

INSTRUCTIONS

This form is to be completed in DUPLICATE by the *direct* supervisor of the employee being appraised. A check mark (✓) is to be placed in the appropriate column. If, due to the nature of the duties, certain factors do not apply, check the N/A column. Refer to the "Supervisor's Guide for Appraising Employee Performance."

Name (print) __Pat Green_____ Position_____

Branch_____Ministry_____ Location _____

CODE: N/A—NOT APPLICABLE; E—EXCELLENT; G—GOOD; S—SATISFACTORY;
B—BORDERLINE; P—POOR

1. QUALITY OF WORK	N/A	E	G	S	B	P
Knowledge of the job					✓	
Ability to plan work						✓
Accuracy in work performance					✓	

2. QUANTITY OF WORK	N/A	E	G	S	B	P
Ability to complete work on time						✓
Volume of work completed					✓	

3. EFFECTIVENESS	N/A	E	G	S	B	P
Ability to carry out instructions					✓	
Ability to work independently						✓
Ability to work under pressure					✓	
Ability to deal adequately in an emergency	✓					
Ability to adapt to new procedures						✓

4. ATTITUDE	N/A	E	G	S	B	P
Attitude to the job				✓		
Attitude toward supervisor						✓
Attitude toward the Ministry				✓		

5. PUBLIC RELATIONS	N/A	E	G	S	B	P
Appearance on duty					✓	
Manner toward the public	✓					

6. WORK HABITS	N/A	E	G	S	B	P
Attendance record						✓
General health			✓			
Co-operation					✓	
Safety attitude and practise				✓		

COMMENTS (related to Section 1 to 6) __Pleasant to work with_____

_____

_____

Figure 6.1. Employee Appraisal Form

TABLE 6.4
Experiment 12: Employee Reference (spoken)

Condition	Content	Sender	Receiver	Context	Sum
Nonconflict Condition					
Female: <1.0 sec.> (Pleasantly, fast:) Yes Pat's a VERY good employee.	-1.69	-1.37	-1.08	-1.09	-5.23
Male: <0.5 sec.> (Sounding inexperienced but sincere:) Um ... yes he IS a good employee, w-- his record shows.	-.90	.33	-.73	-.86	-2.16
Female: <0.5 sec.> (Pitch rising at end of word:) YEAH! ... (Faster:) Ah-- um VERY very good.	.35	-1.11	1.19	-.81	-.38
Male: <0.3 sec.> (Somewhat hesitantly, then more confidently:) Ah ye-es ah, our--our RECORDS SHOW that he's--ah performing satisfactorily.	-.48	1.06	.25	-.27	.56
Male: <0.9 sec.> (Hesitantly at first, then stronger but still as if surprised:) Ah, ye-es, according to her EVALUATION sheet she is (then softly:) yes.	.39	1.39	.43	-.84	1.37
Female: <1.6 sec.> (Brightly, pitch rising at end:) UM! (Then slowing and less sure:) Yeah, it APPEARS to be so.	1.44	-.22	1.16	.64	3.02
Conflict Condition					
Female: <0.7 sec.> (Brightly:) Ahm! (With some emphasis:) She's SATISFACTORY. (Somewhat less confidently:) SHE'S been with our OUTFIT for a while, and she's a SATISFACTORY employee.	-.84	-.63	-1.12	-.63	-3.22

Male:	<0.5 sec.> (As if forcing himself to speak:) Ah. ... He's a ... FAIRLY good employee.	-.15	-.36	-.80	.04	-1.27
Female:	<0.5 sec.> (Confidently:) AHMM. Well I have a RECORD of-- (then less confidently, almost as an aside:) of what she's done here and (then as if an admission:) seems that there's SOME problems.	-.09	.74	.27	.11	1.03
Male:	<1.2 sec.> AHH ... tsk. (repeating the words back mechanically:) is Pat a good. employee? Tsk. (Then stalling:) AH ... in-ah ... OVERALL, or in certain AREAS?	.31	.33	-.80	1.68	1.52
Male:	<1.3 sec.> (In a monotone at first, then rising pitch:) Well, um, that's DEPENDS on what y' call a good EMPLOYEE.	.52	.13	.01	1.58	2.24
Female:	<1.0 sec.> (Brightly:) Umm. (then almost crestfallen:) about AVERAGE.	1.14	-.29	1.21	.44	2.50

Summary Statistics

Reliability (intraclass R) =	.96	.94	.97	.98	
Nonconflict mean =	-.15	.01	.20	-.54	-.47
Conflict mean =	.15	-.01	-.21	.54	.47
t =	.56	.05	.78	2.36	.62
p (one-tailed) =	n.s.	n.s.	n.s.	<.02	n.s.

own replies — which by no means simply repeated back information given to them. There were only slight quantitative effects on most dimensions, but the difference between groups on the Context dimension was statistically significant.

Two particular messages — the first in each condition — are noteworthy. Both of these two messages have very low Sum scores and illustrate the qualitative aspects of clarity on all four dimensions. For example:

Female: [1.0 sec.] (Pleasantly, fast:) **Yes Pat's a VERY good employee.**

The content is definite and unqualified, and the unhesitating tone of voice leaves no question what the speaker's opinion is. What the judges noticed most on the Receiver dimension was "employer talk," that is, a manner consistent with two personnel officers talking about an employee: some formality, with definite information about the employee. Finally, the answer is low on the Context dimension because it virtually echoes back the structure of the question asked.

The second-lowest Sum value was found in the first message in the conflict condition:

Female: [0.7 sec.] (Brightly:) **Ahm!** (With some emphasis:) **She's SATISFAC-TORY.** (Somewhat less confidently:) **SHE'S been with our OUTFIT for a while, and she's a SATISFACTORY employee.**

This message has all of the qualities of the first example, although to a slightly lesser degree. What makes the message unusual is that it is completely false. The term "satisfactory" was one choice on the rating sheet, and Pat Green was consistently rated *below* satisfactory in this condition. Other messages use elastic terms such as **"FAIRLY good"** and **"about AVERAGE,"** but this message is unequivocally false. As such, it was a rare occurrence in our research (one that will be explored further in the next chapter). The usual solution to the conflict was equivocation, rather than a false message or a clear truth.

If the above two messages are kept in mind as examples of the qualitative characteristics of messages low on each dimension, the highest messages can be seen to contrast sharply. For example, the two messages highest on the Content dimension are cloaked in vagueness:

Female: [1.6 sec.] (Brightly, pitch rising at end:) **UM!** (Then slowing and less sure:) **Yeah, it APPEARS to be so.**

Female: [1.0 sec.] (Brightly:) **Umm,** (then almost crestfallen:) **about AVER-AGE.**

Note that the first of these is actually from the nonconflict condition. The message highest on the Sender dimension is also from this condition:

Male: [0.9 sec.] (Hesitantly at first, then stronger but still as if surprised:) **Ah, ye-es, according to her EVALUATION sheet she is** (then softly:) **yes.**

The message highest on the Receiver dimension is, according to our judges, too vague and informal to suit a professional exchange between personnel officers:

Female: [1.0 sec.] (Brightly:) **Umm,** (then almost crestfallen:) **about AVER-AGE.**

Finally, the two mesages with the highest values on the Context dimension throw the question back to the asker:

Male: [1.2 sec.] **AHH . . . tsk,** (repeating the words back mechanically:) **is Pat a good, employee? Tsk.** (Then stalling:) **AH . . . in-ah . . . OVERALL, or in certain AREAS?**

Male: [1.3 sec.] (In a monotone at first, then rising pitch:) **Well, um, that's DEPENDS on what y' call a good EMPLOYEE.**

It is important to reemphasize that, while there was a statistically significant difference on the Context dimension in this experiment, the overall effect of experimental condition was not strong—equivocal messages occurred in both conditions. The reader may have noticed, as have we over the course of this program of research, that when we start a series in a new format, the effect is often initially weak but gets stronger over the series. This is probably because we learn a great deal from both the participants and the judges about how to set up a scenario and phrase a tight question in order to produce conflict. A good example is a problem with the Sender dimension in this experiment: In retrospect, we should have used a question that explicitly asked for the *speaker's* opinion (e.g., **"What do YOU think of PAT as an EMPLOYEE?"**) rather than a general evaluation (**"Is PAT a GOOD employee?"**). Because the evaluation sheets were in fact the source of the information, referring to them was not equivocation, and such references occurred frequently in the nonconflict condition.

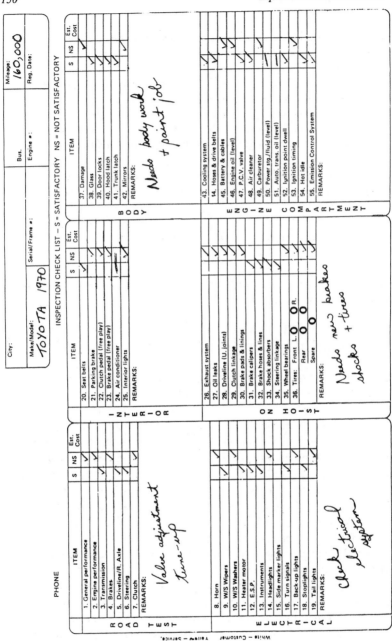

Figure 6.2. Inspection Check List

EXPERIMENT 13: CAR FOR SALE (SPOKEN)

This was the second of the "uncoded information" experiments, in which the participants were given detailed information about the car they were selling, rather than being told by us that it was in good or bad condition. We supplied a photograph of the car and an itemized mechanical checklist about its condition. In the conflict condition, the photograph showed an older car with a lot of damage and dents; the checklist revealed numerous major problems (see Figure 6.2). In the nonconflict condition, the car was much newer, looked good, and had only two minor problems. The specific instructions were as follows:

You have a car that you're trying to sell because you need the money. I'm going to give you a picture of the car and a mechanical checklist of its condition that I'd like you to read over.

The participant then had time to examine all of the information and to ask questions, if any, before Experimenter 1 continued:

Your brother has told a friend of his that you are selling your car. This friend will be calling you in a few minutes and will ask you a question which we'd like you to respond to, [etc.].

Experimenter 2 (who was anonymous to the participant, as usual) then buzzed and said:

HELLO, is this *[participant's FIRST NAME]*? **Your BROTHER has told me you have a CAR for SALE. What kind of SHAPE is the CAR in?**

Notice that we heightened the conflict, compared to the written version, by making the caller someone with whom there is an indirect personal relationship rather than a complete stranger reading car ads. Misrepresentations to a friend of your brother might come back to haunt you.

The data for one person, who misunderstood the instructions, were replaced by adding a thirteenth participant, so the final N was 12. The messages and their quantitative characteristics are given in Table 6.5. All means differed in the predicted direction, and the differences for Content, Context, and Sum were statistically significant.

The first message in the nonconflict condition is a good example of clear, specific, and detailed content:

TABLE 6.5
Experiment 13: Car for Sale (spoken)

Condition	Content	Sender	Receiver	Context	Sum
Nonconflict Condition					
Female: <0.7 sec.> (Softly, matter-of-factly:) It's in ... PRETTY good condition. (Said as if "you know?":) It's got 60,000 miles on it? (Then helpfully, with assurance:) And it's a Honda Civic 1975.	-1.92	.77	-1.42	-.36	-2.93
Female: <0.4 sec.> (Matter-of-factly:) Um, it's in really good SHAPE actually. No DENTS, no nothing.	-.40	-.02	-.36	-.91	-1.69
Female: <0.5 sec.> (Sounding assured:) It's in very GOOD shape.	-.44	-.40	.25	-.90	-1.49
Female: <0.5 sec.> (Very fast:) Ah it's in REALLY good shape.	-.34	-.46	.45	-.87	-1.22
Female: <0.5 sec.> (Very fast:) It's really GOOD shape.	-.09	-.38	.50	-.90	-.87
Male: <1.0 sec.> (Briskly:) Excellent. IT'S— (then, more softly:) there's nothing wrong with it.	-.25	-.21	.57	-.66	-.55
Conflict Condition					
Male: <1.7 sec.> (Hesitantly:) UM ... (then in a tone usually accompanied by "actually":) it's NOT bad shape. (Then helpfully:) It needs WORK; it's an OLD car; it's twelve years old.	-.23	.39	-1.06	.51	-.39

Male:	<1.2 sec.> (With some authority:) Well--it NEEDS-- ah, a little bit of MINOR repairs-- ah. Basically it RUNS, ah-- I--that's what I USE it for. ... So, ah, otherwise it's-- it needs a FEW minor repairs you know, I-- ... it's not in PERFECT condition.	.91	-.25	-.42	.92	1.16
Female:	<0.5 sec.> (As if sighing:) UM ... IT'S a ... (almost reluctantly:) MEDIOCRE type car. (Then in a nasal tone and with some sarcasm:) 'S nothing FANTASTIC.	.08	.08	-.02	1.43	1.57
Female:	<0.6 sec.> (Reluctantly, drawn out:) WELL ... it's NOT in-- (then as if admitting:) it's not in really GOOD shape. (Muffled laugh?)	.54	.37	.63	.34	1.88
Male:	<0.6 sec.> (Noncommittally:) Oh, it's in ... FAIR condition.	.63	.54	.48	.29	1.94
Female:	<1.2 sec.> (Emphatically:) WELL ... "Tsk." (Then almost as if confiding:) It DEPENDS how you want to LOOK at it. Actually, it's NOT really that good.	1.53	-.41	.40	1.11	2.63

Summary Statistics

Reliability (intraclass R) =	.95	.41	.85	.96	
Nonconflict mean =	-.57	-.12	.00	-.77	-1.46
Conflict mean =	.58	.12	.00	.77	1.47
t =	3.08	.97	.01	7.37	5.41
p (one-tailed) =	<.01	n.s.	n.s.	<.001	<.001

Figure 6.3.

Female: [0.7 sec.] (Softly, matter-of-factly:) **It's in ... PRETTY good condition**. (Said as if "you know?":) **It's got 60,000 miles on it?** (Then helpfully, with assurance:) **And it's a Honda Civic 1975.**

Whereas this message uses more words to say less:

Male: [1.2 sec.] (With some authority:) **Well— it NEEDS— ah, a little bit of MINOR repairs— ah. Basically it RUNS, ah— I— that's basically what I USE it for. . . . So, ah, otherwise it's— it needs a FEW minor repairs you know, I— ... it's not in PERFECT condition.**

Our judges could not tell from this message exactly what condition the car is in, and several of them thought that **"Basically it RUNS, ah— I— that's basically what I USE it for"** is a particularly vacuous description. They were also amused by the possibilities opened up in another message (which is reminiscent of **"DEPENDS on what y' call a good EMPLOYEE"**):

Female: [1.2 sec.] (Emphatically:) **WELLL ... Tsk.** (Then almost as if confiding:) **It DEPENDS how you want to LOOK at it. Actually, it's NOT really that good.**

Notice, however, that the above message is low on the Sender dimension, because of its confiding tone. The other messages low on this dimension were so placed because of tone of voice as well. Those sounding self-assured have low values, while a lack of commitment resulted in a high value:

Male: [0.6 sec.] (Noncommittally:) **Oh, it's in . . . FAIR condition.**

There was, overall, little variation among messages on either the Sender or Receiver dimensions. Just as tone of voice determined the Sender value, the appropriateness of both words and tone to the relationship of "selling a car to a friend of your brother" determined the value on the Receiver dimension. Helpful details about the car were appropriate:

Female [0.7 sec.] (Softly, matter-of-factly:) **It's in . . . PRETTY good condition.** (Said as if "you know?":) **It's got 60,000 miles on it?** (Then helpfully, with assurance:) **And it's a Honda Civic 1975.**

Lack of details about the car as well as strange paralinguistic aspects made the following message seem unfriendly and therefore inappropriate to the relationship:

Female: [0.5 sec.] (As if sighing:) **UM . . . IT'S a . . .** (almost reluctantly:) **MEDIOCRE type car.** (Then in a nasal tone and with some sarcasm:) **'S nothing FANTASTIC.**

Messages in the two conditions differ sharply on the Context dimension. All of the nonconflict replies answer the question, **"What kind of SHAPE is the CAR in?,"** and none of the conflict messages do. Looking over the latter replies, the reader can see that they are all vague non-answers, so cryptic or so heavily qualified that no question would be answered well by them.

This was the last experiment in our "spoken message" series. The five sets of spoken messages extended our conflict experiments into verbal-plus-nonverbal communication and confirmed our prediction that equivocation, when it occurred, would pervade a message and be found in both its verbal and paralinguistic aspects. The highly equivocal messages in these experiments were ambiguous both in their words and delivery. Tone of voice was especially important in indicating sender and receiver, but the verbal content mattered as well. Verbal and nonverbal aspects were largely congruent; there were few cases where one was clear and the other unclear.

EXPERIMENT 14A: CAR FOR SALE (FACE-TO-FACE)

The last pair of experiments in this series using our standard conflict/non-conflict design elicited and recorded face-to-face communication. The speakers were videotaped while talking in person to Experimenter 2 (a long way from writing notes to someone who was not there). Thus, the participants had available virtually all verbal and nonverbal possibilities: In addition to the words and paralinguistic aspects just studied, there were facial expressions, direction of gaze, hand and arm gestures, and body or head movements. This experiment used a pair of back-to-back scenarios that replicated previous spoken versions in every other respect, so that the parallel sets of messages could be compared.

We have an excellent video lab — a large, bright room with compact, remotely controlled cameras. In other projects, we had learned that it is unnecessary to conceal the camera or to deceive the participant about it, as long as it is introduced naturally and without undue emphasis. So the instructions began:

> *What you're going to be doing today is to have a couple of brief conversations with another person. I'm going to tell you about a situation that I want you to try and imagine yourself in. Then the other person will come into the room and ask you a question. After that, I'll come back into the room. While we're doing this, we'll be recorded on videotape. There will be two different situations. Before I describe the first one, do you have any questions?*

If a participant asked any questions about being videotaped, these were answered fully and in a manner implying that this was a positive experience; for example:

(enthusiastically:) **YES, you'll get to SEE us on videotape later!**

After the experiment was over, the participant viewed his or her tape while Experimenter 1 explained our theory and predictions and answered questions. It was pointed out that, although names would be kept confidential, no one could be anonymous in a videotape; so the experimenter asked for signed permission to keep the tape and to show it to judges for scaling.

There were two different Experimenter 2's (both female), who were randomly assigned to participants and to scenarios. They were told immediately before each session which scenario they would be in; they were not told which experimental condition the participant was in.

This was an uncoded information experiment; the procedure was exactly like that of Experiment 13, except that the brother's friend was to drop by in person rather than calling. Twelve participants were randomly assigned both to experimental condition and to Experimenter 2. Seventeen people actually participated, but five had to be replaced — one because of experimenter error and the rest for an odd variety of reasons (e.g., one started talking about the car before Experimenter 2 had even asked the question; another had a large rip in his pants that he was not aware of, so we erased his tape because we did not want to show it to the judges).

The messages and their scale values are shown in Table 6.6. In the table, we have not attempted to convey *all* of the visual aspects of the message, because even a much longer description could not recreate the message for the reader. However, along with our usual paralinguistic description, we have always indicated the direction of the speaker's gaze and have also added salient aspects of the respondent's behavior, such as smiles or gestures, particularly if they were noted by the judges.

The difference between conflict and nonconflict messages was in the predicted direction for Content, Sender, Context, and Sum; this difference was significant for Content, Context, and Sum. There was a nonsignificant reversal of direction for the Receiver dimension — as usual, the weakest dimension. Because two different individuals had been randomly assigned to the role of Experimenter 2, we also analyzed the data for experimenter effects; analysis of variance showed neither a significant effect of experimenter nor an experimenter-condition interaction.

The qualitative features of the Content dimension can be illustrated with the first and last messages, which have the lowest and highest values, respectively. The differences are essentially the same kinds as were found in written and spoken messages: The first message is verbally clear and consistent (**"Oh, it's in TERRIFIC shape. I never have ANY problems with it at all"**); the nonverbal aspects are consistent with the verbal message and with each other. The message forms a coherent, animated whole. In contrast, the last message (in the conflict condition) ranges from contradictory (**"needs— . . . um, a lot-of— . . . a LITTLE work"**) to empty (**"You'd probably LIKE it, IF IT'S what you're looking for"**). The nonverbal aspects of this message are also contradictory: the tone of voice seems to apologize and reassure at the same time, while the facial expressions move from concern, to almost agitated head movement, to a patently false smile at the end.

TABLE 6.6
Experiment 14A: Car for Sale (face-to-face)

Condition	Content	Sender	Receiver	Context	Sum
Nonconflict Condition					
Female: <0 sec.> (Looking at the other person, but head is sharply tilted to the side.) (Spoken very fast, with conviction, while raising head and gesturing at the other:) **Oh, it's in TERRIFIC shape.** (While shaking head:) **I never have ANY problems with it at all.** (Smiles.)	-1.20	-1.41	.17	-1.14	-3.58
Female: <.56 sec.> (Looking mostly at the other person, with occasional glances to either side; smiling almost constantly.) (Pitch descending; all in a very "nice" tone, with lips often pursed:) **Ahh, it's in PRETTY good shape.** (Almost inaudibly:) **Yea—mhm ...** (then louder:) **it-ah ...** (grimace, very slight laugh) **... needs—ah a new rear TAIL light— ah—BULB ... and the parking brakes should be CHECKED.** (Then forced, as if running out of breath:) **But it's in pretty good shape apart from that.**	-.77	.36	-.58	-.19	-1.18
Female: <.80 sec.> (Looks quickly off to the side, then towards the other person but somewhat defocused; hands are supporting chin and partly covering mouth; nods constantly.) (Nasally, pitch descending:) **Ahh** (then fast but firm tone:) **it's in REALLY good shape** (still nodding).	-.45	.34	.61	-1.16	-.66
Male: <.20 sec.> (Looking slightly downwards.) (Pleasantly confident and businesslike tone:) **It's in VERY good shape. There's ONLY—** ... (gestures "you know?" and grimaces slightly) **a FEW minor problems with it.**	-.35	-.06	.27	-.28	-.42

Female:	<.86 sec.> (Looking mostly at the other person.) (Nodding head; perky, enthusiastic tone, sounding almost surprised:) It's ACTUALLY in pretty GOOD shape. Um-- (then becoming more businesslike; tilts head slightly:) THERE's just a couple of MINOR things but other than that-- its--its REALLY in VERY good shape INDEED.	.30	-.54	.26	.13	.15
Male:	<.80 sec.> (Not clear whether he's looking at the other person or down.) (Warm, somewhat enthusiastic tone:) OHH--. it's pretty GOOD. (Quick smile.)	.25	-.04	1.01	-.55	.67

Conflict Condition

Male:	<.96 sec.> (Begins by looking down; figits, uncrosses legs, and then continues to play with his finger.) (In a nasal, flat tone:) Ah, NOT-- it's-in-- PRETTY good shape. (Looks back up with slight smile.) With a little WORK, (twitches head) you could-- LIKELY fix it UP ... into a good car. (Ends in slightly questioning tone, then tightens mouth.)	-.33	.29	-1.29	.50	-.83
Male:	<.74 sec.> (Raises head to look directly at the other person.) (Fairly clear and serious tone:) TERRIBLE ... (then looks down and smiles) to be absolutely honest. (Very slight laugh; ends with "I give up" or "I can't help it" gesture.)	.76	-1.17	1.87	1.02	.44
Male:	<.50 sec.> (Looking in direction of other person, but slightly downwards.) (Almost regretful tone:) WELL ... it NEEDS a lot of-ah BODY work. the PAINT'S a bit rusted and-ah. ... (Juts chin out quickly.) The BRAKES need some-- ... NEED to be fixed.	-.05	.29	-.30	.61	.55

TABLE 6.6 Continued

Behavior description					
Female: <1.10 sec.> (Looking at the other person.) (Starts by leaning head and shoulders left then right; then in casual, off-hand tone:) WELL, it's not BAD. It's an older CAR. (Stops and looks as if "you know?".) And there's all the (nodding confidently and wrinkling nose) things that go wrong with older CARS, but-ah ... OTHER than that, (raises eyebrows) it's not too BAD. (Then, wide-eyed and shaking head throughout) Bit of WORK and it'd probably be all right.	.49	.52	-.94	.81	.88
Female: <1.00 sec.> (Looking at the other person; except when nodding head as emphasis; smiling almost constantly.) (As if conceding a point:) WELL—it's not the GREATEST shape. (Then explaining pleasantly:) It needs a ... fair bit of WORK and TUNING UP ... and-ah, replacing the TIRES and whatnot.	.50	.37	-.48	.51	.90
Female: <.42 sec.> (Looking at the other person with glances to the side; somewhat concerned facial expression; head nodding and moving increasingly.) (Apologetic, reassuring tone:) WELL—WHEN you SEE it, you'll SEE that it—the BODY needs— ... um, a lot-of-... a LITTLE work. But if you're HANDY, or you know someone that's handy, you know ... wash up, paint job 'n ? ... (Quietly, then sounding pleased:) You'd probably LIKE it, IF IT'S what you're looking for. ("Posed" smile at end.)	.97	1.27	-.60	1.79	3.43

Summary Statistics

Reliability (intraclass R) =	.79	.88	.96	.96	
Nonconflict mean =	-.37	-.23	.29	-.53	-.84
Conflict mean =	.39	.26	-.29	.53	.90
t =	2.54	1.15	1.15	2.50	2.08
p (one-tailed) =	<.02	n.s.	n.s.	<.02	<.05

Both words and delivery were important in conveying the sender's opinion. The first message uses "**I**" and is delivered with enthusiastic animation; the latter quality is also present in another message:

(Nodding head; perky, enthusiastic tone, sounding almost surprised:) **It's ACTUALLY in pretty GOOD shape** [etc.]

But one of the conflict messages was even more clearly the speaker's own opinion:

(Fairly clear and serious tone:) **TERRIBLE** ... (then looks down and smiles) **to be absolutely honest.** (Very slight laugh; ends with "I give up" or "I can't help it" gesture.)

The phrase "**to be absolutely honest**" is apparently equivalent to saying "**this is my true opinion.**" In contrast, the last message (in the conflict condition) keeps putting the onus on the other person ("**WHEN you SEE it,**" "**if you're HANDY,**" "**you'd probably LIKE it**"), and also looks and sounds far from enthusiastic and convinced.

Position on the Receiver dimension was determined primarily by whether the speaker looked directly at the other person and whether the message was "car talk," that is, contained details appropriate to a potential buyer. All of the messages with negative values had these two properties to some degree; in some cases, the word "**you**" was also used. The message with the highest value ("**TERRIBLE**") did not seem to our judges to be, either in content or manner, the sort of thing one would say to a person to whom one is trying to sell a car.

The same message, however, was a clear answer to the question "**What kind of SHAPE is the CAR in?**" and so had a low value on the Context dimension, as did most of the other messages that described the car. Messages moved up the continuum as they added extra information or qualifications, and the highest message (again the last in the conflict condition) answered at least two entirely different questions, namely, "**WHAT will I think when I SEE the car?**" and "**IS it a car I can get fixed UP?**"

This was our third and last use of the Car Ad scenario, each time in a different format (written, spoken, face-to-face). In all three formats there were significant differences between conflict and nonconflict conditions, and the qualitative differences in verbal content were also similar. The two versions described in this chapter elicited nonverbal equivocation as well, but the overall effect is still an integrated ·message — thoroughly clear or thoroughly equivocal.

EXPERIMENT 14B: CLASS PRESENTATION (FACE-TO-FACE)

Immediately after the car scenario, Experimenter 1 returned and introduced the class presentation scenario, which was exactly like Experiment 10 except that the other student dropped by instead of calling to ask about her presentation. The experimental condition was the opposite of whatever had been randomly assigned for the first half of the experiment (the car sale), and a different Experimenter 2 played the role of the other student.

The replies of the 12 participants are shown in Table 6.7, which also has the quantitative data and an indication of what the speaker's position was in Table 6.6. The last experiment in this format was a good one to end on: The differences between conflict and nonconflict conditions were significant for all four dimensions and their Sum. No experimenter effects or interactions were significant. As in Experiments 11A and B, the participants changed from equivocal to clear replies solely as a function of experimental condition. Indeed, the person who gave the clearest message in 14A gave the most equivocal message in 14B, while the person who was most equivocal in 14A became the clearest in 14B. In both cases, the Sum was over +3 in the conflict condition and over −3 in the nonconflict condition, indicating a dramatic change in clarity of communication within a few minutes.

The first three messages in the table are clear on the Content dimension. They are well (though far from perfectly) constructed. In contrast, the highest value on this dimension went to the following message, in which a gestural emblem of uncertainty is juxtapositioned with an ambiguous verbal evaluation:

Male: [3.4 sec.] (Looking at the other person most of the time.) (Purses lips, then ducks head to the side while lifting hands in classic "What can I say?" gesture.) (Then, in guarded voice while smiling and nodding:) **Pretty GOOD.**

(A few judges interpreted the gesture as "balancing" or "weighing" alternatives, which still indicates uncertainty.)

Messages low on the Sender dimension use the words "**I thought**" or, alternatively, portray enthusiasm nonverbally (for example, the "Hooray" gesture in the third message). At the other end, the sender's own opinion is avoided by indirect phrasing, such as "**it didn't seem to**" or "**I-I NOTICED**

that-ah that it wasn't-ah, THAT well RECEIVED." The message with the highest value gave no opinion at all: **"Well HOW do you THINK you DID?"**

The position of a message on the Receiver dimension was determined both by whether the speaker is looking at the receiver and by the phrasing. For example, the approach taken in the message just given above, as well as in the third and fourth messages in the conflict condition, was seen as more appropriate to a teacher-student than a peer relationship.

The clearest messages on the Context dimension echo back the structure of the question asked:

"HOW did I DO on my PRESENTATION?"

"YOU DID [whatever]"

Other messages so strongly imply the structure of the question by their intonation, phrasing, and quickness of response that they were also judged low on this dimension; for example,

Female: [.73 sec.] (Looking at the other person; smiling and nodding constantly.) (In a pleased and proud tone:) **REALLY well,** (softer:) **really WELL.**

Messages high on the Context dimension answered different questions, added irrelevant material, or answered the question with a question.

The class presentation scenario had now been used in all of our formats (forced choice, written, spoken, and face-to-face) and each time had produced the predicted effects. As with the car ads, both our theory and measurement of equivocation generalized across mode of communication. Each of the messages in these experiments is unique, yet their properties were detectable by the same scaling method, with the same results.

RESPONSE LATENCY:
TWO THEORETICAL ALTERNATIVES

Recall that our theory (Chapter 3) is an adaptation of Lewin's conflict theory, which proposes that, in an avoidance-avoidance conflict, the negative aspects of the available options lead to vacillation, as the individual approaches each alternative, is repelled by it, turns to the other option, and so on until forced to choose or until it becomes possible to leave the field. This psychological process would take some time, and for this reason increased latency of response is a classic prediction for avoidance-avoidance

TABLE 6.7
Experiment 14B: Class Presentation (face-to-face)

Condition	Content	Sender	Receiver	Context	Sum	Order[a]
Nonconflict Condition						
Female: <1.10 sec.> (Looking directly at the other person, with head slightly tilted, nodding in emphasis.) (Pitch descending at first, in pleased and emphatic tone, almost as if pleasantly surprised:) **YOU did REALLY WELL. You REALLY did. I mean I-was-- I-was--** (slight shrug and hand gesture toward the other person.) **I thought it was VERY GOOD.** (Gestures quickly toward the other person.) (Rapidly, as if cutting off the other person:) **YOU should feel GOOD about it TOO.**	-1.09	-1.17	-.52	-.90	-3.68	12
Male: <.46 sec.> (Looking directly at the other person most of the time.) (Warmly, with mild enthusiasm:) **Oh it was GOOD. You did really WELL. ya--** (rubs nose, then gestures out towards other person) **AHM-- ...** (looks down briefly; then in labored tone, with head bouncing, and gestural "beats" accompanying each stressed word:) **DESCRIBED all the POINTS that ya-- NEEDED to, to get the PROPER ... perspective ACROSS. 'n I thought it was GOOD.**	1.01	-.92	-.59	-.92	-3.44	7
Female: <.73 sec.> (Looking at the other person; smiling frequently.) (While shaking head, in tone of restrained warmth:) **You did GREAT.** (Both hands come up into "Hooray" gesture, then slap down on legs.) (Begins to nod; with staccato delivery:) **You did REALLY WELL. Everybody was REALLY pleased.**	-.99	-.42	-.97	-1.02	-3.40	11

Speaker	Description						
Female:	<.12 sec.> (Looking directly at the other person; smiling and nodding constantly.) (In a pleased and proud tone:) REALLY well, (softer:) really WELL.	.56	-.47	-.58	-.89	-1.38	10
Male:	<.11 sec.> (Looking at the other person.) (Quietly, in somewhat restrained but positive tone:) Oh, REALLY WELL. (Slight smile with head nod and almost inaudible:) Mhm. (Then confidently:) Everybody seemed to LIKE it. Seemed pretty SMOOTH. (Slight smile.)	-.28	.21	-.52	-.74	-1.33	9
Male:	<1.20 sec.> (Looking down except for two glances at the other person during first and last phrases.) (Begins with quick "What can I say?" gesture; then gently, with no enthusiasm:) I thought it looked REALLY GOOD—ah—. (Same gesture.) ... Seemed to be organized WELL, and—uh. ... (Prolonged gesture with both hands. "What else can I say?") SEEMED to go over QUITE well. (Slight shrug.)	-.10	-.50	.14	-.17	-.63	8

Conflict Condition

Speaker	Description						
Female:	<2.10 sec.> (Looking away from the other person until the end of the message; smiling somewhat stiffly throughout.) (Looks up at ceiling and takes a deep breath:) AHM—— mh—— (grimaces, looks down at floor, and laughs, which makes next statement virtually unintelligible:) That's a really hard one. ... (Deep breath, then clearer but fast and somewhat jerkily:) It—the—I feel that the MATERIAL you HAD was probably GOOD, (now looking up at the other person) but your MANNER in which you presented it could PROBABLY have needed a lot more work. (Jerks head back sharply.)	.11	.19	-.06	.57	.81	2

165

TABLE 6.7
Continued

Male:	<3.40 sec.> (Looking at the other person most of the time.) (Purses lips, then ducks head to the side while lifting hands in classic "What can I say?" gesture.) (Then, in a guarded voice while smiling and nodding:) Pretty GOOD.	1.43	.45	.23	.20	2.31	4
Female:	<1.29 sec.> (Starts by leaning back and looking away from the other person; then, looking at the other and in a surprised and thoughtful tone:) OH! WELL. (then more matter-of-factly:) It didn't seem to go OVER as WELL as-- ... you THOUGHT it MIGHT. Ahh ... (then faster, in helpful tone:) MAYBE we can get together and TALK about-- ... SOME of the areas that I-- ... (slows down:) think, MAYBE we could-- ... IMPROVE on.	.58	.81	.55	.60	2.54	3
Female:	<1.23 sec.> (Looking mostly at the other person.) (Takes a big breath; then in a regretful, sympathetic tone, while nodding frequently:) WELLLL, I think there were PROBABLY a few PROBLEMS that-ah, MAYBE we could have IRONED out BEFOREHAND, if we'd-- (then, with circling gesture and nodding) maybe RAN over-the whole THING. ... BUT-ah ..: the-the (with circling gesture again) INFORMATION was GOOD but--. (Both hands move to portray disorganization.) (Begins smiling, as tone becomes almost whining:) you just didn't SEEM to ORGANIZE it right.	.05	-.08	.66	.41	1.04	5

Male:	<2.19 sec.> (Looking away from the other person for the first part of the message.) (Sighs; then in descending pitch:) AAAHN ... tsk ... (Sighs.) ... (Very long pause.) (Smile; other person tilts her head and gives slight sympathetic laugh.) (Speaker sighs again.) (Another very long pause.) (Then looks at the other person, and in warm but reluctant tone:) I—I NOTICED that—ah that it wasn't—ah, THAT well RECEIVED. ... (Then, very softly:) And—it—ah— it—— (then, sounding curious, almost questioning:) S-SOME of the REFERENCES I GAVE you, you DIDN'T—you didn't seem to have looked UP.	.60	.58	1.08	1.02	3.28	6
Female:	<.66 sec.> (Looking at the other person, with head very tilted.) (Raises and lowers head in patronizing way while answering in a pleasant but brittle, "teacher" tone:) Well HOW do you THINK you DID?	.14	1.34	.49	1.85	3.82	1

Summary Statistics

Reliability (intraclass R) =	.91	.90	.83	.98
Nonconflict mean =	-.49	-.55	-.51	-.77	-2.31
Conflict mean =	.49	.55	.49	.78	2.30
t =	2.82	3.90	4.63	5.68	6.29
p (one-tailed) =	<.01	<.001	<.001	<.001	<.001

a. Speaker's position in Table 6.6 (Experiment 14a).

conflicts (Barker, 1942). Extending Lewin's theory to communicative behavior, one would predict that people in the conflict condition would take longer before beginning their replies than people in the nonconflict condition. This can be measured either as the time until the first utterance (as shown in the tables in this chapter) or as the time until the first meaningful word; the latter would treat mere sounds, such as "**Ahh,**" as part of the vacillation. The data and significance tests for both measures of latency for all of the experiments in this chapter are given in Appendix B. Whichever way latency is measured, it is longer in the conflict than the nonconflict condition in our experiments, and this difference is often significant — even though we are dealing with very short time intervals. These data are perfectly consistent with Lewin's theory.

However, we have reservations about this interpretation, arising from the differences (noted in Chapter 3) between Lewin's original theory and our adaptation of it. We are trying to build a social model of communicative behavior, independent of cognitive processes. The Lewinian interpretation of latency is inevitably an intrapsychic one: it "gets inside" the individual's mind and attributes the delay to his or her struggle with the alternatives. In this view, latency is not part of the message but only a by-product of the internal conflict. We have sought another, purely communicative interpretation of these silences. They can be seen as an aspect of equivocation itself, that is, another way of being unclear. Pauses before (and during) a message make it less direct and responsive, just as other nonverbal aspects of the message do. They soften the negative aspects of the message, just as fuzzy phrases do. We interpret these silences, then, not as evidence of a psychological process but as an intrinsic part of the message itself: "Well-timed silence hath more eloquence than speech" (Tupper, 1838-1842).

Therefore, tempting as it is to fit our latency data neatly into Lewinian theory, we choose not to do so — not only for the sake of theoretical consistency, but for the more important sake of giving the message primacy over mental processes. Eschewing intrapsychic explanations can free us from traditional models and let us see in new ways.

SUMMARY

A series of seven experiments conducted either on the telephone or in person studied the nature of equivocation in messages with both verbal and nonverbal aspects. In each experiment, people in an avoidance-avoidance conflict gave significantly more equivocal replies than people in a non-conflict, control condition. This included scenarios in which the participants were given uncoded information from which they had to infer the conflict as well as generate a message. Finally, equivocal messages were not discrepant or incongruous; as our integrated message model predicted, their verbal aspects were as hesitant and vague as were their nonverbal aspects.

7

Truths, Lies, and Equivocations

That can the Subtle difference descry
Betwixt AEquivocation and a Lye.
(Randolph, *Poems*, 1634; in Hazlitt,
1875/1968, p. 568)

As we pointed out in Chapter 1, nonstraightforward communication has heretofore been of interest to only a small minority of researchers. The majority have passed over these "odd" messages, often regarding them as errors to be ignored or reinterpreted. So most of our research was conducted well off the beaten tracks of research in communication, social psychology, and related disciplines. This changed, however, as we began to work with the messages described in the previous chapter, which have both verbal and nonverbal aspects. At this point, our research began to intersect another line of research, on deception or lying.[1] There is a sizable literature in social psychology and communication on the topic of verbal versus nonverbal deception, and many who do research on this topic would consider equivocation a form of deception. We do not share this opinion and propose instead that equivocation is neither a false message nor a clear truth, but rather an alternative used precisely when both of these are to be avoided. To show this, we will first examine deception theory and research from our own perspective. Then we will describe the research we have conducted in order to clarify the distinction between truths, lies, and equivocations.

DECEPTION THEORY AND RESEARCH

In a sense, deception research has been "detection" research, focusing on how well people function as human lie detectors, that is, on whether people can tell when someone is lying to them. The recent scholarly literature on deception owes a great deal to an early article by Ekman and Friesen (1969) in which they proposed that, while individuals may be able to deceive other people verbally, they may not be so successful when their nonverbal behavior is examined. Quoting Freud's dictum:

> he that has eyes to see and ears to hear may convince himself than no mortal can keep a secret. If his lips are silent, he chatters with his finger-tips; betrayal oozes out of him at every pore (1905/1959, p. 94).

Ekman and Friesen went on to refine the common belief that "nonverbal behavior reveals how people feel, even when they wish to conceal their feelings" (Ekman & Friesen, 1974, p. 288). Specifically, these authors posited that we are much less able to control some nonverbal behaviors than others. Their proposed hierarchy ranged from maximum control of words, less of the face, even less of the hands, to least control of the legs and feet. In other words, a person might be able to lie with his or her speech and facial expression, but fidgety hands or feet would give away the truth.

Ekman and Friesen (1969) also proposed a useful distinction between *deception clues* and *leakage*. Nonverbal leakage is behavior revealing what the speaker is attempting verbally to conceal or deny. Deception clues are indications that the speaker is lying. Such clues do not reveal *what* the speaker is hiding but only indicate that he or she is attempting to deceive; they are presumed to be caused by anxiety about lying.

Subsequent research has focused on how deceivers behave and how observers might detect deception: With what accuracy can lay people detect deception? What clues do people say they use? Which clues really help? Is accuracy in detecting deception a function of access to different nonverbal "channels," such as tone of voice, body, or facial expression? A typical study would induce participants to lie, record their replies, and then ask other participants to identify the liars. The latter might be done by showing only the face or body of the speaker, in order to look for nonverbal leakage. Reviews of this literature can be found in Knapp and Comadena (1979), Miller and Burgoon (1981), Zuckerman, DePaulo, and Rosenthal (1981), and Ekman (1985). No firm conclusions can be drawn yet, because different studies with different variables sometimes do and sometimes do not agree in their findings.

Treating Deception as Discourse

In our view, there is a fundamental problem in current treatments of deception, namely, deceptive communication is not treated as communication in the ordinary sense but as something apart from discourse. Yet lies are speech acts; "saying something" is a necessary and sufficient condition for a lie to occur. We will examine here three important ways in which deception has *not* been treated as discourse, along with our suggestions for an alternative, discourse-based approach.

DEFINITIONAL PROBLEMS

In our view, a crucial weakness in deception research is that there are no definitions (conceptual or operational) that can consistently distinguish between deceptive and nondeceptive messages. This is because, although deception theorists (such as Ekman, 1985, pp. 41-42; Knapp & Comadena, 1979, p. 271; Miller, 1983, pp. 92-93; Zuckerman et al., 1981, p. 3) agree that a formal definition must focus on the *misrepresentation of information* by the deceiver (a discourse-based definition), virtually all of them add other, *noninformational* criteria as well. Knapp and Comadena (1979) discussed this practice and its implications, noting that most theorists start out in a straightforward manner:

> Many of the studies of lying and deception seem to operationalize the act as: *the conscious alteration of information a person believes to be true in order to significantly change another's perceptions from what the deceiver thought they would be without deception.* (p. 271; italics in original)

This is a discourse-based definition: A message is encoded so as to convey false information. The problem is that

> a central component of this perspective is the treatment of information — adding or subtracting from the perceived truth. But as the following review of related lines of research suggests, *information treatment is not always a distinguishing factor for identifying lies and truth.* (p. 271, italics added)

Knapp and Comadena went on to identify three noninformational criteria used to define whether lying has occurred:

> (1) the actor's motivation; (2) the degree to which the actor was aware of what he or she was doing; and (3) the effects of the act on the parties involved. (p. 275)

None of these refers to the discourse itself — to what was said. As a result, what is considered deceptive communication may sometimes include:

white lies, cover-ups, bluffing, euphemisms, masks, pretenses, tall-tales, put-ons, hoaxes, and other forms of falsehoods, fabrications, and simulations. (p. 270)

But at other times, in other circumstances, many deception theorists *exclude* deceptive acts "of loving concern," as well as "pseudo-agreement and [the] false praise of ingratiation," "euphemisms and exaggerations," and "vagueness and ambiguity" (pp. 271-272). For example, "where there is little or no perceived harm . . . , the act may not even be considered a lie" (p. 276).

The problem that Knapp and Comadena identified in research predating their review is still present in deception theories. For example, Ekman's (1985) primary definition of lies is quite broad. He equates lies with deceit (an informational definition) and includes "two major forms of lying: concealment, leaving out true information; and falsification, or presenting false information as if it were true" (p. 41), plus several other minor forms (pp. 41-42). However, in order to exclude some acts that fit the primary criterion, he adds two secondary, noninformational criteria, which emphasize *choice*, by both parties: In Ekman's view, a liar can choose not to lie; he therefore excludes paranoid delusions, pathological liars, and those who believe their own lies. On the other side, the target of the lie cannot have chosen to be misled: "It would be bizarre to call actors liars. Their audience agrees to be misled, for a time; that is why they are there" (p. 27). Unfortunately, taken to its logical conclusion, the latter criterion would also exclude virtually all experimentally elicited deception, because the experimenter (or confederate) has consented — and even carefully arranged — to be misled.

Critics such as Austin (1969), Hopper and Bell (1984), and Keith (1984) have argued for a considerably broadened concept of deception — perhaps called *pretending* — that both includes and differentiates among concealment, misleading, teasing, put-ons, satire, practical jokes, hoaxes, and so forth. Their point is that speaking or acting in a manner contrary to the truth characterizes many other actions not ordinarily called *lies*. They suggest that the study of deception has been distorted by a too-narrow focus on lying.

In our view, these serious definitional (and therefore measurement) problems arise because of efforts to align formal definitions of deception with intuitive conceptions of the moral issues involved. The focus in traditional treatments of lying and deception has been on the liar rather than the lie, that is, on the speaker rather than the discourse and on detecting and protecting ourselves from unwanted lies rather than on studying deception itself. Perhaps understandably, a strong moral tone underlies theory and research on deception, one that contrasts honesty with dishonesty and responsibility with reprehensibility, so that its theorists struggle to define lying in a way that includes "bad" lies and exculpates "good" lies. But it is this quasilegal approach that has made adequate scientific definition virtually impossible, as the primary, discourse-based definition (the veridicality of information in the message) is arbitrarily expanded or narrowed by noninformational criteria such as the motivation, justification, or effects of the message. Moreover, because these criteria necessarily invoke personal ethical judgments, there is little possibility of consensus, much less of an operational definition. In brief, there exists at present no independent and objective means for identifying certain messages as lies or truths.

A related problem with traditional approaches to deception is that they ignore its subtlety as discourse. For example, most deception theorists would treat as lies equivocations such as the following reply to a question about a class presentation (from Experiment 6):

> **You should've spent more time preparing. It wasn't really clear as to what you were getting across. I'll explain more during our lunch break.**

This reply would be considered a lie because it does not tell "the truth, the whole truth, and nothing but the truth," namely, "**I think you did a very bad job.**" Yet no competent user of the language could miss the meaning of this equivocal reply, which is that the presentation was not good and that the writer is trying to be kind and helpful. We propose (and will show) that receivers understand this meaning as easily as they understand other indirect speech acts such as:

> **Can you reach the salt?**

when it means:

> **Please pass me the salt.**

(See Searle, 1975; see also Chapter 1, this volume.) If equivocations are lies, then so are indirect speech acts. No current definition of lies or deception can cope with this distinction, again because there is no means of identifying lies.

As noted above, most of the difficulties in defining deception arise from an unsuccessful struggle to make a distinction between acceptable and unacceptable lies. Because the very terms *lie* and *deception* are saturated with moral connotations, users of these terms feel compelled to go past the discourse itself to ask whether we would condemn the message. The solution to this dilemma is to recognize explicitly the *multidimensional* nature of intuitive conceptions of deception and to begin a systematic identification of the various dimensions being invoked.

We propose that the primary definition must be informational, that is, based on the truth or falsity of the information represented in the message. This dimension, for which an operational definition will be presented below, can be called *truthfulness-falsity*, or distance-from-the-truth. Other researchers could add (and devise measures for) other dimensions not related to the discourse itself such as intention to mislead, consent of the receiver, perceived justification, harmful effect, and so forth. If in fact there is an intuitive consensus about what constitutes a lie, it would undoubtedly be located at some intersection of several of these dimensions. A multidimensional approach is the only hope for unraveling the current tangle of definitional problems. In the meantime, we are avoiding even using the term *lie* (except when quoting or paraphrasing other theorists) and will focus on the truthfulness-falsity of a message.

SEPARATION OF VERBAL AND NONVERBAL ASPECTS OF MESSAGES

As mentioned at the outset, deception researchers have been particularly interested in nonverbal leakage or deception clues. The assumption that, when people lie verbally, there will be evidence in their nonverbal behaviors arises from an even more basic premise: that there are verbal and nonverbal "channels" of communication, which operate independently and are under different degrees of control. Researchers as disparate as linguists and specialists in nonverbal communication typically share this same premise, that nonverbal behaviors constitute a separate, nonlinguistic system. Both imply that nonverbal actions should be tallied, not decoded.

(This separation may even be the reason that deception is so seldom seen as discourse: If the verbal part of the message is a lie, then it is not "real" — that is, not good — communication. And if the nonverbal aspects of the message are either inadvertent leakage of information or equally unintentional clues that deception is occurring, then they too are not communication. Taken apart in this way, deception can make no claim to being communication.)

We will leave the arguments for a separate, nonlinguistic role for nonverbal behaviors to the proponents of such a view and confine ourselves to two rebuttals. First, McNeill (1985) has offered a convincing array of evidence that hand gestures made during conversation are linguistic. That is, they are part of the same process that generates words; they are highly integrated with words; they develop in children and disappear in aphasia like words; and they have linguistic structure and functions comparable to words. Chovil (1989) has shown that facial expressions have many different syntactic and semantic functions, most of which are integrated with words. In face-to-face communication, language is not limited to speech. Our second argument will be empirical, as we examine whether separate "channels" of communication actually function independently (including incongruently). If not, then we should be treating verbal and nonverbal acts as an *integrated message* of considerable linguistic complexity and precision.

SITUATIONAL CONTEXT

A salient characteristic of discourse analysis is to see discourse as situationally grounded, as intimately related to its immediate social circumstances. In contrast, deception seems to have only one "context" — the weak moral character of the deceiver: People lie because they are devious, self-serving, or afraid. This focus on the liar not only ignores the lie as discourse but also neglects the situation in which the discourse occurs.

Yet the situations that present people with the option of lying are both fascinating and varied. Recall Turner, Edgely, and Olmstead (1975) who pointed out that, in situations requiring "tact," a hurtful truth to a person one cares about is a relationship lie in that it implies that one does not mind hurting the other person, and this is *not* true. So, in different situations, the effect of a false message may be protecting a friend from pain, or keeping one's job, or getting oneself out of an unwelcome social obligation, or getting away with a crime, or making a surprise party successful. Each of these situations is different in ways that have as yet scarcely been explored, and these differences undoubtedly affect the properties of the messages evoked in each situation. For example, the politician who does not want to tell a certain truth on nation-wide television must also consider the need to have "plausible deniability" in case what he is hiding comes out later; a tangential response might be better suited to this particular situation than active misrepresentation. In contrast, someone planning a surprise gift for his or her spouse can falsify thoroughly, enthusiastically, and even extravagantly, because all of this will later be seen as a confirmation of the effort put into carrying out the surprise. Needless to say, with our interest in the situational specifics bearing on communication, the indifference of deception researchers to an analysis of the situational particulars that elicit deception is most frustrating. Like most discourse analysts, we believe that the best (and most interesting) approach is to pay extremely close attention to both the situation and what is said.

AN ALTERNATIVE VIEW

In summary, we find in deception research several implicit and explicit assumptions with which we disagree:

1. There is usually a simple division of messages into truths and lies, which implies that this single property is sufficient to characterize any instance. As noted above, we think that several dimensions are necessary to capture the diversity of messages in this broad domain. We are particularly interested in two distinct coordinates on which messages can vary: truthfulness and equivocality. *What* is said can range from true to false; *how* it is said can range (as we have seen throughout this book) from clear to equivocal. These two coordinates are represented in Figure 7.1, which proposes that both true and false messages may be clear or equivocal.

2. Deception research seems based on the assumption that people often lie. In contrast, we propose that, given the choice, people will not lie but rather will equivocate truthfully. Recall that the theory we set out in Chapter 3 identified situations in which any clear, direct message has negative consequences — regardless of whether the message is true or false — so clear messages will be avoided. An unclear, equivocal message is a better route. Figure 7.2 describes such avoidance-avoidance conflicts schematically and shows how an equivocal truth is the only way to avoid the other, negative alternatives.

Some of the experiments described in Chapter 4 provided strong evidence for our proposal that equivocation will be chosen rather than a false message. Recall that in Experiments 1, 2, and 3, one of the choices offered was both clear and false (e. g., **"The gift is perfect; I really love it"**). As summarized in Table 7.1, the false message was rarely chosen in those experiments. Of the 371 people in avoidance-avoidance conflicts who were offered the three classes of choices, a little more than 6% chose the false message. Between 3% and 4% chose a clear truth, while more than 90% chose an equivocal message. This is particularly surprising because of the number of factors that would seem to favor false messages in these experiments: the false message was already prepared, so that the subjects did not have to think of it themselves; it would avoid a bad consequence (hurting someone); and there was no chance of detection, because the choice was completely anonymous. Yet when equivocation was an alternative, the false message was seldom preferred.

3. Another assumption in the literature on deception research is that participants in such studies were in fact induced to lie when the researchers intended them to. Our reading of this research is that, because of inadequate

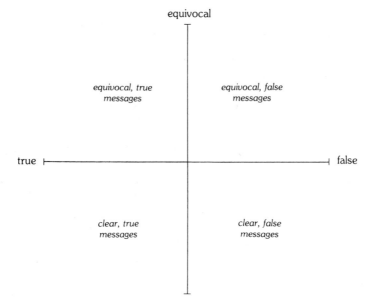

Figure 7.1. Proposed Independent Coordinates of Truthfulness and Equivocation

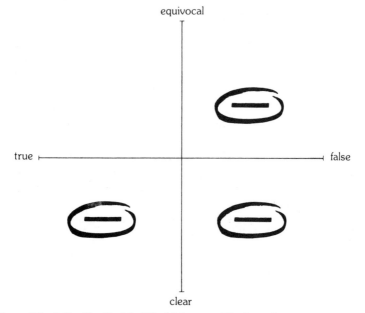

Figure 7.2. A Conflict Model of Truthfulness and Equivocation

TABLE 7.1
Frequency of Choice of True, False, and Equivocal Messages
in Experiments 1–3

	Message Type		
	False	True	Equivocal
Experiment 1			
Class	3	5	48 + 39 = 87
Employee	0	2	66 + 28 = 94
Gift	11	4	5 + 76 = 81
Experiment 2 (Conflict Condition Only)			
Class	0	1	13 +10 = 23
Gift	4	0	20
Experiment 3 (Conflict Condition Only)			
Class	4	1	13
Gift	1	0	17
Totals	23	13	335
	6.2%	3.5%	90.2%

definition of lying and the lack of analysis of the messages themselves, what have been treated as lies may often have been equivocal truths. For example, Zuckerman et al. (1981) suggested that the participants' *verbal* responses are empirically the most replicable yet least understood effect in deception experiments. We will examine this issue empirically using data from our equivocation experiments and a new measure, which could be applied in deception experiments as well.

4. We also reject the deception researchers' model of separate "channels" of communication and propose in its place an integrated message model, in which the whole message is the minimum unit, with verbal and nonverbal components inextricably interwoven and working together to produce the ultimate message.

A major assumption of the "separate channels" model is that the nonverbal channel is less well controlled, so that while people may be able to lie verbally, they will either "leak" the truth nonverbally or manifest nonverbal deception clues. Because we doubt that the verbal aspects of a message are under different and better control than the nonverbal aspects, we do not believe that the nonverbal reveals what the verbal conceals. Specifically, we propose that the nonverbal aspects of a message do not "leak truth"; they are just as capable of lying (or equivocating) as are the verbal aspects.

EVIDENCE DISTINGUISHING BETWEEN FALSE AND EQUIVOCAL MESSAGES

The Truthfulness of Participants' Own Messages

Although the evidence from the forced-choice experiments strongly suggests that people distinguish between equivocal and false messages, it is not conclusive. Because people seldom communicate by choosing among messages written by someone else, we needed to know whether the messages people had themselves generated in our conflict conditions were truthful (Bavelas et al., in press).

At this point, a surprising difficulty appeared: There existed no direct, objective measure of truth or lying. We believe the twin reasons are — as discussed above — that there is no satisfactory definition of lying and that deception researchers pay little attention to the content of the deceivers' messages. Nor will the interested reader find a record of what participants in these experiments actually said, should she or he wish to verify that some messages were lies. Instead other, more indirect means are relied upon, as will be illustrated by several typical examples. Ekman and Friesen (1969) defined truth in their study as what psychiatric experts said about a patient (rather than her own assertions). In another study, Ekman and Friesen (1974) instructed their subjects to lie, gave them good reasons to, and assumed that they did unless they "confessed." Kraut (1978) asked subjects to lie and then asked them to watch their own videotapes and to indicate when they were lying and when they were not. Zuckerman, DeFrank, Hall, Larrance, and Rosenthal (1979) told subjects to give their actual opinions sometimes and to give false opinions at other times, but they did not assess independently whether or to what degree this was actually done. DePaulo and Rosenthal (1979) asked subjects to say, sometimes falsely and sometimes truthfully, whether they liked or disliked someone; these messages were then rated for whether liking and disliking was being indicated. This is a potentially better, more objective procedure, but there was a possible confounding problem in their procedure. As is common in deception research, the raters knew that lying was a possibility. In this case, the raters knew because they had been subjects; that is, the subjects themselves rated all of the tapes except their own. Therefore, it could well be that they were looking for lies (or deception clues) rather than just rating liking versus disliking. It can be argued that, whenever raters know that lying is a possibility, ratings based solely on what the message represents are not possible.

Our measure of truthfulness is based on a fundamental property of messages: they represent or portray realities to receivers. A truthful message portrays reality accurately (or as the sender believes it to be). A false message portrays reality as different from what it is (or what the sender believes it to be). Therefore, if we ask people what the message tells them, we can later compare this decoded meaning to the reality the message should represent. The farther the decoded meaning is from the true state of affairs, the more false the message is. It is important not to mention the possibility of deception to these decoders. They are to treat each message as both true and real and to tell us what it means. Our model is one of decoding, not detection; the truth or falsity of the message is not judged directly but by a comparison between its decoded meaning and the meaning it should have, that is, with the reality it should represent.

So we measure truthfulness by asking naive raters (not our trained equivocation judges) what a message says and later matching their ratings to the true meaning. If what the message means to the decoder is close to what the real state of affairs is (or what the speaker believed it to be), then the message is true. If the message is closer to the opposite state of affairs, then it is false. Implicit in our proposal is the assumption that truth and falsity form a continuum, not a dichotomy. If a student receives an F in a course and says, "**I got a D**," this is false, but saying "**I got an A**" is even more false. Even in cases where there are only two possibilities (e.g., one is pregnant or not), the content of a message may induce some doubt in the listener's mind as to which is true (e.g., "**I think it may be just barely possible than I am sort of pregnant**").

RATING PROCEDURE

In order to assess empirically the degree of truthfulness or falsity in the spontaneous messages in our experimental conflicts, we asked people to rate the meaning of the messages in the written, spoken, and face-to-face experiments (described in Chapters 5 and 6). The raters were students recruited from various classes (usually in the linguistics department); they were seen individually and paid for their time. Using a magnitude estimation scale printed on a single sheet of paper, the rater indicated what the message was saying. We used the average across raters for each message to indicate what that message conveyed, and our objective measure of truthfulness came from a comparison of this meaning to what the message should have conveyed.

As will be seen, we also gave the raters the option of putting any message off the scale (i.e., not rating what it meant); we did so for several reasons: First, we wanted to limit the amount of inference that raters would make, in order to focus them on the surface meaning of the message — a decoding rather than a detection orientation. Second, it was possible that some messages might be so equivocal that they would not convey any meaning at all. Finally, some definitions of lying include "lies of omission" (e.g., Miller, 1983, pp. 93-96; Ekman, 1985, p. 41) as well as active falsification. Because such messages would not convey any information about the topic at hand, they would be put off the scale, where we could identify them.

The general instructions were as follows:

We are interested in communication and what we'd like you to do is to rate some messages that we have obtained from some experiments. More specifically, we'd like you to rate messages on this scale.

The participant is given the scaling sheet for the first set of messages, which began:

Please rate the [N] messages on the following scale. Draw a slash through the point on the scale where the message belongs and then write the number of the message underneath the slash. If a message does not really fit or belong on the scale, then write the number of the message on the line following the scale.

The scale was a 16-cm line with two endpoint descriptions just below it at the far left and right.

The rest of the instructions were phrased specifically in terms of the set of messages raters were about to scale. For example, when the messages were from the Car Ad scenario, the experimenter went on to say:

Messages describing a car that is in good condition would be scaled at this end point [which read "good condition"], whereas messages describing a car that is in bad condition would be scaled at the other end [where the endpoint read "bad condition"]. This line is a continuum, so the poorer the condition of the car, the further down the scale the message would go. Any questions?

The endpoints always corresponded exactly to the descriptions originally given to the experimental subjects in the conflict and nonconflict conditions;

that is, these endpoints were the respective truths for the two experimental conditions.

Raters were then told to limit the inferences they made and to put messages off the scale if necessary:

> *With some of the messages, you'll have to make some minimal inferences about the car's condition. For example, if the message says that the car needs some repairs, you can infer that it is not in perfect condition. However, if you have to make so many inferences that you can't really judge what the general running condition of the car is, then simply put the number of the message on the line below the scale. This line is for messages that don't really fit or belong on the scale.*

Finally, the experimenter said (for this particular set of messages):

> *All of the messages are in response to the question, "What is the general running condition of the car?" Here are the 18 messages that you will be rating. Read through each message and then rate the condition of the car. Rate each message on its own; don't try to compare it to the others. Any questions?*

The meaning of a message was determined by averaging over all of the raters who rated that message. These averages (e.g., 4.2 cm) represent a point on the continuum corresponding to the meaning the message had for decoders (e.g., the car is in fairly good but not perfect condition). We expected that these measured meanings would differ in the two different experimental conditions, because participants would have been truthful in both conditions. Comparison of the means of the ratings would test this hypothesis.

We also wanted a quantitative measure of how truthful (or false) the content of a message was, independent of its specific meaning. Such a number can be calculated by taking the difference between the average rating of meaning just described and the value of the appropriate truthful endpoint. When, for example, the car was in good condition, the truth about its condition was at zero. When it was in bad condition, the truthful endpoint lay at 16 cm. Subtracting each message's (or condition's) mean rating from its truthful endpoint, and ignoring the sign, gives us the distance from the truthful endpoint, or *degree of truthfulness*, of the content of that message.

WRITTEN MESSAGES: EXPERIMENTS 6, 8, AND 9[2]

The meaning scale for Experiment 6, the Class Presentation, was defined by the endpoints, "Very well done, well prepared, and well delivered" on the far left and "Very badly done, poorly prepared, and poorly delivered" on the right. Eight people rated the 20 messages — a matrix of 160 ratings. For 14 of these 160 ratings, the decision was to put the message off the scale. The intraclass reliability based on the remaining ratings was .93. (The sums of squares required for the reliability coefficient were obtained by one-way analysis of variance for unequal n.)

The meaning of a message was determined by averaging over all of the raters who rated that message. These meanings differed significantly for experimental conditions, as we had predicted: The mean rating of the nonconflict messages was 5.3 cm, that is, toward the "very well done" end, whereas the mean rating of conflict messages was 10.2, nearer to the "very badly done" end ($t = 4.83$, $df = 18$, $p < .001$). The rated meanings differed as predicted.

For Experiment 8, the Bizarre Gift scenario, the endpoints were "the gift was carefully selected with the writer's tastes and interests in mind" and "the gift is quite bizarre, so the writer isn't clear if it's meant as a joke or to be taken seriously." The intraclass reliability for eight raters of the 18 messages was .94. This excluded the 14 times that any rater placed a particular message off the scale. The mean rating of the nonconflict messages was 4.2 cm, while the mean of the conflict ratings was 11.2 cm. This difference was statistically significant ($t = 5.08$, $df = 16$, $p < .001$).

Finally, the Car Ad messages (Experiment 9) were rated, using "good condition" and "bad condition" as the endpoints. Altogether, the eight raters of 18 ads placed a message off the scale four times. The intraclass reliability for the remaining ratings was .93. The mean ratings were 6.9 cm for the nonconflict condition and 11.4 cm for the conflict condition ($t = 4.83$, $df = 16$, $p < .001$).

The data for these three experiments can also be presented in a form that connects them directly to our theory. Recall that we propose two independent coordinates on which messages can vary: equivocality and truthfulness (Figure 7.1). Furthermore, we proposed that in avoidance-avoidance conflicts messages would become equivocal but not untruthful (Figure 7.2). Now we have real messages with quantitative values for truthfulness and for equivocation — values that can be actually entered on these two coordinates. Figure 7.3 uses this format to present the results of the three written-message experiments, as follows.

The equivocation Sum values for each condition are on the vertical axis, in the same negative-to-positive scale used throughout this book. Truthfulness is represented on the horizontal axis. The ratings of meaning were transformed (as described above) to produce values for "distance from the truth" (about the presentation), ranging from completely true to completely false. For the nonconflict condition of the Class Presentation experiment, the

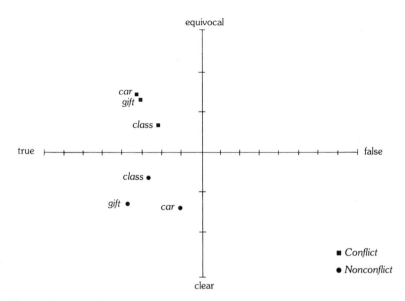

Figure 7.3. Truthfulness and Equivocation in Subject-Written Messages

mean was 5.3 cm away from its truthful endpoint of 0 cm. For the conflict condition, the truthful endpoint was 16 cm, so that the distance was 16 minus 10.2, or 5.8 cm from "perfect truth." The transformed means for the Bizarre Gift and Car Ad experiments are entered in the same way. These results make it obvious that neither group generated false messages: The "false" half of the figure is empty. All means fall in the "true" half; they differ only on the equivocation dimension, as predicted.

SPOKEN MESSAGES (EXPERIMENTS 10 THROUGH 13)[3]

The same eight raters used the same rating procedure for the five sets of spoken messages, which they heard on audiotape.

The endpoints for the messages from Experiment 10, the Class Presentation, were the same as for the written version of the same scenario, given above. Intraclass reliability was .86 for eight raters of 12 messages, excluding five instances where messages were put off the scale. The mean rating for the nonconflict condition was 4.2 cm, and the mean for the conflict condition was 11.2 cm ($t = 5.39$, $df = 10$, $p < .001$).

The messages from Experiment 11A, the Bizarre Gift, were scaled using the same endpoints as the written version, given above. The intraclass reliability was .95 for eight raters of the 12 messages, excluding two instances

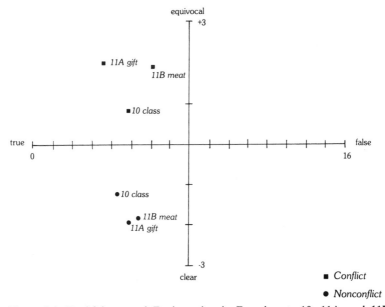

Figure 7.4. Truthfulness and Equivocation in Experiments 10, 11A, and 11B (Spoken)

where messages were put off the scale. The mean rating for the nonconflict condition was 4.7 cm; the mean for the conflict condition was 11.6 cm ($t = 4.72$, $df = 10$, $p < .001$).

The second set of messages from this experiment, the Meat Market (11B) was scaled with the following endpoints: "fresh, good quality meat" and "old, poor quality meat." The eight raters rated the 12 messages with a reliability of .92; this excluded the four times messages were put off the scale. The means of the nonconflict and conflict conditions differed as predicted: 5.3 versus 9.8 cm ($t = 3.12$, $df = 10$, $p < .01$).

The group means for these three experiments are entered on the coordinates of equivocation and truthfulness in Figure 7.4 (which is set up exactly as Figure 7.3). Again, all means are in the "true" half, with the nonconflict and conflict groups differing only in equivocation.

Because in Experiments 12 and 13 we gave subjects uncoded data from which they would have to infer the conflict and generate messages, we gave the raters the same uncoded data as endpoints. Thus, for the scaling of messages from the Employee Reference scenario (Experiment 12), there were no written endpoints below the scale. Instead, the raters were shown the two evaluation sheets used to induce the nonconflict and conflict condi-

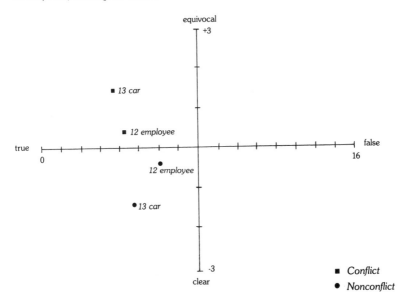

Figure 7.5. Truthfulness and Equivocation in Experiments 12 and 13 (Spoken, Uncoded Data)

tions and were told that the former was the left-hand endpoint and the latter was the right-hand endpoint. This left the raters to imagine other evaluation forms, between these two extremes, which might correspond to the messages they would hear. Despite the potential ambiguity of defining the continuum in this way, the intraclass reliability was still high at .91 for eight raters of 12 messages. There were only three instances of a message being put off the scale. The mean ratings were 6.0 for the nonconflict messages and 11.7 for the conflict messages ($t = 4.68$, $df = 10$, $p = .001$). The truthfulness and equivocation values are plotted in Figure 7.5.

The messages from the Car Ad experiment with uncoded information (Experiment 13) were scaled in the same way. That is, the mechanical checklists for the nonconflict and conflict conditions were the left and right endpoints, respectively. However, the year and make of the car were removed from the checklist and the raters were not shown a picture of the car, because some of the messages mentioned these details. (We wanted the raters to focus on representations about the condition of the car rather than just identifying which car was being described.) Again, despite the increased complexity of their task, the eight raters of 12 messages had high intraclass reliability, .95. In only two instances was a message put off the scale. The nonconflict

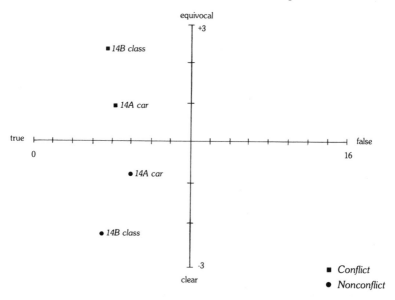

Figure 7.6. Truthfulness and Equivocation in Experiments 14A and 14B (Face-to-Face)

messages had a mean of 4.7, the conflict messages 12.3 ($t = 10.22$, $df = 10$, $p < .001$). The truthfulness and equivocation values are plotted in Figure 7.5.

All of the above results show that the participants in the spoken experiments told the truth. The conflict and nonconflict messages only differed in the degree of equivocation, not in the degree of truthfulness.

FACE-TO-FACE MESSAGES (EXPERIMENTS 14A AND 14B)[4]

Finally, we obtained ratings of the two experiments in which subjects' messages included all verbal and nonverbal possibilities. These messages were rated on videotape using the same procedure as was used for the previous experiments.

The endpoints for the face-to-face Car for Sale scenario (Experiment 14A) were the same as for the uncoded, spoken version (just described above), and the results were virtually the same as well. The eight raters scaled all 12 messages, putting none off the scale; intraclass reliability was .96. Nonconflict messages had a mean of 4.9, conflict messages had a mean of 11.8, ($t = 7.95$, $df = 10$, $p < .001$). These groups are entered on both equivocation and truthfulness coordinates in Figure 7.6.

The messages from the Class Presentation (Experiment 14B) were rated by a different set of raters (for reasons to be explained in the next section), with an intraclass reliability of .96 for five raters of the 12 messages. Messages were put off the scale four times, including the same (conflict) message three times; this message (the last message in the Conflict condition in Table 6.7) was excluded from further analysis. The means of the non-conflict and conflict conditions were 3.28 and 11.78 ($t = 5.32$, $df = 10$, $p < .001$). Figure 7.6 gives the positions of these two groups on truthfulness and equivocation.

In summary, truthfulness ratings of the 10 different sets of messages from previous experiments produced consistent results: Messages from the conflict and nonconflict conditions did not vary on truthfulness but rather on equivocation. These two aspects of communication functioned independently in people's messages. When the distinction is made, it is evident that these participants had spontaneously avoided false messages, just as others had done in the forced-choice experiments.

Are Equivocations Lies of Omission?

Our rating method was also designed to test the hypothesis that equivocations might be mostly "lies of omission." As the reader would expect, we are uncomfortable with that term because it is both pejorative and an oxymoron, and we will translate it into an empirical description here: It is possible that, while the equivocating speaker does not misrepresent information, he or she responds with irrelevant information, thereby avoiding the unpleasant information altogether. Because our raters were instructed to put messages off the scale if they could not find the relevant information in them, the number of times a message was put off the scale can be used to identify possible "lies of omission." (This would also test another alternative explanation, which is that the messages in the conflict condition were lies but that nonverbal leakage or deception clues rendered them too ambiguous to be rated.)

If either possibility were so, there would be more unrateable messages in the conflict than the nonconflict condition. The numbers do not support this interpretation. First, the number of decisions that a message was unrateable was very low. A total of 1,084 ratings were made of the ten sets of messages; 52, or, less than 5%, were placed off the scale. (A disproportionate number of these were placed off the scale by one individual rater.) Second, these decisions were not limited to messages from the conflict condition: 31 were in the conflict condition, 21 in the nonconflict condition. This difference was tested for significance by treating the two conditions as correlated observations within each experiment. The number of messages placed off the scale in each experiment did not differ significantly by condition (correlated $t = 1.15$, $df = 9$, $p < .14$).

Is Equivocation Nonverbal Leakage?

Given that equivocal messages were rated rather than put off the scale, it might still be argued that these messages were verbally false but contained contradictory, "leaked" information nonverbally. If this leakage were sufficiently detectable, the result would be a message that would be scaled as contradictory (equivocal) but from which raters could decode "the truth." In other words, leakage theorists could argue that, because our raters had seen or heard the whole message, they had inferred from its nonverbal aspects what the speaker sought to hide. (Note that this criticism assumes that the raters disregarded our instructions *not* to make such inferences. Nor will it explain the ratings of written messages, where only verbal information existed, or the forced-choice results.)

This alternative explanation can be tested by varying the nonverbal information available to those who rated the meaning of the messages. So we presented the messages from the visual Class Presentation experiment to seven different groups of raters in seven different versions, ranging from purely verbal to purely nonverbal. If the participants had lied verbally, the ratings of the verbal versions should reveal effective deception — the raters should decode a message that is not true. If leakage occurred, there should be a systematic *change* in rated meaning over the seven versions, with the ratings moving toward the true meaning as nonverbal information is added. Recall that we ask the raters to decode meaning, not to detect deception, so their ratings are an independent, objective test of the leakage hypothesis.

Thirty-six (paid) raters from psychology and linguistics classes were randomly assigned to one of the seven different versions, using the same endpoints as for all earlier versions of the Class Presentation scenario. One rater was replaced because she forgot to scale one of the messages, leaving the planned *n* of five per version. The seven versions formed a continuum defined by the availability of nonverbal information:

1. *Verbal, edited.* All messages were transcribed, then paralinguistic disfluencies were edited out. The resulting messages had complete sentences and no hesitations or stammering.

2. *Verbal, transcribed.* Each message was transcribed literally, including its para-linguistic aspects.

3. *Audio without latency.* The video messages were copied onto audiotape. Because hesitancy before answering has been described as a major paralinguistic clue that deception is occurring, response latency was removed in this version by removing the preceding question.

4. *Audio with latency.* Same as above, but the latency was added by including the question on the tape.

5. *Video without latency.* The video version was used but with the latency clue removed, as above.

6. *Video with latency.* This was the video of the message as it was actually delivered.

7. *Video without sound.* Only visual nonverbal information was available, with no verbal content.

For purposes of analysis, then, this was a 2 x 7 design, with two experimental conditions (conflict and nonconflict) and seven different levels of nonverbal information.

Between one and six messages were put off the scale in each version, including one message (**"Well HOW do you THINK you DID?"**) that most raters found unrateable regardless of the version in which they read, heard, or saw it; this message was eliminated from further analysis. For the rateable messages, the reliabilities of the first six versions ranged from .86 to .98. However, the reliability of the video-without-sound version was .33; raters using purely nonverbal information did not agree at all on the meaning of the message, so this version was excluded from further analysis.

If the equivocations obtained in the conflict condition were really "leaky lies," then the decoded meaning should change as more nonverbal information is added. This hypothesis was tested by analysis of variance contrasts (on the conflict condition only) in the form of a monotonic decline; $F (1, 24) = .001$, $p > .89$. Our own prediction that both the conflict and nonconflict messages are truthful was tested as a main effect of condition. This analysis revealed a strong effect of experimental condition; $F (1, 24) = 612.26$, $p < .0001$; eta-squared = 91% of the variance. There was no effect of the version in which the message was rated and no interaction between condition and version.

Equivocations are not leaky lies. No different meaning is decoded from their nonverbal than their verbal aspects. In whatever form they are rated, they are truthful.

EXPERIMENT 15: THE LOCAL MUSICAL – A DIRECT TEST OF THE NONVERBAL LEAKAGE HYPOTHESIS

As discussed at the beginning of this chapter, a major premise of the deception model (indeed, of most views of nonverbal behavior) is that nonverbal behavior is a "channel" of communication separate from and less well controlled than verbal communication. The nonverbal leakage hypothesis echoes this premise and proposes that the nonverbal channel is much less effective at lying than is the verbal. Some authors (e.g., Ekman & Friesen, 1969, 1974) have been more specific and have proposed that people are better able to control their speech than their more peripheral nonverbal actions. In this model, words can deceive better than tone of voice, which in turn can deceive better than bodily actions.

Suppose we obtain and present our raters with some messages that are, in fact, false. Suppose further that we vary their access to the verbal and nonverbal components of these messages. If the leakage hypothesis is accurate, then raters with access to only verbal channels should decode a different message than those who view the nonverbal aspects as well. The former should be (unknowingly) deceived by the well-controlled verbal channel and should rate the message as meaning something that is not true. The other raters, with access to the entire message, should be more likely to decode the true meaning, because it would be revealed on the nonverbal channel. In contrast, our model of integrated verbal and nonverbal aspects proposes a "whole message" with no unique or different information in the nonverbal components of a message. Therefore, the ratings should *not* differ as a function of channel availability. (Note that the derivations for the two models follow the same reasoning as, and are parallel to, the predictions for equivocation in the last section.)

Design

In order to obtain false messages, we added a third experimental condition to our usual conflict/nonconflict design. Subjects in this condition were given a good reason to lie spontaneously to another person, face-to-face. The resulting messages were rated for meaning in the seven different versions used for the Class Presentation data (and also, of course, scaled for equivocation in their actual version).

The difficult part of setting up this experiment was getting people to lie! The many pilot scenarios we exhausted before we succeeded in obtaining false messages added to our conviction that people seldom choose this route when equivocation is possible. We finally found a role-playing situation in which people were very likely to lie spontaneously. This situation used a commonly accepted reason, namely, a "surprise party." In these circumstances, a direct truth would spoil the other person's birthday surprise. A false message, on the other hand, would preserve the surprise and even add to the fun when disclosed later. In theoretical terms, this is a *nonconflict* situation in which a *false* message has a positive valence. By appropriate variations, we created our usual conflict and nonconflict conditions as well. The latter will now be called the nonconflict-*true* condition to distinguish it from the new nonconflict-*false* condition.

In addition to the three experimental conditions, there were seven rating conditions (the same versions as were used for Experiment 14B above). We predicted that rating and scaling of the resulting messages should reveal three groups—false messages, equivocal truths, and clear truths—and that the meaning of these messages would not be affected by the verbal or nonverbal information available to the raters.

Procedure

Our subjects were 22 students recruited by posters around campus during exam period and paid $5.00 each for participation.

When each individual arrived, Experimenter 1 began by saying:

What I'm going to do is to describe a situation that you are to imagine yourself in. Then I'm going to leave the room, and someone else will enter and ask you a question that we'd like you to respond to. While all of this is going on, we'll be videotaping, so you get a chance to see all of this on television later. Any questions?

For the nonconflict-false condition, the instruction continued:

The situation is: You saw a [local] performance of the Broadway play, "Cats," and you really enjoyed it—the singing, the dancing, the whole production was just great. Your favorite cousin's birthday is on Saturday, and you decided this would make a great surprise party. So you got all of his friends organized to go along, you bought a whole block of tickets, and everyone is excited about the surprise.

That is the situation. Now I'm going to leave the room, and someone else will come in. Imagine that the person who is entering the room is the cousin you are having the surprise party for. He is on his way to pick up a ticket to the Friday performance (which is a day before you bought the tickets for), and he wants to ask you how you liked it.

When Experimenter 2 entered, he said:

> **HI, [participant's first name] ! I'm ON my way downtown to get a TICKET for "CATS." HOW did you LIKE the PERFORMANCE?**

In the nonconflict-true condition, there was no mention of a party for the cousin. Instead, after the production was described as great, Experimenter 1 said:

> *Your favorite cousin is dating the director but hasn't seen it yet.*

> *That is the situation. Now I'm going to leave the room, and someone else will come in. Imagine that the person who is entering the room is the cousin who is dating the director. He is on his way to get a ticket to the Friday performance, and he wants to ask you how you liked it.*

The reader may by now have anticipated the conflict version. It was identical to the nonconflict-true script just given, except that:

> *You saw a performance of the Broadway play, "Cats," and you really hated it — the singing, the dancing, the whole production was just awful. Your favorite cousin is dating the director but hasn't seen it yet. . . .*

The question asked by Experimenter 2 was the same in all conditions. Thus, the subjects had to respond spontaneously to a situation in which a false description was appropriate, or a true description was appropriate, or where both true and false responses were to be avoided.

Four participants' data were replaced — two because they did not understand the instructions and two because they did not attempt to falsify their description. We eliminated the latter two replies because we were no longer interested in *whether* people would generate false messages but in *how* they would do so. This left the planned N of 18 ($n = 6$).

Analysis and Results

The messages were scaled for equivocation in the usual way, but in two sessions because of the number and length of the messages. In each of the sessions, the same six judges scaled nine messages (three from each experimental condition). The messages are presented in Table 7.2 with their equivocation values, and the statistical tests are presented in Table 7.3. The Sum

Figure 7.7.

shows the predicted result, with clear messages in the nonconflict-true and nonconflict-false conditions and equivocal messages in the conflict condition. The results on the other dimensions revealed that the nonconflict-false messages were sometimes intermediate in clarity, that is, significantly different from the nonconflict-true as well as the conflict messages.

The messages were also rated for meaning in the seven different versions. Thirty-five students, paid for their assistance, were randomly assigned to one of the versions ($n = 5$). The endpoints were "the person really enjoyed the play and thought the whole production was great" (at 0 cm) and "the person really hated the play and thought the whole production was awful" (at 13 cm). The reliabilities for the first six versions ranged from .97 to .99; the Video Without Sound version had a reliability of .88 and so was left in the analysis. Overall, messages were put off the scale between zero and nine

(continued on page 203)

TABLE 7.2

Experiment 15: Performance of "Cats" (face-to-face)

Condition	Content	Sender	Receiver	Context	Sum
Nonconflict-True Condition					
Female: <0.2 sec.> (Usually looking at the other person; either smiling or looking ready to smile most of the time. Shakes head to emphasize every word; her gestures flow from one into the next, and they too "beat" in time with her speech.) (Intensely and enthusiastically:) Ah! FAN-TASTIC ... singing, dancing (moves hand back and forth like a conductor) just GREAT (moves fingers smoothly toward the other person; then, in a tone that sounds almost as if overcome with emotion:) Just--RIGHT ON (shakes closed fist).	-.94	-.65	-.89	-.96	-3.44
Male: <0.9 sec.> (Looking mostly at the other person, occasionally up or to the side during pauses; tilting and shaking head often.) (In a warm, praising, but restrained tone:) OH I thought it was WELL DONE. (Slight smile.) The-- SINGING was EXCELLENT, then smiling more and in a somewhat more enthusiastic tone:) And I just en-ENJOYED the-- ... the SETS, the-- SCENERY ... ahhhh ... the COSTUMING. EVERYTHING about it was just GREAT.	-1.35	-.61	-.31	-1.00	-3.27
Male: <0.5 sec.> (Initially looking at the other person.) (In a fast, throaty, definite tone:) OH it was FA--- (looks down, closes eyes, smiles slightly, and makes "OK" gesture) a--good SHOW. EXCELLENT, (then looking at the other person; nodding; much softer:) excellent.	-1.00	-.36	-.33	-.87	-2.56
Male: <0.2 sec.> (Eyes darting toward the other person and away throughout; looking as though he is about to smile.) (In a smooth and warm but not very enthusiastic tone:) I ENJOYED it--it WAS--ah--... (Shrugs shoulders and draws mouth down) MUSIC was good, DANCING was good. It WAS ah--... ALL in ALL a good PRODUCTION, (very softly:) I guess.	-.72	-.14	-.18	-1.16	-2.20

-.33	.17	-.53	-.29	-.98

Female: <1.0 sec.> (Looking directly at the other person. Unsmiling throughout.) (Starts by squinting and looking pained, though tone is pleasantly matter-of-fact:) OH-AHHHH-- ... really I wasn't that GOOD, really. I wouldn't-- really GO if I were you. (grimaces) It wasn't that GOOD, really. (Shaking head: more softly:) It's NOT that good. (End with mouth quite downturned.)

-.55	-.61	.32	.09	.75

Male: <0.5 sec.> (Begins by looking away from the other person.) (Unsmiling and in a flat, unenthusiastic, almost world-weary tone throughout:) UM. (then looks back at the other) It wasn't as GOOD (both hands gesture slightly toward the other person) as I had EXPECTED-- (looks away) it to BE. (Hand gestures vaguely and returns hand to knee with an audible slap; then he looks at the other person.) I've SEEN ... (gestures vaguely) quite a few OTHER Broadway PRODUCTIONS, and it wasn't (tilts head, then slaps eg lightly) NEAR as good as most of the OTHERS. soo-- ... I don't KNOW ... it WASN'T (draws finger across chin then flips hand quickly) really WORTH-- ... buying a ticket for.

.11	-.45	-.68	.49	-.53

Male: <2.0 sec.> (Looking mostly at the other person and usually smiling as if he's trying not to.) (Begins by taking a big breath, smiling, looking down, and shifting far forward in his chair; then, very softly:) WELL ... (sighs; then looks up at the other person and, in a disapproving tone:) I've SEEN it done BETTER (juts chin slightly). I've-AH-- ... (then thoughtfully and somewhat slower:) I don't know if I'd RECOMMEND it. I SAW it in New YORK and it WAS-- ... (flips fingers out towards the other person) QUITE a bit BETTER (same gesture). I'd WAIT-- ... wait .... (then holding both palms out toward the other and in a firmer, "friendly advice" tone:) but DON'T spend your MONEY on it.

TABLE 7.2
Continued

	.70	.67	-.20	.30	1.47

Female: <0.5 sec.> (Looking mostly at the other person. Face looks somewhat concerned, with knitted brows and just a suggestion of a smile.) (In a matter-of-fact, slightly diffident tone of voice.) I WASN'T too impressed MYSELF, but-- (interrupting herself, considerably faster and brighter, while pointing hands quickly toward the other person.) YOU might like it. (Looks almost expectantly at the other, then returns to her original tone, considerably slower.) But--AH ... (scowls and shakes head) WELLL ... I just-- I just wasn't IMPRESSED with it.

	1.18	-.13	.27	1.32	2.64

Male: <2.8 sec.> (Eyes roll up, shift, then almost close; starts confidently, then stops abruptly:) WELL, I--...-- (looks at the other person and, while nodding and smiling, in a somewhat reluctant tone:) IT was pretty GOOD overall. (Looks away then back; said with a slight sneer and almost as if confiding a secret:) AHHH, there's a FEW things-- --a few ROUGH edges that need-- ... HONING UP. (Then, while looking down, said as if stalling:) AHHM ... I would SAY that--ah, (then, looking back, nodding frequently; speeds up and sounds more confident:) IT'LL probably get BETTER with TIME. IN FACT YOU'LL get probably ... ah ... (looks away) YOU'LL probably go to a BETTER SHOWING than I did (smiles). (Shrugs; then, smiling more, sounding reassuring and still confident:) I was DISAPPOINTED, but that doesn't MEAN that, you know, that YOU'LL be left out in the COLD.

	.97	1.22	1.08	.92	4.19

Male: <2.5 sec.> (Initially smiles and looks away, then, pleasantly, AHHH (looks at the other person and smiles broadly) it-was--... (rotates head and says with a slight laugh:) INTERESTING. (then looks down and stops smiling) AH ... (Long pause, chews lips; then, thoughtfully:) Well ACTUALLY, ah. ... (Long pause, then looks up, winces, and says faster while laughing;) To tell you the TRUTH, I didn't (smile did appear and tone becomes serious:) EN-ENJOY it--(nods, while smiling, and says in a very soft, gentle voice:) completely.

-1.20   -.94   .89   -.84   -2.09

Male: <0.3 sec.> (Mostly looking off to the side or down; shaking head frequently; has a "wide eyed" look.) (In a warm, gentle voice:) It was— ... REALLY well done. I THOUGHT the—ah, (raises eyebrows) CHOREOGRAPHY was EXCELLENT. (Shakes his head left and right.) The MUSIC was OUTSTANDING. (Raises his eyebrows twice.) Ah VERY well PERFORMED and—ah the ACTING (looks to his right and then shakes his head) was SUPERLATIVE.

-.74   .72   1.39   -.85   .52

Male: <0.5 sec.> (Looks down and to the side, never at the other person. Very solemn and thoughtful facial expression; tone of voice is subdued throughout, almost to himself.) (Nodding slightly; looking and sounding as if surprised to hear himself saying this:) I was GREAT. (Long pause, during which he raises eyebrows, lowers corners of mouth, and turns thumbs and intertwined fingers out toward the other person, all as if "what else can I say?".) (Then in a more matter-of-fact but slightly strangled tone:) The—ah ... the WHOLE performance, SINGING, dancing, CHOREOGRAPHY ... (takes a breath and raises eyebrows; then in "why do you ask?" tone:) was ALL fine.

Nonconflict-False Condition

.00   -.83   -.87   -.33   -2.03

Female: <1.0 sec.> (Begins by looking up to one side then closes her eyes and swings her head down to the other side, with a very broad grimace.) (Speaking very fast and confidently throughout:) Well I'll TELL you you know (now looking directly at the other person, but with face still turned aside; smiling slightly) I didn't THINK it was THAT GOOD (nods very slightly in emphasis). (Mouth turns down but expression is not unpleasant.) I mean I— (looks upwards then back at the other person) I thought it was really OVERRATED. (Then, as if debating what to advise:) Ahm ... PROBABLY? ... (Turning head away with exaggerated scowl:) I WOULDN'T bother going— if I were YOU.

TABLE 7.2
Continued

Male: .19 .07 −.84 .70 .12

<0.5 sec.> (Looking obliquely at the other person, occasionally down or away.) (Initially smiling and in a mildly surprised tone of voice.) Oh-yeah, I just SAW it. it's—(grimaces and makes a "so-so" gesture; then in a tone implying something distasteful:) it's o—... KAY. (grimaces again; then in a dubious tone:) I dunno. I—I dunno ... if I'd SPEND that much MONEY to go and see it, I mean—("so-so" gesture again; then more firmly:) ... it's OVERRATED in MY point of view. (Looks up at the other person.)

Male: .34 .62 −.43 .02 .55

<0.9 sec.> (Looking away at first.) (While pursing lips in exaggerated manner and moving head right then left; in rising pitch, almost a question:) MMMH. (Starts smiling and looks at the other person; then rapidly, staccato:) I don't KNOW. (Even more rapidly:) I thought it PROBABLY wasn't worth GOING to.

Conflict Condition

Female: .26 .01 .50 .04 .81

<1.5 sec.> (Often looking obliquely away from the other person; emphasizes "I" each time it is said; pleasant but unsmiling expression.) (Shaking head and in a soft, somewhat reluctant but composed voice:) I ... wasn't ALL that THRILLED with it, (then, much softer:) I'm afraid. (Long pause.) It wasn't—ALL (shifts to a more upright and forward position in her chair) that I was HOPING it would be. (Then, in a more conversational tone:) I've heard a LOT (gestures with both hands open toward the other person) of good THINGS about it, but— ... (grimaces; nods, then shakes head; speeds up:) I wasn't all that THRILLED.

Female: <1.8 sec.> (Mostly looking at the other person; nodding and inclining toward the other person; smiling throughout.) (Begins by taking a deep breath, then exhales her first word through pursed lips, in a lilting tone which ends with a light laugh and big smile:) Welll ... (then, still smiling, and in a warm, well-modulated tone:) I didn't LIKE it all the MUCH. (Then gestures toward self while adding hastily:) But that's just MY opinion. (Lifts and drops folded hands) SO— .... I would SEE it ANYWAY.

    .76   -.25   .21   .33   1.05

Male: <1.0 sec.> (Often looking up and to the side, seldom at the other person.) (Begins by looking away and, with intonation that sounds like "Oh NO!":) Ohhh—OH! (raises eyebrows and puffs out cheeks; then in reluctant, hesitant manner:) ....ahhh... IT was (lifts hand to gesture toward the other person and then slaps leg) NOT—, (then, very fast:) I don't know I'm NOT— ... very (tilts head, wrinkles face into a scowl, and makes same gesture ending in a slap; then, more fluently but sounding disappointed:) TOO into MUSICALS that much, so AS far (same head tilt and gesture) as the music would GO, I would SAY— (shrugs with slight scowl) you— know it was—, not too BA—AD? (Ends by bobbing head in a nod.)

    1.57   1.49   .77   2.04   5.87

Summary Statistics

Reliability (intraclass R) (Trial 1) =	.97	.74	.76	.96	
(Trial 2) =	.93	.90	.89	.98	
Nonconflict-true mean =	-.99	-.33	.10	-.95	-2.17
Conflict mean =	-.04	.17	-.51	.11	-.60
Nonconflict-false mean =	.91	.50	.44	.83	2.67

TABLE 7.3

Experiment 15: Mean Equivocation Values for Conditions and Statistical Analyses

	N	Content	Sender	Receiver	Context	Sum
Condition						
Nonconflict-true	6	-.99	-.33	.10	-.95	-2.17
Conflict	6	.91	.50	.44	.83	2.67
Nonconflict-false	6	-.04	-.38	-.49	.11	-.79
Reliability[a]						
Trial 1		.97	.74[b]	.76[b]	.96	
Trial 2		.93	.90	.89	.98	
ANOVA (planned contrasts)						
F (1, 15)		43.17	8.37	4.21	24.36	30.49
p		<.001	<.01	n.s.	<.001	<.001
Bivariate t-tests (df = 10)						
Conflict vs. Nonconflict-true		9.07***	2.17	.87	5.66***	4.82***
Conflict vs. Nonconflict-false		4.14***	2.25*	3.57***	2.01*	3.90***
Nonconflict-false vs. Nonconflict-true		5.57***	.14	1.46	6.00***	2.04

a. Because 12 is the upper limit of visual messages that can be scaled by judges in a single session, the 18 messages in Experiment 15 were split into two scaling trials (n = 9). There were an equal number of conflict, nonconflict-false messages in each trial.

b. The low intraclass reliability is due to curtailment of range.

* p < .05, one-tailed, not adjusted for alpha inflation.

** p < .05, one-tailed, adjusted for alpha inflation.

*** p < .05, two-tailed, adjusted for alpha inflation.

times out of the 90 ratings (5 raters times 18 messages) in each version. This included one message (the last message in the nonconflict-false condition in Table 7.2) that was subsequently excluded from analysis in three versions because it was put off the scale by 3 out of 5 raters. Meaning values were obtained for each version by averaging over its set of 5 (or fewer) raters.

The meaning values were converted to distances-from-the-truth in the usual way, by subtracting from the true endpoint for the condition, that is, from 0 cm for the nonconflict-true and nonconflict-false conditions and from 13 cm for the conflict condition. The results are summarized graphically in Figure 7.8. A leakage model must predict that the nonconflict-false messages would drop from false towards true as nonverbal information was added. This hypothesis was tested and rejected by applying a set of (analysis of variance) contrasts to this condition that described a monotonic decline over the seven versions; $F(1, 32) = 1.17, p = .29$. Thus, there was no effect of the availability of nonverbal information in the nonconflict-false condition. Indeed, the raters decoded a false meaning even in the Video Without Sound version, whereas in the other two conditions the averages for this version went to the center of the scale (had no systematic meaning). Our prediction (which was that, regardless of version, participants in the nonconflict-true and conflict conditions would reply truthfully, while participants in the nonconflict-false condition would reply falsely) was tested and confirmed by the appropriate contrasts $(-1, -1, +2)$; $F(1, 102) = 393.52, p<.001$, accounting for 75% of the variance.

Finally, the three experimental conditions are located on coordinates in Figure 7.9, which summarizes this experiment: As predicted, the transformed truthfulness means show that conflict and nonconflict-true messages were truthful but the nonconflict-false group were not, and the conflict messages were equivocal while the nonconflict-true and nonconflict-false messages were clearer. In different situations, people produced messages that were true or false, equivocal or clear, depending on which was appropriate.

As the reader may have noticed in Table 7.2, the qualitative differences between the conflict and nonconflict-true messages are very similar to those found in previous experiments, particularly the face-to-face messages described in Chapter 6. The nonconflict-true messages are well (though by no means perfectly) put together. They show some enthusiasm, and they focus entirely on the question asked with no other references. The Conflict messages give contradictory opinions, wander in and out of other topics, and answer a variety of different questions, such as **"Are you INTO musicals?"** or **"Will it get BETTER?"**

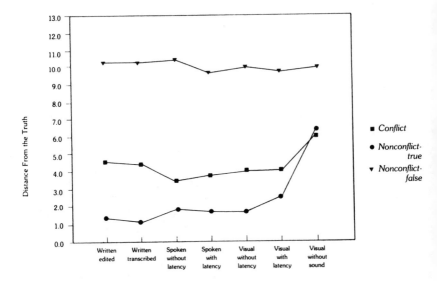

Figure 7.8. Experiment 15 — Mean Truthfulness Ratings

The nonconflict-false messages take a different form — one which we interpret as suited to the problem they had to solve. These messages are just as clear as the nonconflict-true messages on the Sender dimension and actually even clearer on the Receiver dimension: These speakers looked the other person straight in the eye and appeared to give a personal opinion.

Where they are equivocal is on the Content and Context dimensions. Our judges saw them as somewhat hesitant and indecisive and noticed that they always include the answer to another question as well. In our view, these characteristics make sense when the messages are seen as part of the situation in which they were elicited: The speaker's problem was to steer the other person away from buying a ticket. The question provides a means to this end, namely, the opportunity for the speaker to express an opinion about the production. However, it would seem odd if the speaker leaped into a scathing attack on the production; it might even become too "obvious" that he or she is steering the other person away from it. So the criticisms that our "liars" made are understated, almost off-hand. They have a guarded neutrality and feigned objectivity that sometimes pretends to decide before our very eyes, though reluctantly, that the production was not *quite* all that it might have

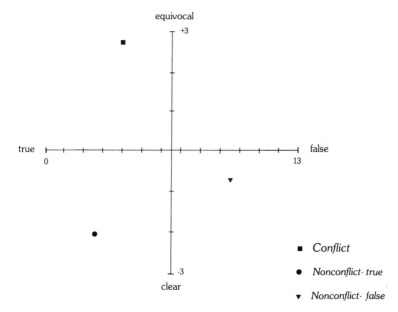

Figure 7.9. Truthfulness and Equivocation Condition Means in Experiment 15 (Face-to-Face)

been. This quality accounts for the ambiguity that judges noticed on the Content dimension.

These messages are also relatively high on the Context dimension, because they always add the answer to an additional, unasked (although somewhat related) question: "**Should I GO?**" Each one mentions (and discourages) the speaker's buying a ticket, spending money, or going to the show. In our view, equivocation on this dimension arises because the speaker must "plant" an answer to an unasked question. Thus, the lies combine a low-key, credible criticism with the hint that the ticket has not yet been — and perhaps should not be — purchased.

The latency data (in Appendix B) are consistent with this interpretation. They show an essentially linear pattern, with the nonconflict-false messages intermediate between the conflict and nonconflict-true messages, which were respectively high and low as usual. If latency reflects internal ambivalence or preparation time, then producing false messages created less ambivalence or required less preparation than did equivocation. On the other hand, if latency encodes lack of enthusiasm, as we propose, then the latencies are consistent with the understated reluctance that the speakers affected in this condition, as well as with the softened truths of the conflict condition. Unencumbered praise is quick off the mark; hesitation speaks volumes.

Implications for Deception Research

These data confirm that communicative situations can be varied, as predicted, to produce messages varying in truthfulness and equivocation. Our measures of these two dimensions may be useful to deception researchers by permitting them: (1) to verify objectively the truth or falsity of their messages; (2) to examine whether equivocation is occurring in their experiments; (3) to test for nonverbal leakage, unconfounded by deception clues; and (4) to check for "lies of omission."

In pointing out that we did not obtain evidence for nonverbal leakage, the specific characteristics of our situation should be noted: A false message had a very positive valence in this situation. Moreover, the information being hidden was not something "bad" (about the speaker, the listener, or anything else) but was instead praise. This would tend to separate nonverbal leakage from deception clues, which have been confounded in most previous designs by having the speakers only hide negative information. Finally, the subjects had a short time to think about their reply as Experimenter 2 entered the room. It would be very interesting to vary these situational parameters systematically.

We suggested earlier that the primary definition of deception must be information-based, but that other dimensions could be added. Here, we have added the dimension of equivocality and have shown how situational valences push messages around on these two dimensions. Following our lead, other aspects of deception could also be measured and studied from a situational point of view. In specified situations, do people produce messages that are rated as, say, false but not harmful? Do messages produced for a receiver who consents to being deceived differ from those produced when there is no consent by the receiver? Under what conditions could perfectly unequivocal false messages be obtained?

SUMMARY

A distinction is made between truthfulness and equivocation, that is, between *what* a message says (whether it is true or false) and *how* it is said (whether it is equivocal or clear). Deception theories assume that people often lie but are likely to be given away by their nonverbal behavior (nonverbal leakage). We obtained ratings of truthfulness for all of the messages elicited in previous experiments and confirmed that equivocal messages are unclear but true. A new experiment that induced false messages showed that such messages are empirically distinct from equivocations. Ratings also showed that equivocations are not "lies of omission" and that neither equivocations or false messages "leak the truth" nonverbally.

NOTES

1. Most authors use *deception* to mean *deceptive communication* (rather than other deceptive actions, e.g., Hyman, 1989) and use both as synonyms for lying.

2. Originally described in Chapter 5, Experiment 6: Class Presentation (Written) and Experiment 8: Bizarre Gift (Written). The Member of Parliament scenario (Experiment 7) is not included here because it was not a "truth versus lying" conflict.

3. Reported in Chapter 6, Experiment 10: Class Presentation (Spoken), Experiment 11A: Bizarre Gift (Spoken), Experiment 11B: Meat Market (Spoken), Experiment 12: Employee Reference (Spoken), and Experiment 13: Car for Sale (Spoken).

4. Described in Chapter 6, Experiment 14A: Car for Sale (Face-to-Face) and Experiment 14B: Class Presentation (Face-to-Face).

8

Children's Equivocation: Exploratory Studies

Kids get bad press. They are portrayed in cartoons as unwittingly giving away family secrets, passing on overheard insults, and generally endangering relationships. When they are not blurting out unwelcome truths, they misspeak, miscommunicate, and misinterpret. We wondered whether, when children misspeak, they may do so deliberately and for the same reasons as adults do. That is, they may be aware of the social consequences both of falsehoods and of truths and may sometimes be able to solve such dilemmas by avoiding direct communication. Equivocation, when used by a child as a strategy to escape an avoidance-avoidance conflict, would require both social perception and communicative ability. For example, the child would have to realize that, while a falsification is not a good idea, a straightforward truth may have adverse consequences on the relationship. Having recognized that truth is the better course, the child must still find a way to modify it, to soften its bluntness.

This chapter reports our initial explorations of children's abilities to use ambiguous language for social reasons. We did not study children as intensively as we have adults, and the results were not as clear-cut. Even so, the picture we put together from the previous literature and our pilot studies suggests that, while children may lack the sophistication of adults, there can be greater subtlety in their use of language, in terms of its impact on others, than popular depictions suggest. We hope that some readers will also be convinced that further work in this area would be fruitful and will take up where we left off.

PREVIOUS RESEARCH ON CHILDREN'S
UNDERSTANDING AND USE
OF AMBIGUOUS LANGUAGE

In order to estimate the age at which children might be able to produce a deliberately equivocal message, we consulted the current literature on children's communication. Unfortunately, equivocation as a developmental topic has not been studied; however, there were some studies on the broader topic of ambiguous language. Just as we found for adults, the researchers who have not treated ambiguity as defective language (and therefore dismissed it) are in the minority. But research by this minority has demonstrated an impressive array of the kinds of ambiguity children are able to handle.

Humor often relies on linguistic ambiguity. Hirsh-Pask, Gleitman, and Gleitman (1978) carried out an extensive study of children's ability to recognize the subtlety of ambiguous language used in humor, and they were able to outline some of the difficult linguistic structures that young children have mastered. A sample of children from Grades 1 through 6 were first asked to rate jokes as very funny, a little funny, or not funny at all; they were then asked to explain the jokes.

The researchers selected jokes in several categories of language ambiguity, with all of the punch lines hinging on some kind of play on words. For example, phonological ambiguity occurs when two words sound alike, with a difference in only one phonological segment:

If you put three ducks in a box, what do you have?

A box of quackers. (p. 118)

Lexical ambiguity occurs when the same word has two different meanings:

How can hunters in the woods best find their lost dogs?

By putting their ears to a tree and listening to the bark.
(p. 118)

As one might expect, older children understood more jokes and were better able to explain the jokes than were younger children. The children's ability to respond accurately was also related to verbal ability (as measured by reading skill), but all children found certain kinds of ambiguities harder to explain than others. For example, children had special difficulty when the task required breaking up a language unit, the polysyllable morpheme; for example:

How do trains hear?

Through their engine ears. (p. 118)

"**Engineers**" is a lexical unit that must be forced apart to be heard as "**engine ears.**"

The ability to detect alternative interpretations of a word was present much earlier than the ability to explain the resulting ambiguity. Children as young as 6 and 7 years old often "got" a joke but had difficulty explaining it. It seems that speaking and understanding do not require metalinguistic ability (the conscious reflection on "language as an object"), which explaining the ambiguity does require. The authors concluded:

> In sum, what must logically be there in the brain for the purposes of perceiving language is not necessarily always or wholly there in the mind for the purpose of relecting on and commenting about language. The subject does not know *about* everything he knows *how to do* with language. (p. 127)

Another kind of ambiguous communication is *sarcasm*. Ackerman (1982) compared adults' abilities to recognize and understand sarcasm with those of first and third graders. He found that first graders can interpret sarcastic utterances — but only when the integration of context and utterance information is facilitated. In other words, the sarcastic statement must be "set up" to be accurately interpreted. Specifically, they found that children could interpret the sarcasm correctly if the contextual information immediately followed the sarcastic utterance, as in the following example:

> It was ten o'clock and reading time in school. Billy turned the page in his book. The teacher said, "**You're very quiet today, Billy.**" Billy had been talking out loud to his friends disturbing everyone. He sat up in his chair. (p. 1077)

Because the contextual information, "**Billy had been talking out loud ... **", immediately followed the sarcastic message, the children could understand the sarcasm.

Ackerman's studies elucidated the cognitive processes involved in the comprehension of sarcasm:

> To understand a sarcastic utterance a listener has to note the contradiction between the utterance and the contextual information, infer that the speaker is aware of this contradiction in using the utterance and integrate the contextual and utterance information. (p. 1)

It seems amazing that children comprehend sarcasm at all!

Green (1979) studied the comprehension of *speaker uncertainty* by children from 5 to 17 years old. One of these studies used a toy schoolhouse, a three-inch doll (the same gender as the subject), and a toy chair. One wall of the schoolhouse folded down to reveal the interior. The subject was told:

> *This little doll sometimes can't quite make up its mind about what to do next, and other times it already has its mind made up. The doll is going to tell you some things from this [pointing to tape recorder]. Listen carefully to what it says. If the doll has already decided what to do next, if it's already made up its mind, then you can move it outside, like it was going to really go do it [experimenter demonstrates]. But if the doll isn't really sure what it's going to do next, if it hasn't already decided yet, then put it over here in its Thinking Chair where it goes to make up its mind [experimenter demonstrates]. (p. 669)*

The child listened to the doll "speaking" tape-recorded messages and decided whether the doll had made up its mind about what it was going to do next. The messages varied in how clear versus uncertain they were (as judged by adults), for example:

I might go outside.

Maybe I'll ride my bicycle.

I may visit a friend.

I'm not sure if I should go outside.

Perhaps I'll take a walk.

Maybe I might ride my bicycle.

Perhaps I might go swimming.

I've decided what to do next. (p. 669)

If the child recognized the indecision of the doll from the message, he or she was identifying speaker uncertainty. As noted above, the accuracy of recognition of speaker uncertainty in a message was scored by comparison to adult judgments of the same statements.

In a second task, the child was asked to say which of two children in photographs "took longer to make up its mind," judging from the statements attributed to the children. For example,

I'll probably play a game.

versus

Maybe I might play a game. (p. 670)

Choosing between such messages required the child to recognize different *degrees* of speaker uncertainty. Again, these judgments were evaluated against the same comparative judgments by adults.

Green was interested in relating the children's judgments to Piagetian cognitive stage. The results of the first study showed that recognition of speaker uncertainty appeared at Piaget's concrete operational stage (about 11 years of age in this sample). The second study showed that children's judgments about the more subtle quality of degree of speaker uncertainty were more consistent at the level of formal operations (about 16 years in this sample) than at lower levels of development.

Carrell (1981) compared children's understanding of *indirect requests* with adults' understanding of the same material. She was interested in two issues: How well are young children (between 4 and 7 years of age) able to comprehend various syntactic forms conveying indirect requests, and how does the relationship between the type of request and ease of comprehension change from childhood to adulthood? Each child was given a red crayon, a blue crayon, and a sheet with uncolored circles on it. The experimenter read one of a series of sentences, and the child was to color one of the circles red or blue according to what he or she understood to have been requested. Each of the 40 different sentences conveyed a request, varying in indirectness, to color the circle either red or blue. Each kind of request had a positive and a negative version; for example:

I would love to see the circle colored blue.

I would hate to see the circle colored blue. (p. 332)

The following is an example of an interrogative request and its corresponding negative:

Does the circle really need to be painted blue?

Doesn't the circle really need to be painted blue? (p. 332)

Some of the sentences were extremely difficult to understand for syntactic reasons, for example:

I'll be very happy unless you make the circle blue. (p. 332)

The children had an average total test performance of 77.2% correct; their performance improved over the four grade levels. With some exceptions, there were more errors on interrogative forms, such as:

Should you color the circle blue? (p. 332)

and every negative request was more difficult to understand than its positive counterpart. Finally, these findings were compared to Clark and Lucy's (1975) findings for adults doing the same test. There was a high and statistically significant correlation (across sentences) between the adults' and children's ease or difficulty with the same requests. In other words, the adults made mistakes on the same sentences that the children found difficult to understand. Had the results been confined to the children's performance, we might have attributed all of their errors to their stage of development and not discovered that there are some difficulties inherent in the statements themselves.

It is interesting to note that one kind of declarative form that posed difficulty for the children was exactly the kind of statement that children often hear when parents or teachers try to get them to do something by appealing to their sense of fair play, for example:

Johnny will be sad unless you give him back his pencil.

Carrell's results suggest that this kind of request will leave a child wondering whether Johnny wants his pencil.

The studies described above show that children are developing the ability to recognize and interpret ambiguity at fairly young ages. Next, we will examine two studies of the interpersonal aspects of ambiguity, in which children had to deal with the impact of their own communication on another person.

Figure 8.1.

Robinson and Robinson (1978a, 1978b, 1981, 1983) have done extensive research into children's ability to recognize *ambiguous instructions*, including their own. Specifically, they have studied the extent of children's understanding that a listener needs clear information and that communicative failure can sometimes be attributed to the person speaking. Through interactive tasks with the child, they assess whether he or she understands that a speaker (including oneself) can be responsible for a listener's failure to understand something. Children who understand this possibility (and therefore do not always blame the listener) may communicate more effectively. For example, Robinson and Robinson (1983) showed, with children between 5 and 7, that "speaker blamers" gave clearer and better instructions than did "listener blamers."

Even closer to our interests is one of their studies (Robinson & Robinson, 1978b) in which children were asked to give *poor* as well as good instructions. The children (between 5 years 4 months and 9 years 10 months) had six cards, each with a line drawing of a man that differed slightly from the others in some small detail. The experimenter had an identical set of cards and was to choose one according to the child's instruction. As part of the game the child was asked, "**Now give me an easy [message], so I know just which one to pick**" or "**Now give me a very hard one, so I don't know which one to pick**" (p. 221). Easy messages were quite specific, such as:

A man with a blue flower and he's got three buttons. (p. 223)

Examples of hard messages are:

A man with a flower [which described four cards]
A man with a flag [which described two cards]. (p. 222)

The children were able to give deliberately ambiguous messages, that is, they could produce clarity or unclarity on request. This was particularly true for the "speaker blamers," whereas few of the "listener blamers" could do so. Thus, deliberate ambiguity requires some metalinguistic insight into communication as an interpersonal process involving both speaker and listener.

Bates (1976) used a comprehensive and creative research strategy to study the development of communicative abilities in *politeness*, which is often indirect and less than clear. (For example, compare "**Take out the garbage**" with "**Would you like to take out the garbage?**") In a first, longitudinal study, she analyzed the audiotaped interactions of two children in their homes for two years, from approximately 15 months to 3 1/2 years of age. She wanted to see how children used language to get their parents to do something for them. These two children appeared to change what they said according to how it had been received by the adult and to modify it into a more acceptable version in order to achieve a goal (e.g., to get the adult to play a game with them). In effect, they seemed to be trying to make the adults "an offer they couldn't refuse." The earliest polite form (by adult standards) appeared as young as 18 months; this was a change to interrogative form when an imperative form had failed:

We play this game!

was often modified to

We play this game? (p. 277)

These longitudinal observations were followed up with a cross-sectional study designed to test the ability of young children to produce and judge different forms of polite requests. Children at six different age levels (from 2 years 10 months to 6 years 2 months) were tested in schools in Rome. A bowl of candies was placed beside a puppet of an elderly, grey-haired woman named Signora Rossi. The children were told that, if they asked her, Signora Rossi would give them a candy. After the child had made the request, the experimenter pretended to whisper with the puppet and then told the child:

Mrs. Rossi said that she will surely give you a candy. But, you know, she's a bit old, and she likes it when children are VERY, very nice. Ask her again EVEN MORE NICELY for the candy. (p. 297)

The child was given a candy regardless of his or her next response and was told that a second one would be given if he or she asked "**EVEN MORE NICELY.**"

Then, in the second part of the study, the child was put in charge of Signora Rossi's candy. Two frog puppets asked the child for candy, and the child was to put it in the mouth of the one who spoke in the nicest way. There were eight different forms of request presented in two different random orders. Afterwards, the child was asked why he or she thought the chosen request was "nicer."

The first task (Signora Rossi) was designed to find out whether the child was able to *produce* responses that varied on a politeness dimension. Judgments of the frog puppets' requests was designed to reveal whether the child could *recognize* differences on a politeness dimension. Asking the children why the one they picked was nicer was a way of finding out whether the child could *articulate* (metalinguistically) the reasons for such differences.

The results provided several insights into children's interpersonal use of language. The ages at which children could produce the various polite forms was the same as the order of acquisition in the longitudinal study. When told to ask "**even more nicely**," younger children knew fewer polite devices than older children, but children of any age were able to increase politeness in some way. Thus, a dimensional concept of politeness was well established by age 3, and further increases in skill were manifested by more sophisticated forms of politeness.

Bates also asked adults to rank order the children's statements on relative politeness. She discovered that the order of acquisition for various polite forms paralleled adult judgments of relative politeness. That is, requests that adults deemed to be more polite appeared later in development.

As for judging politeness, the youngest age group recognized saying "please," whereas the use of the conditional or of formal address were only recognized by the oldest group in the study. The ability to give reasons for their judgments was not a precondition of the children's ability to make correct judgments about (i.e., to recognize) polite forms. Younger children could make correct judgments but could not explain their judgments. Once again, we see that children know more than they know they know.

Bates's theoretical interpretations of these data reinforce our propositions that communication need not always be clear, direct, and efficient to be "good" communication and that the interpersonal impact of a message plays a major role in the form it takes. She pointed out that, when polite forms begin to appear:

> there is a crossover from efficiency in communication (expanding messages which fail) to politeness (diminishing the force of messages which fail), a shift that must involve the knowledge that some speech forms are unacceptable. . . . (p. 332)

In other words:

> Polite devices do not render requests more informative, at least not with respect to the speaker's [explicit] goal and/or the course of action recommended to the listener. Instead, they render requests less offensive. (p. 319)

From all of the above studies, it seemed clear to us that children know quite a bit about communication, including recognizing various kinds of ambiguity and being able to deliver an ambiguous or unambiguous message when instructed to do so. They know how to make a message nonstraightforward and, in the case of politeness, will select such a message for its social effects. This led us to ask whether children might be able to recognize a communicative conflict, that is, a social situation that requires problem-solving communication, and be able to select or produce equivocal messages in such a situation.

EXPERIMENT 16: GIFT (FORCED CHOICE)

Our exploration of these issues began with two simple experiments. We revived the multiple-choice format (specifically, Experiment 3: Control for Unpleasantness, described in Chapter 4, with conflict versus unpleasant nonconflict conditions) to answer the initial questions: Would children choose an equivocal message as providing a way out of an avoidance-avoidance conflict, as our theory proposes?

It happened that two groups of Grade 7 students with an interest in psychology visited our university for a day. With their teachers' permission, we took the opportunity to ask for the children's responses to our avoidance-avoidance conflicts, in exchange for an explanation and discussion of the experiment with the students. One group saw the Gift scenario; the other saw the Class scenario (Experiment 17, below). Pilot testing had shown that children of this age — between 12 and 13 — could easily understand these two situations.

The format and procedures were virtually identical to the Gift scenario of Experiment 3, with conflict and nonconflict conditions randomly ordered. The only difference was that, instead of all possible random orders of response options, a fixed order was used in each condition, with our predicted choice for that condition appearing last. So if the children tended to choose the first messages they came to, the order would be stacked against our hypothesis. The instruction, scenario, and choice of responses were typewritten on a full sheet of paper.

The experimenter described the procedure, emphasizing that this was not a test, that they should imagine themselves in the situation, and that they should limit themselves to the replies given. The 43 children were then asked to turn over their sheets, where they read the following:

Try to imagine the situation described below, as vividly as possible. Then read all the choices and indicate which you would write *in this situation.*

Remember . . . (1) try to really put yourself in the situation, and also (2) limit yourself to just the choices given. (3) We are not interested in what you think you should say, but in what you think you actually would say.

You have received a birthday gift from someone you really like a lot. This person's birthday is on the same day as yours, and you had sent a gift too. The gift you received is awful, and you don't like it at all.

The friend, who lives in another province, expects a thank-you note telling how you like the gift. So you are going to write a short note about the gift you received (without mentioning the one you sent). Which of the following would you say?

I really like the gift you sent.
Thank you very much.

I don't like the gift you sent.

Thank you very much for the gift,
it was very kind of you.

So the child had a choice of a pleasant false message, a hurtful truth, or an equivocation. In the (unpleasant) nonconflict condition, the key sentences of the third paragraph read:

> *This person's birthday is on the same day as yours, but you completely forgot it this year and you sent nothing. The gift you received is great, and you like it very much.*

The order of alternatives for this condition was:

Thank you very much for the gift,
it was very kind of you.

I don't like the gift you sent.

I really like the gift you sent.
Thank you very much.

After everyone had completed the form, the experimenter explained the procedures and hypothesis and answered all questions.

The children's choices, summarized in Table 8.1, were significantly different from chance, with the equivocation preferred in the conflict condition. We also tested the difference between children's and adults' choices, using the frequencies from Table 4.7 for (proportional) expected values and the children's choices here as observed values; chi-square = .509, df = 2, not significant. Thus, these children, around age 13, responded identically to adults, choosing equivocation specifically in an avoidance-avoidance conflict.

EXPERIMENT 17: CLASS PRESENTATION (FORCED CHOICE)

The 44 children in the other Grade 7 group saw the Class scenario from Experiment 3, with format and procedures exactly as described above. The scenario was as follows:

TABLE 8.1

Experiments 16 & 17: Frequencies of Choice in Conflict and Nonconflict Condition (Class and Gift with Children)

Situation	Message	Sum	Condition[a]	
			Conflict	Nonconflict
Gift	I really like the gift you sent. Thank you very much.	-1.57	1	15
	I don't like the gift you sent.	-1.58	0	0
	Thank you very much for the gift, it was very kind of you.	3.13	20	7
Class	I think you did fine.	-2.06	4	17
	I think you did a bad job.	-2.29	6	0
	Not bad.	4.36	10	4

a. Chi-square for the first two versus third message (as listed above) in the conflict and nonconflict conditions: Gift = 18.5, $df = 2$, $p < .001$; Class = 16.6, $df = 2$, $p < .001$.

You are in a class which meets three times a week for the entire year. Each student has to make an individual presentation to the class. Today you and another student gave your presentations, separately—first you, then him. You were both very scared. Yours went really well. You were ready, not nervous, and generally did a very good job.

The other student, after you, did very badly—his presentation was poorly prepared and poorly delivered. After he sits down again, he passes you a note: "How did I do?" You have to jot something down and pass it back to him. Which of the following would you write?

I think you did fine.

I think you did a bad job.

Not bad.

Again the choices were a pleasant falsehood, a hurtful truth, and an equivocation. In the (unpleasant) nonconflict condition, the presentations were described as follows:

Yours went terribly. You were not ready yet, too nervous, and generally did a very bad job.

The other student, after you, did very well—his presentation was well prepared and well delivered.

As before, the order of alternatives was against our hypothesis:

Not bad.

I think you did a bad job.

I think you did fine.

Three children's sheets could not be used (two had circled more than one choice and one had crossed out all three), leaving an N of 41. The results, given in Table 8.1, were significantly different from chance, but their pattern did *not* confirm our hypothesis. While a straightforward truth was preferred in the nonconflict condition, equivocations were chosen by only half of the children in the conflict condition. These results differed significantly from the adults' pattern, given in Table 4.7 (chi-square = 26.61, $df = 2$, $p < .001$), primarily because children chose a hurtful truth (**"I think you did a bad job"**) more frequently than did the adults. Thus, children of the same age and from the same population chose differently in the Class than in the Gift scenario. There were many specific differences in the two situations, some of which might explain the lack of generality of the results; these will be discussed after the next pair of experiments.

EXPERIMENT 18A: NEW HAIRDO (SPOKEN)

In the next two experiments, we obtained even younger children's own spontaneous replies to conflict and nonconflict conditions, using procedures similar to our "spoken" experiments (see Chapter 6) and scenarios adapted from previous experiments with adults. These "back-to-back" experiments used the New Hairdo (18A) and Gift (18B) scenarios, rewritten to be appropriate for children ranging in age from 6 to 10. Again, these experiments should be considered pilot studies.

The subjects were 12 children in the experimenter's neighborhood (two males and ten females) of 6, 8, and 10, with four in each age group. Within each age level, the children were randomly assigned to either a conflict or nonconflict version of the New Hairdo scenario.

With the parents' permission, the experimenter went to the home of each child and explained the experiment in the child's own room. The experimenter had a toy walkie-talkie set that was connected to the tape recorder. One end of the walkie-talkie was in the child's room; the other end, connected to a tape recorder, was in an adjoining room. Thus, the experimenter could go into the adjoining room and buzz the child for a "telephone call."

The experimenter explained the procedure to the child and told her or him that the conversation on the "phone" would be tape-recorded. The instructions for the New Hairdo scenario were as follows:

> *I'm going to tell you a story, and I want you to try and pretend that you are the person in the story and that what happens is happening to you. This is the story:*
>
> *You are out shopping with your Mom, and you see your best friend coming out of a hairdresser's shop with a new hairdo that doesn't suit them at all. It makes them look like a boy [girl]. They wave to you and you wave back, but you quickly walk in the other direction because you don't want them to ask you if you like their hair.*
>
> *Later, when you are at home, you get a call from this friend. I am going to go out of the room and call you on the phone. I am going to pretend that I am your friend with the new hairdo, so talk to me just as if I am that friend.*

Notice that we underscored the conflict by implying that the child initially would have wanted to avoid the question.

The nonconflict version was the same until the description of the hairstyle, which was described as:

really nice—it made them look a lot better.

Again, the child did not talk to the friend at the time (although not because he or she wanted to avoid being asked); hence the phone call.

Then the experimenter went to the other room, buzzed the walkie-talkie to signal the child, and said:

HELLO, is this [child's name]?

[Then, after the child had said "**Yes**"]

I SAW you downtown; HOW do you LIKE my HAIR?

The child's answer to this question was the message of interest.

The order in which the messages were presented to judges for scaling was random with respect both to age group and experimental condition. The results are shown in Table 8.2, in which the messages, their scale values, reliabilities, and *t*-tests are given. There was no significant effect of condition on any of the four dimensions. It is obvious, examining the Sum values of messages in the table, that a highly equivocal message occurred in the nonconflict condition, and three clear messages (two true and one false) occurred in the conflict condition. Again we will defer discussion of why the results were not as predicted until we have the results of the final experiment as well.

EXPERIMENT 18B: GIFT (SPOKEN)

After the child had answered the question about the hair and the experimenter had finished the conversation (in role), she went back into the other room, assured the child that he or she had done a good job on the first story, and gave the scenario for the second part of the experiment. As in our previous "back-to-back" experiments, each child's experimental condition was reversed from 18A. The story for the Gift scenario was:

A relative who lives out of town—let's call her Aunt Bertha—sends you a present in the mail. You are expecting it to be a T-shirt. So you get it, open it, but [for girls:] it's one of those thin shirts with the holes in the sleeves and a hockey player on it.

TABLE 8.2

Experiment 18A: Hairdo (spoken)

Condition	Content	Sender	Receiver	Context	Sum
Nonconflict Condition					
Female: <1.2 sec.> (Enthusiastically, as if a (8) restrained shout:) **It's GREAT.**	-.76	-.86	-1.04	-.48	-3.14
Female: <sec.[a]> (Very fast, somewhat forced:) (10) **I-think it's GREAAAT.**	-.07	-.64	-.43	-.73	-1.87
Female: <1.5 sec.> (Brightly, smoothly:) **It's** (10) **NICE.**	-.44	-.50	-.45	-.35	-1.74
Female: <0.8 sec.> (In a lilting, slightly (8) "precious" voice:) **It's PRET-ty.**	-.39	-.09	-.15	-.53	-1.16
Female: <1.0 sec.> (In a slow, almost (6) mechanical pace, but with warmth:) **It looks SU-per.**	-.29	.13	.36	-.09	.11
Male: <1.0 sec.> (Sounds as if spoken by (6) three different people. At first, forced out breathily:) **I--** ... (then higher, almost sung:) **UMMM** ... (then lower, hesitantly, and almost completely flat:) **GOOD.**	1.53	1.25	1.26	1.33	5.37
Conflict Condition					
Male: <2.0 sec.> (Softly but intensely:) **I** (6) **HATE it.**	-.75	-.82	-.62	-1.07	-3.26
Male: <2.0 sec.> (Almost coyly:) **I LIKE-it.** (6)	-.58	-.54	.25	-.93	-1.75
Female: <2.5 sec.> (Starts with long intake of (8) breath; then frankly, as if "biting the bullet":) **I, THINK it doesn't really SUIT you.** (Exhale.)	-.53	-.88	-.10	.41	-1.15

Female: (8)	<1.0 sec.> (In a reassuring but restrained tone:) IT'S o-KAY.	.62	.48	.21	.37	1.68
Female: (10)	<4.3 sec.> (Muffled laugh) .... (then, slurred and reluctantly but in a sweet tone:) well-looks PRETTY nice.	.39	1.21	.16	-.93	2.69
Female: (10)	<1.5 sec.> (Hesitantly:) Ahhh .... (then, almost sourly, as if being forced to concede:) it's o-KAY, I guess.	1.25	1.27	.54	1.14	4.20

Summary Statistics

Reliability (intraclass R) =	.88	.93	.68	.91	
Nonconflict mean =	-.07	-.12	-.08	-.14	-.41
Conflict mean =	.07	.12	.07	.14	.40
t =	.29	.46	.41	.49	.47
p (one-tailed) =	n.s.	n.s.	n.s.	n.s.	n.s.

a. Due to recording difficulties it was not possible to time the latency for this message.

Now I am going to call you on the phone and I will be Aunt Bertha. You just pick it up again when it buzzes.

For boys, the T-shirt

has a little fluffy kitten on it with a pink bow on its head.

In both cases, the description of the shirt was delivered with grimaces and intonation to reinforce the inappropriateness of the gift. In the nonconflict version, the children were simply told that they had received a T-shirt as a present from Aunt Bertha and that it was really nice, it was one they wanted.

Then the experimenter left the room, buzzed the child on the walkie-talkie, and said:

HELLO, is this [child's name]?

[Then, after the child had said "**Yes**"]

This is Aunt BERTHA calling; HOW do you LIKE the PRESENT I sent you?

After the child had given his or her response, the experiment was explained in detail appropriate to the age group; the parent or parents were given a complete explanation and asked for signed permission to keep and analyze the audiotape.

The children's replies were scaled as usual, randomly ordered for age and experimental condition. The results, given in Table 8.3, showed that the two experimental conditions differed significantly on all four dimensions and the Sum. The messages that the children gave in the conflict condition were less clear, less expressive of their own opinions, less addressed to the receiver, and less directly related to the question than were the messages in the nonconflict condition.

On the Content dimension, the two messages scaled as the clearest are:

Female (10): [0.5 sec.] (Enthusiastically, with great relish:) **Oh I LOVE it. It's NEAT.**

Female (10): [0.5 sec.] (Warmly and enthusiastically:) **OH, it's GREAT, I always WANTED one.**

In these messages, both the words and the delivery clearly convey enthusiasm. The message rated most equivocal is:

Male (6): [0.3 sec.] (Abruptly, with no inflection:) **GOOD.**

This message was judged as both too brief and too flat to be clear. Also very unclear in Content is:

Female (10): (Quickly, matter-of-factly:) **I think it's — NEAT.**

Our judges said that the slight hesitation before the adjective, combined with the neutral, matter-of-fact intonation, could mean either positive *or* negative feelings, making the ultimate meaning of the message indeterminate. Another message:

Female (6): [0.8 sec.] (In a subdued, mechanical tone:) **It was NICE.**

was heard as insincere. The tone did not match the words but sounded forced and was therefore judged to be ambiguous in content.

On the Sender dimension, the message that sounded most definitely the speaker's own opinion was the first message in the nonconflict condition, which had a very enthusiastic and convincing tone, along with strong words ("I LOVE it, it's NEAT"). The two most equivocal messages on the Sender dimension were the last two in the conflict condition, both of which were flat and expressionless, as well as giving the minimum amount of information possible. Examination of the message values on the Sender dimension shows that the presence of "I" is not their sole determinant; intonation can override the personal pronoun, as was true of the adult spoken messages.

The judges rated the messages on the Receiver dimension according to whether they were appropriate communication with an aunt, such as:

Female (10): [0.5 sec.] (Warmly and enthusiastically:) **OH, it's GREAT, I always WANTED one.**

The laconic message:

Male (6): [0.3 sec.] (Abruptly, no inflection:) **GOOD.**

was seen as inappropriate for a child talking to his aunt.

On the Context dimension, messages giving a personal opinion of the shirt (such as the first four in the nonconflict condition) were judged most responsive, as was a negative opinion:

TABLE 8.3
Experiment 18B: Gift (spoken)

Condition	Content	Sender	Receiver	Context	Sum	Order[a]
Nonconflict Condition						
Female: (10) <0.5 sec.> (Enthusiastically, with great relish:) Oh, I LOVE it. It's NEAT.	-1.00	-1.48	-.73	-1.19	-4.40	12
Female: (10) <0.5 sec.> (Warmly and enthusiastically:) OH, it's GREAT, I always WANTED one.	-.66	-.92	-1.22	-.54	-3.34	11
Male: (6) <0.8 sec.> (In a shy but warm tone:) I LIKE it.	-.53	-.40	-.38	-.97	-2.28	8
Male: (6) <0.6 sec.> (In an off-hand though pleasant tone:) I LIKE it.	-.72	-.17	.01	-.72	-1.60	7
Female: (8) <1.0 sec.> (Warmly, contentedly:) It was NICE.	-.30	-.22	-.35	.13	-.74	10
Female: (8) <1.5 sec.> (Not very enthusiastically:) It was NICE.	.38	.40	-.15	.28	.91	9
Conflict Condition						
Female: (10) <1.1 sec.> (In an adult tone, not very convincing:) Oh, it's very NICE.	-.07	.04	-.58	.04	-.57	3
Female: (8) <1.7 sec.> (Drawled out, apologetically:) WE-LLL ... I DON' really LIKE it.	.60	-.47	.69	-.40	.42	1

	.52	.35	.15	.29	1.31	5
Female: (6) <0.8 sec.> (In a subdued, mechanical tone:) It was NICE.						
Female: (8) <1.2 sec.> (At first hesitantly and haltingly:) Well--IT'S ... it-- ... (then in almost a questioning tone:) it's a BOY'S shirt.	-.32	.57	.58	1.83	2.66	4
Female: (10) <sec.[a]> (Quickly, matter-of-factly:) I think it's-- NEAT.	.64	1.03	.38	.70	2.75	2
Male: (6) <0.3 sec.> (Abruptly, no inflection:) GOOD.	1.45	1.28	1.45	.64	4.82	6

Summary Statistics

Reliability (intraclass R) =	.83	.89	.85	.93	
Nonconflict mean =	-.47	-.47	-.47	-.50	-1.91
Conflict mean =	.47	.47	.45	.52	1.90
t =	2.50	2.50	2.80	2.59	3.69
p (one-tailed) =	<.05	<.05	<.01	<.05	<.005

[a] Due to recording difficulties it was not possible to time the latency for this message.

Figure 8.2.

Female (8): [1.7 sec.] (Drawled out and apologetically:) **WE-LLL...I DON'
really LIKE it.**

High on this dimension was the patently nonresponsive message:

Female (8): [1.2 sec.] (At first hesitantly and haltingly:) **Welll-IT's ... it − ...**
(then in almost a questioning tone:) **it's a BOY'S shirt.**

Also high on the Context dimension was the laconic and oddly intonated
"GOOD," a response that was seen as a strange and ambiguous answer to
the question.

When scaling the messages, the judges were paying attention to subtle
paralinguistic clues. Some messages with similar words are quite different

when heard rather than read. Examining the conflict messages (and the last of the nonconflict messages), we might speculate whether children show the kind of verbal-nonverbal incongruence that we did not find in adults. It is obvious (even without systematic ratings such as were done in Chapter 7) that four of the conflict messages are verbally false:

Oh, it's very NICE.

It was NICE.

I think it's— NEAT.

GOOD.

So much for children's reputation as blurters of truths! However, the para-linguistic aspects of these messages are unconvincing or incongruent. This incongruency was also found in a *true* message:

WE-LLL . . . I DON' really LIKE it

which is delivered without conviction. Although the sample is very small, we may ask whether children show nonverbal leakage (which adults do not) or whether they simply cannot yet integrate the verbal and nonverbal aspects as well as adults can. We doubt both of these interpretations and suggest an alternative, which is that incongruence may be a communicative strategy used at younger ages. When we pretested the New Hairdo scenario, one articulate 10-year-old said:

I would say that I sort of liked it but not very expressively, so that the friend would understand that it was okay but not great.

In other words, children's incongruence may not be error but may instead be a "stage" they go through. This would be analogous to different stages for the expression of negation (Bellugi, 1967, described in Tager-Flusberg, 1989), from **"No like"** to **"I no like it"** to **"I don't like it,"** where earlier forms (with no auxilliaries) are like other children's although not like adults'.

DISCUSSION OF EXPERIMENTS 16, 17, 18A, AND 18B

How can we understand the mixed effects obtained in these studies? The reader has undoubtedly noticed several possible differences among the four studies, which might account for their different results. The simplest explanation, and the one we are inclined to accept, is that the results depend on the scenario: In both of the Gift scenarios, children equivocated in the conflict and not in the nonconflict condition, just like adults. In the other two scenarios (Class and New Hairdo), they did not. Before elaborating on this interpretation, let us consider some other possibilities.

The first pair of experiments were in forced-choice format with older children (12 to 13), while the second pair were in spoken format with younger children (6 to 10). Because one experiment in each pair produced the predicted results (and one in each pair did not), neither age nor format can be the reason for the difference. (Also, although the number at each age level in the 18A/B sample was too small for separate analysis, mere inspection of the tables suggests no consistent age effect within the range studied.)

In the Class and New Hairdo scenarios, the other person involved was a peer, while in the spoken Gift scenario, she was an adult. However, the forced-choice Gift scenario left the age of the other person ambiguous. If the children assumed that this person was an adult, then adult-versus-peer might be an explanation for the different effects. But there is no compelling reason to suppose that all of them made this assumption.

There are many specific aspects of Experiments 17 and 18A that might seem to supply explanations but can be discounted because they were not true of both, or because they were also true of 16 and 18B. For example, in Experiment 17 we departed from our usual random order of alternatives and used a fixed order that went against our hypothesis—but we also did so in 16. There were two different samples for 16 versus 17—but the same sample was used in 18A and 18B. And so forth . . .

The most straightforward explanation is that children respond to avoidance-avoidance conflicts by equivocation in the "unwanted gift" scenario but not necessarily in others. Receiving gifts (including unsuitable ones) is already a familiar experience for children, and their parents may have explicitly instructed them never to hurt the giver's feelings. The implication of our interpretation is that children up to ages 12 and 13 do not have a *generalized* ability to recognize and handle communicative avoidance-avoidance conflicts communicatively. Recall that our results for young adults in University were consistent even when we used scenarios with which they had probably had no personal experience (e.g., the Meat Market or Employee Reference). So we can speculate that generalization must develop in adolescence.

These findings suggest to us a whole new equivocation project, with children. Over what ages does recognition of a specific situation change to recognition of a general structure? What is the nature of situations that children master earlier versus later? Recall also the suggestive possibility (especially in 18B) that children's equivocations may be nonverbally incongruent combinations of truth and falsity. If this is so, when do they acquire the wider techniques we find in adults? We hope that readers whose primary interest is in development will forgive us for not spending another 10 years on these new questions and that some will even go on to answer them for all of us.

SUMMARY

The literature reviewed showed that young children not only recognize and understand ambiguous language but can sometimes use it strategically for interpersonal reasons (such as politeness). Our exploratory studies tested whether children would equivocate in avoidance-avoidance conflicts as adults do. The results were mixed and apparently depended on the specific scenario. Children equivocated in response to an unsuitable gift but not in other scenarios. We consider these studies only a tantalizing beginning of a full understanding of when and how children equivocate.

9

Field Studies of Political Interviews

In Chapter 3, we proposed that when people are in communicative avoidance-avoidance conflicts, in which all direct replies lead to negative consequences, they will equivocate instead. The rest of the book has presented experimental evidence for this theory. Here, this evidence will be extended in two ways: First, we left the lab and went to the field, to test out theory in a real political setting. Second, through subsequent nonexperimental work (observations and interviews), we extended our theory to dyadic interaction between reporter and politician. As in Chapter 8, we consider the work described here more a promising beginning than a final word.

WHY POLITICAL COMMUNICATION?

After working our way carefully from highly controlled to richer and more spontaneous experiments, we were ready at last for a study of naturally occurring equivocation. There were several possible sources of data. For example, we could try to obtain letters of reference for potential graduate students whose academic records were either excellent or poor. Presumably, people writing references for the latter students would be in an avoidance-avoidance conflict, caught between deprecating the student and denying the poor record. It would, however, be very difficult to obtain such data in anonymous form, with no identification of the applicant or the referee. Another possibility would be actually to make subjects do well or poorly on a presentation and then to ask other subjects to comment on the performance. Most of the studies we would imagine, such as these, were not acceptable to us for ethical reasons. Although painful avoidance-avoidance conflicts may be part of everyday life, we did not feel that, as researchers, we had a right either to gain access to such information or to create real conflicts, merely to test our theory.

On the other hand, what if the situation is voluntarily entered into and the resulting communication is intended for the public? This is the nature of political communication. The participants (politicians and reporters) seek the vicissitudes of political communication, and they intend their messages to be publically disseminated. They are actors on a public stage, so while our scrutiny of their communication might risk their disagreement, it does not violate their rights as individuals.

We had already studied one of the avoidance-avoidance conflicts that may be inherent in political communication. Recall the laboratory experiment (Chapter 5, Experiment 7: Member of Parliament [Written]) in which we asked undergraduate subjects to imagine themselves as a Member of Parliament. A highway was being planned for the home riding (electoral district), and two routes were being considered. Subjects in the conflict condition were told that both routes had advantages and disadvantages and that their constituency was equally divided as to which route was better. Their problem, then, was to avoid offending the supporters of either route. In the nonconflict condition, subjects were told that one route was clearly better and favored by their constituents. All subjects had to respond by telegram to a hometown reporter's question, **"Which route do you prefer, Route A or Route B?"** The subjects in the conflict condition solved their avoidance-avoidance conflict, as our theory predicted, by equivocation, specifically on the Content and Context dimensions: their replies were vague and did not answer the reporter's question. Their messages (Table 5.2) are remarkably like political cliches; we almost felt that the subjects were deliberately satirizing politicians. In any case, it was obvious that one does not have to be a politician to produce such "political" messages.

It could be argued, though, that real politicians are equivocal for their own reasons. The popular stereotype is that they come out of the womb equivocating, that is, that the fault is not in the situation but in them as individuals. They are seen as vague and evasive by nature, without reference to their communicative situation. The scholarly literature is usually pejorative as well, focusing on dishonesty and furtive intentions (e.g., Ekman, 1985; Graber, 1976; Spero, 1980). We have to admit that we implicitly accepted this stereotype until we thought about the contradiction it implied, namely, that politicians should be blamed for their equivocation while the rest of us are seen as only responding to a difficult situation. The logical alternative is to attribute the politician's equivocations to his or her situation, just as our theory does for everyone else: Equivocal messages are inevitable reactions to communicative avoidance-avoidance conflicts.

To illustrate this point, we offer (instead of an equivocation), an example of a politician *not* equivocating. In an interview by broadcaster Roger Mudd of candidate Gary Hart during the 1984 primaries, the following exchange occurred:

Mudd: [0.2 sec.] (Looking at Hart, smiling throughout:) **Ah . . . and a FINAL question.** (Jokingly:) **Would you do your Teddy Kennedy IMITATION?**

Hart: [0.1 sec.] (Looking at Mudd with a serious expression and a slight nod; emphatically:) **NO.**

Mudd: [1.3 sec.] (Looking at Hart, smiling throughout; pleasantly:) **I've HEARD it's hilarious.**

Hart: [0.2 sec.] (Looking at Mudd, with slight frown; seriously:) **I don't THINK so.**

Hart's replies are clear in content, spoken strongly and seriously as his personal opinion, addressed directly to Mudd, and directly answer his questions. If politicians were inherently equivocal, such replies would require an explanation as much as equivocations do. The study to be described next was aimed at explaining both.

EXPERIMENT 19: A FIELD STUDY

We conducted a study of our conflict theory of equivocation at the July 1984 Liberal Party leadership convention (Bavelas, Black, Bryson, & Mullett, 1988). Pierre Trudeau had announced his intention to resign as Prime Minister of Canada and leader of the (governing) Liberal Party. In the Canadian Parliamentary tradition, the person chosen to succeed him at this convention would automatically become Prime Minister and, soon after, lead the party in a national election. There were several candidates for the leadership, including John Turner as the front-runner and Jean Chretien as a very popular second choice. One of our research group, Lisa Bryson, was going to attend the convention as an alternate delegate. Because she probably would not be voting, she would have the time and opportunity to conduct a field experiment with the regular delegates.

We devised a question intended to present a conflict for certain delegates and not for others:

Do YOU think the LIBERALS can WIN the next election under JOHN TURNER?

This question, put to delegates who already favored Turner, should create no conflict for them; they could answer "**Yes**" and perhaps give their reasons. The same question should put Chretien supporters in an avoidance-avoidance conflict, with two bad alternatives: Saying that the party could win under Turner would be publically conceding a major point to the candidate they opposed; saying that the Liberals could not win under Turner would appear disloyal to their party. Thus, instead of experimentally imposing a conflict, we formulated a question that would interact with the individual's political alignment to create a conflict (or not). The Chretien supporters would be in the conflict condition, the Turner supporters in the nonconflict condition.

The question was asked at the beginning of a brief interview, recorded on audiotape, at the convention site (Ottawa Civic Centre) the day before formal voting for party leader. The scene in which these interviews were recorded was close to chaos, as anyone who has attended or seen television coverage of a political convention can imagine. There were milling crowds, constantly on the move, lots of noise, intensely excited and partisan people, and almost around-the-clock activity.

The interviewer approached delegates who were wearing either exclusively Turner or exclusively Chretien buttons, hats, and so forth. She introduced herself (truthfully) as a student conducting a study of political communication and asked if the delegate would answer some questions. If the delegate consented and spoke English, she began the interview (which had to be conducted in English so that our judges could scale the messages). The first questions identified the individual's status and commitment:

Which CANDIDATE are you COMMITED to?

and

Are you an ELECTED delegate?

Then the key question was asked:

Do YOU think the LIBERALS can WIN the next election under JOHN TURNER?

After the answer, several more questions were asked, on potentially conflict-inducing topics, in case our main question did not work out. A total of 38 delegates were interviewed. These included 25 males and 13 females; 13 were bilingual Francophones (i.e., French was their first language) and 25 were Anglophones; 12 supported Turner, and 26 supported Chretien.

Later, back in Victoria, we examined the tape carefully to find respondents who met our criteria. Six of the Turner replies were excluded for the following reasons: two were not elected delegates, one indicated only wavering support, and the interviewer had (understandably, in the circumstances) asked the question slightly differently in three cases, for example, "**Can the LIBERALS WIN the election under TURNER?**" We had learned from previous experiments that any answer is tightly connected to the wording of the question. For example, not including "**Do YOU think**" in the question would change the kinds of answers that might be elicited (see Chapter 6, Experiment 12: Employee Reference [Spoken]). Moreover, if more than one version of the question were used, which question would we give judges for scaling on the Context dimension? For similar reasons, ten of the Chretien replies were excluded: three were not elected delegates, the responses of two were obscured by background noise, one indicated wavering support, and there were slight variations in four of the questions.

This screening left us with 6 Turner (nonconflict) and 16 Chretien (conflict) messages. For scaling purposes, this was rather a large N. As we have made clear earlier (in Chapter 5), we prefer small samples, both out of consideration for our judges and because we have been able to demonstrate strong effects without requiring large N's. Also, the condition n's were quite unequal, which is statistically undesirable. Moreover, the two groups were not (proportionately) comparable on two potentially confounding variables: first-language and gender.

So we created equal, comparable n's by stratified random sampling from the larger (Chretien) group. We randomly selected two male Anglophones who supported Chretien from the total of six available, because there were two male Anglophones in the Turner group. We randomly selected two female Anglophones who supported Chretien from the total of four available, because there were two female Anglophones in the Turner group. And for the same reasons, one man was randomly selected from the four male Franco-phones and one woman from the two female Francophones. This left six in each group, exactly matched for gender and first language. The selection of speakers was completely random and could not be affected by whether the messages seemed to confirm our hypothesis.

The 12 messages were scaled by judges in the usual way; they are presented in Table 9.1 along with their scale values, reliabilities, and *t*-tests. There were significant differences on the Sender and Context dimensions as well as the Sum. The delegates in a conflict did not state their own opinions as unequivocally and did not answer the question as directly as did the delegates not in a conflict. Thus, political delegates participating in an important political event equivocated only when put in an avoidance-avoidance conflict. When there was no communicative conflict, their messages were clear.

Qualitative analysis reveals by-now familiar features of clear versus equivocal messages. Clarity on the Content dimension is achieved by putting ideas together coherently, even though there may be a slight speech error:

> *Male:* (French) [0.6 sec.] (Gently, very slightly slurred:) **I'm SURE of it. NOT only we wi-will we WIN, but we'll have a majority GOVERNMENT, I think.**

The least clear message on the Content dimension is long and incoherent, reminiscent of Mr. R (see Chapter 1), skipping from point to point with unfinished sentences:

> *Female:* (English) [2.1 sec.] (As if surprised:) **Ah, NO. I really DON'T. Ah …** (then more deliberately:) **CERTAINLY … NOT … in the WEST … ah …** (then faster:) **because Mr. TURNER represents BAY Street and everything that is FEARED, in-ah ALBERTA, certainly and-in the OIL patch, and-ah.** (Then still fast, with more feeling:) **So I would SAY — any HOPE we HAVE. We would have such — such RESPECT to GO with Mr. Chretien that-ah, with Mr. TURNER we could WRITE-OFF A-Alberta, as far as GETTING members ELECTED.** (Then slower:) **And I'm REEA-LLY concerned about the EAST … for that same REASON.** (Then faster and brighter:) **I don't think the easter would —, I DON'T think the east would VOTE FOR Mr. Chretien because he's FRENCH, I think it would JUST be BECAUSE of his PARTY loyalty and his PERFORMANCE, and THOSE are the exact same reasons that of course the WEST respects him.**

On the Sender dimension, values were influenced by the presence of "**I think,**" "**I'm sure,**" or "**I believe**" (for example, the first four messages in Table 9.1) and also by conviction in the tone of voice. The message our judges rated highest, as least representing the sender's own opinion, lacks both of these elements:

TABLE 9.1
Experiment 19: Liberal Leadership Convention

Condition		Content	Sender	Receiver	Context	Sum
Nonconflict Condition						
Male: (French)	<0.6 sec.> (Gently, very slightly slurred:) I'm SURE of it. Not only we wi-will we WIN, but we'll have a majority GOVERNMENT, I think.	-.94	-1.05	-.31	-.26	-2.56
Male: (English)	<1.4 sec.> (Smoothly, matter-of-factly:) I THINK so, YES. I THINK with the MOMENTUM of the CONVENTION and-- .... (speeding up:) fairly SOON-- an election fairly SOON. I think that's POSSIBLE.	-.12	-.78	-.75	-.43	-2.08
Female: (French)	<0.5 sec.> (Solemnly:) Yes, I THINK so. It's WHY I-I-I my vote will-ah-- ... to John TURNER.	.11	-.73	-.07	-.71	-1.40
Female: (English)	<0.8 sec.> (Carefully, almost sing-song:) I BELIEVE so yes. They can ESPECIALLY attract the WEST.	.28	-.23	-.26	-.26	-.47
Female: (English)	<0.4 sec.> (Firmly:) Yes I DO.	-.01	-.04	.93	-.98	-.10
Male: (English)	<0.8 sec.> (Confidently, pleasantly:) Sure DO.	.53	.22	.72	-.75	.72
Conflict Condition						
Female: (English)	<0.7 sec.> (With sharp pitch rise:) Under John TURNER? (Then well modulated but fast throughout:) Ahm. I think that the LIBERALS are in a GOOD position right now to WIN under a STRONG leader, and I think John Turner WOULD BE a strong leader. but-ah. (then as if smiling:) of course I'm BIASED. I think ah--it-it would have a STRONGER chance of winning under Jean CHRETIEN.	.02	.03	-1.15	.92	-.18

Male:
(French)

<1.1 sec.> (Sounding increasingly chatty and self-assured:) Ahh ... I think the LIBERALS have a good chance of WINNING ... ELECTIONS with-- either Mr. CHRETIEN or Mr. TURNER, so-ah, I think THAT-- ... the LIBERALS ... are BOUND to win the next ELECTIONS, the way THINGS are going NOW, so-- I think EITHER, if they have Mr. CHRETIEN or Mr. Turner, their CHANCES are good. S-the reason why I'm for Mr. CHRETIEN is that-- I think he-HE's the candidate of can-continuity and that's what I'm LOOKING for, so-ah-- ... (then softer and mumbled:) THAT'S why I support him.

−.43   −.12   −.50   1.09   .04

Male:
(Eng-
lish)

<1.0 sec.> (Monotone, almost guarded:) WE could win. YES.

−.42   .71   .13   −.25   .17

Female:
(French)

<1.4 sec.> (Doubtfully:) WELL-ah (audible exhale) ... maybe they COULD. (speeding up and more enthusiasti-cally:) but I think it would be BETTER to have CHRETIEN. Chretien's my MAN and I think-ah-- he's-ah ... (now as if listing off points:) everybody LIKES him, and-ah he's BEEN ... in the House of Commons for so LONG. He's got the EXPERIENCE, HE'S the one that can lead us to a VICTORY. DEFINITELY. (As if an afterthought:) Maybe TURNER would do it, but-- Chretien SURE would.

−.24   −.18   .40   .89   .87

Male:
(Eng-
lish)

<1.4 sec.> (As if with reservations:) Yesss.

.13   1.38   .77   −.86   1.42

TABLE 9.1
Continued

Female:
(Eng-
lish)

<2.1 sec.> (As if surprised:) Ah,
NO. I really DON'T. Ah ... (then
more deliberately:) CERTAINLY ...
NOT ... in   the WEST ... ah ...
(then faster:) because Mr. TURNER
represents BAY Street and everything
that is FEARED,   in-ah ALBERTA,
certainly and-in the OIL patch, and-
ah. (Then still fast, with more
feeling:) So I would SAY-- any HOPE
we HAVE. We would have   such--
such RESPECT to GO with Mr. Chretien
that-ah, with Mr. TURNER we could
WRITE OFF A-Alberta, as far as
GETTING members ELECTED. (Then,
slower:) And I'm REEA-LLV concerned
about the EAST ... for that same
REASON.   (Then faster and brighter:)
I don't think the easter would--,
I DON'T think the east would VOTE
FOR Mr. Chretien because he's
FRENCH. I think it would JUST be
BECAUSE of his PARTY loyalty and his
PERFORMANCE, and THOSE are the
exact same reasons that of course the
WEST respects him.

	1.19	.70	.07	1.60	3.56
Summary Statistics Reliability (intraclass R)[a] =	.59	.84	.78	.96	
(test set) =	.98	.90	.98	.97	
Nonconflict mean =	-.03	-.44	.04	-.57	-.98
Conflict mean =	.04	.42	-.05	.57	.98
t =	.20	2.66	.22	2.85	2.56
p (one-tailed) =	n.s.	<.05	n.s.	<.01	<.05

a. Intraclass correlations are highly sensitive to curtailment of range, hence the apparently lower reliabilities of the Content and Receiver dimensions. The same judges' scalings of the more varied message set used in the test set are highly reliable.

242

Male: (English) [1.4 sec.] (As if with reservations:) **Yesss.**

The long message above (the last in Table 9.1) was also rated as equivocal because it was not clear which of the several opinions stated the speaker herself held.

The Receiver dimension, as usual, did not distinguish between conditions. Judges paid attention to political content and a smooth professional manner, appropriate to an interview.

Some of the cryptic messages with high values on the other dimensions were seen as directly answering the question ("**Do YOU think the LIBER-ALS can WIN the next election under JOHN TURNER?**") by echoing its structure; hence:

Female: (English) [0.4 sec.] (Firmly:) **Yes I DO.**

Male: (English) [0.8 sec.] (Confidently, pleasantly:) **Sure DO.**

The message highest on the Context dimension was again the long, last message in Table 9.1, which answered the question initially and then went off into many different topics.

DISCUSSION

We can offer several potential criticisms of this study. First, of course, it is not a true experiment. We did not randomly assign conflict and nonconflict conditions to subjects but rather generated them out of the individual's own political stance. For this reason, our two conditions are completely confounded with leader preference: All of the subjects who were in conflict (and equivocated) were Chretien supporters, and all subjects who were not in conflict (and responded clearly) were Turner supporters. This is the nature of field research; one often trades internal for external validity. However, because the results were virtually identical to those of previous experiments where the confound did not exist, we do not think that hypothetical differences between Turner and Chretien supporters are a plausible alternative explanation. It is more parsimonious to attribute the obtained differences to the conflict induced by the question.

Another criticism of this experiment is that, despite our commitment to studying the entire message as delivered (see, for example, Chapter 5), we made an audio recording of a face-to-face interaction. Again, this was necessitated by field conditions; all we could do was to make sure that the

Figure 9.1.

subjects knew they were speaking primarily for a tape recorder, not just face-to-face.

Also, we interviewed only a small fraction of the approximately 3,500 delegates attending, and our N was even smaller after we had deleted 26 messages. This problem troubles us least of all, because we aimed to conduct a field experiment, not a sample survey of Liberal delegates, and because deletion was not related to the equivocal or unequivocal nature of the message.

Finally, there are criticisms we take more seriously: However far our field study was from the lab, it was still not isomorphic to the usual political interview, for at least three reasons. First, a "student conducting a study of political communication" is not ordinarily one of the participants in the process. Second, the respondents were not politicians in the sense of being candidates seeking office at the time (although some may well have done so in the past or later, in the general election). Third, analysis of one answer to one question may not capture the complexity of what is usually a sequential give-and-take.

In brief, what we found from this study was that we could take our basic design to the field — away from university students and hypothetical conflicts — and still confirm our theory. What we could not know from this study is how the naturally occurring political process generates equivocation. To explore this process, we would have to change method entirely, which is what we did next.

A DYADIC ANALYSIS OF EQUIVOCATION IN POLITICAL INTERVIEWS

Political campaigns dominated the rest of 1984. Turner won the leadership and called a federal election, as expected, and the quadrennial U.S. primary and general elections were held as well. We decided to immerse ourselves in these data, not conducting surveys or experiments but observing and interviewing in the manner of ethnographers (see Spradley, 1982). Our sources of information were quite varied and included the following:

(1) studying television coverage of both the U.S. and Canadian elections, especially televised interviews, press conferences, and "scrums" (in which reporters and technicians crowd around and pursue the politician), but also national and local debates, news analyses, and weekly public affairs programs;

(2) confidential interviews with political candidates (mostly candidates in the Canadian federal election for Victoria area ridings);

(3) similar interviews with reporters for newspapers, radio, and television;

(4) attending live press conferences and interviews;

(5) two days' travelling with and helping a television reporter and crew who were conducting political interviews.

We focused on the political interview (rather than on ads, press releases, or party platforms) because in interviews we can see directly the process by which the messages are generated. What came out of these observations was a dyadic model of equivocation in the political interview, one that includes both reporter and politician in their face-to-face interaction.[1]

We propose that the nature of the political interview with its inherent avoidance conflicts for *both* participants generates equivocation. We will identify the pressures on each of the parties, but our main interest is in how they fit together, in interpersonal interaction, to perpetuate political equivocation.

Focus on Politicians

Politicians readily described their own communication as sometimes "ambiguous," "vague," "whishy-washy," "indirect," and "obscure." They were not apologetic about such responses; from their point of view, the situation often does not allow simple, direct communication. The examples they gave us, and those we observed, suggested that they must cope with avoidance conflicts of many different kinds, as described below. In each case, all direct replies would lead to bad consequences; equivocation is the only escape. Also, recall (from Chapter 1) that Goss and Williams (1973; Williams & Goss, 1975) showed that equivocation *worked*, in the sense that equivocal messages attributed to public figures elicited more agreement and resulted in better character ratings than did clear messages on difficult topics.

A common source of conflict is that there are many controversial issues on which there is a *divided electorate* (as in our Experiment 7). Direct replies supporting or criticizing either position would offend a substantial number of voters and are therefore to be avoided. For example (in a candidates' debate held in New York on March 28, 1984), Dan Rather asked Walter Mondale for his opinion on just such an issue[2]:

> *Rather:* **Do you favor or oppose federal gun control?**
>
> *Mondale:* **I favor control of the so-called Saturday Night Special, snud-nosed — ... snub-nosed guns that are used only to kill police and each other for concealment. There is no excuse for their use.**

The message is obviously equivocal. The content is so tangled that it implies these guns kill each other, as well as police, in order to remain concealed. The message does not answer the question asked, but answers instead a much easier question, **"Do you favor the control of guns that are used only to kill policemen, and do you think there is any excuse for their use?"** Such an answer is unlikely to offend either side of the gun-control issue.

There may be *differences between the party and the constituency*. That is, the policy of the party (and the candidate) may be at odds with the interests of the constituency being addressed. For example, the candidate's party may

Figure 9.2.

favor a cut in military spending, but he or she is running in an area where such funds are an important part of the local economy. To embrace the proposed cuts openly is political suicide, whereas to oppose them is apostasy.

The candidate may be caught in any number of *policy contradictions*: between two aspects of the party platform (e.g., reduce the deficit but do not cut spending); between the candidate's stated position and that of the party (or party leader); between previous party promises and current practice; or between the candidate's own past and present positions, if these have changed. The candidate must avoid appearing inconsistent, or at odds with the party, or insensitive to the contradiction. If asked, the candidate may have to comment on the contradiction without admitting that it is serious and without implying fault in either policy. We took the following example from the 1984 U.S. vice-presidential candidates' debate, when George Bush was President Reagan's running mate. Each candidate was standing at a podium facing the audience on one side and the panel on the other, including the reporter, Norma Quarles, who asked a question about a policy contradiction. (This excerpt is also a good example of what Heritage, 1985, called "talk produced for an overhearing audience," in that Bush often lapses into a speech-making intonation and rhythm.)

Quarles: [1.9 sec.] (Alternates between looking at her notes on the table and at Bush during her question; with a serious expression and no gestures throughout; begins with an audible intake of breath, then in an assertive yet factual tone of voice:) **Vice President BUSH, four years AGO you would have allowed federal financing of ABORTIONS in cases of RAPE and incest** (nods), **as well as when the mother's life was THREATENED** (small nod and eyebrow flash). (Audible intake of breath, then rhetorically:) **Does your position NOW** (big nod) **agree with President REAGAN** (eyebrows raised, then more factually:) **who in SUNDAY'S** (eyebrows lowered) **debate** (eyebrows raised) **came VERY** (eyebrows lowered) **close to SAYIN' that "abortion is murder"?**

Bush: [1.8 sec.] (In a personal manner, with traces of embarrassment:) **You know there has BEEN,** (small nod) **I have to make a confession an-n EVOLUTION in my position. . . .** (looks over the entire audience; then dramatically and dogmatically:) **THERE'S BEEN 15 MILLION ABORTIONS . . .** (slightly less emphasis:) **SINCE 1973.** (Returns gaze to camera and panel; now again personal but with conviction:) **Ahn I** (slight head shake) **don't take that LIGHTLY** (places open hand on chest and then on the podium again; then with conviction and considerable emphasis:) **THERE'S BEEN a MILLION and half this** (nods) **YEAR.** (Small nods throughout; slightly more conversationally:) **The PRESIDENT and I** (raises hand and pinches fingers together) **do FAVOR a human rights amendment. I favor ONE that would have an exception** (shifts slightly to the left) **for for incest and rape and** (nod) **he doesn't.** (While shaking head slightly:) **But we bo-only** (gestures hand with open palm toward Quarles) **for the LIFE of the MOTHER and I agree with him on that.** (More assertively:) **So YES** (bangs hand on podium) **my position has EVOLVED.** (Shifts back to the right; assertively and rhetorically:) **BUT I'd like to see the AMERICAN who faced** (raises both hands and holds them shoulder-width apart) **with 15 MILLION ABORTIONS** (lowers both hands and starts nodding) **isn't rethinking his or her position** (raises right eyebrow). **And I'm-I'll** (raises both hands in an exasperated gesture and looks down to the side) **just STAND with the answer that** (shifts to an erect position; looks at Quarles and camera; with increasing assertiveness) **I** (emphatic nods) **support the President's position. And** (large frown) **COMFORTABLY from a MORAL STANDPOINT.** (Ends with a big grin.)

Quarles: [1.0 sec.] (Nodding and jabbing her index finger toward Bush; rhetorically and with a trace of a "gotcha" tone:) **So you BELIEVE it is AKIN to murder?**

Bush: [0.8 sec,] (Matter-of-factly:) **I gue-I support the PRESIDENT'S position** (nods).

Quarles: [0.2 sec.] (Softly:) **Fine**.

Note that, like this example, all of the above contradictions are made into avoidance-avoidance conflicts by questions put to the candidate. Until the contradiction is raised by someone (usually a reporter), no communicative conflict exists.

Another, less abstract set of conflicts does not involve policy issues but is created by the interview process itself. One is the pressure of *time limits*. If the politician is asked about a complex issue but is forced to answer briefly, he or she has a choice between two unattractive alternatives: reducing the issue to a simple, incomplete answer or appearing long-winded and circuitous (or even being cut off).

When asked about a particular issue, the candidate may have to protect *confidential information*, which cannot be revealed at present. Such information might really be "top secret," or it may merely be knowledge of internal poll results, forthcoming policy changes, ongoing mediations and discussions, and strategically planned political announcements or events. The choice here is between telling a truth that will reveal a secret and concealing (or even denying) the information — a strategy that could be exposed by future events.

The opposite of "the man who knew too much" can also create a problem, namely, when the candidate *lacks knowledge* of the issue being addressed. Not being prepared for a question presents a bad choice between improvising or fabricating an answer (which may not hold together) and admitting "I don't know."

Finally, there are rare instances of *interpersonal conflict* between politician and reporter. Occasionally one "aggressive" reporter pushes the candidate very hard, for example, accusing him or her of lying or equivocating. The candidate cannot comment explicitly on the inappropriateness of a personal conflict in this setting, yet both a counterattack and meek acceptance would have a price.

It is important to note that, with the exception of being well prepared on every conceivable issue, the politician can do little about the other sources of conflict. Inevitably, sometimes, voters will be divided; parties, candidates, and constituencies will disagree; a brief reply will be necessary; the candidate will have to keep a secret; or a reporter will press aggressively. And, most important, the public and press are waiting to seize on any mistake. Over and over, politicians told us that the goal of a campaign was to *avoid making mistakes*: Elections are lost, not won. They told familiar horror stories of the one highly publicized mistake that ended a political career. They resented the press (and, by implication, the public) for punishing imperfection so brutally. But before we switch our blame from a hapless politician to a provocative and irresponsible reporter, we should first examine the reporter's communication and communicative situation in the same way.

Focus on Reporters

IDENTIFYING REPORTERS' EQUIVOCATION

Reporters agreed that politicians often encounter conflicts where equivocation is the least negative option. They also agreed that they too face such conflicts, but they did not see their own communication as highly equivocal. Rather, they applied a different standard because of their special role in this particular communicative setting. That is, they readily conceded that (1) they often use terms that have no clear referent but instead belong to the current jargon of the campaign (e.g., acronyms and "buzz words"); (2) they ask questions and make assertions whose source is not clear; (3) they may sometimes grill a local candidate about something only the national leader can answer; and (4) they typically change the topic repeatedly and abruptly during an interview. But in their opinion, this is the nature of political interviewing, hence, not equivocal.

Since Chapter 2, we have emphasized a model in which equivocation is defined as a departure from clarity in one or more of four essential elements of communication: Content, Sender, Receiver, and Context. We have shown that, in a wide variety of contexts (including the political replies in Experiment 19), these dimensions are sensitive to the kinds of messages evoked in communicative avoidance conflicts. The four practices described in the previous paragraph correspond, respectively, to departures from these four elements. The question is whether it is appropriate to apply our model to the special case of messages by reporters when they are interviewing or questioning politicians.

Surely, it is reasonable to say that the *content* of reporters' comments or questions should be clear and unambiguous, not only to the people immediately involved but to the public for whom the information is being generated. Also, any question or comment should be clearly addressed to the immediate *receiver* (the politician), who is the only one there to answer it.

The problems arise when we consider the other two dimensions. Although he or she is the sender of the message, it is not the reporter's role to offer personal opinions. Instead, the reporter usually raises issues or asks questions that others (e.g., a certain sector of the public or the opposing candidate) might wish answered. Because the reporter is by trade a spokesperson, we cannot measure clarity on the Sender dimension by whether his or her own opinion has been offered. It is appropriate, however, to say that the message should make clear *who it is that the speaker is speaking for*. Is the source of the question a certain political group, another candidate, part or all of the electorate, or common gossip? Beginning a question with "**They SAY you're PRETTY far to the LEFT**" must be counted as equivocal. Similarly, presenting personally held views in the guise of a general-interest question is equivocal, as will be seen in the example below.

Finally, there is the question of Context, which has meant until now that the respondent should answer the preceding (implicit or explicit) question. As politicians are not supposed to ask questions of reporters, this definition has to be modified. Our yardstick can be, instead, that the reporter's next question or statement should be *directly related to the previous speaking turn*. The abrupt discontinuities or rapid-fire questioning must be counted as changes of topic and therefore equivocal on the Context dimension, no matter how common they are in a political interview. That these may be required by the situation does not make them coherent (because the situation may require incoherence). Recall that equivocal messages both make sense and do not make sense, changing in our evaluation like a "reversible figure."

Let us illustrate this modified definition of equivocation with an exchange between a reporter, George Will, and a politician, George McGovern, during the 1984 Democratic primary campaign. (Although the interview was broadcast live, it was not a face-to-face interview. George Will and Peter Jennings were in New York while McGovern was in Washington, so the interview was conducted over the telephone, with the McGovern video feed superimposed during the broadcast. Such techniques obscure even further the sender-receiver relationship in what appears to be face-to-face interaction.) McGovern is finishing his reply to a previous question:

McGovern: [1.5 sec.] (Nods slightly at the end of each sentence and has a pleasant facial expression throughout; matter-of-factly:) **Well ... Ahh LET me say George that I never did THINK that I was out of the MAINSTREAM.** (Slight smile.) **I thought back in '72 I was in the MAINSTREAM.** (Assertively:) **All of my life as an ACTIVE DEMOCRAT I've supported the nominee of the party.** (Reflectively, almost with resignation:) **Even when it was SOMEONE that I didn't 100% ENDORSE. I EXPECTED people to do that when I was the candidate in '72. . . .** Ah (seriously and slightly assertive:) I THINK that what has HAPPENED is that in '83 and '84 people have a— more ACCURATE IMAGE of me. I don't think I've CHANGED the standards that I set in '72— the RULES that I ran on and the IDEAS that I brought FORWARD (then using a more conversational tone of voice) are generally accepted by most Democrats. (Slight smile.) Ahhh JUST about everyone now recognizes that VIETNAM— (frown) for example, was a MISTAKE.

Will: [0.8 sec.] (With a neutral facial expression except as noted; assertively, almost as if accusing:) SENATOR . . . on the night of MAY THIRTY first in BRINKWOOD California, the three CANDIDATES are going to a DINNER and raise one hundred and fifty thousand dollars to WIPE OUT your campaign debt. (Smiles during the next sentence; ironically:) Which in THAT neighborhood can be accomplished before the QUICHE curdles. . . . (Almost conversationally:) AFTERWARDS you've invited them to meet with you to iron THESE differences. (Almost as if accusing:) GARY HART intends to PRESS on those five hundred and eighty seven DELEGATES which he says were FRAUDULENTLY elected with P.A.C. MONEY for Mondale. JESSE JACKSON is SAYING— that HE'S not getting his FAIR share of DELEGATES. He wants to ABOLISH the RUN OFFS in the southern primaries. Those are SUBSTANTIAL differences (slight nod) that YOU are going to have to DEAL WITH that night.

The *content* of Will's question is unclear, partly because of asides such as **"before the QUICHE curdles"** and partly because of private idioms such as **"P.A.C. MONEY"** and **"RUN OFFS."** More broadly, it is unclear in content because it contains a series of loosely connected topics (from the fund-raising dinner to various candidates' complaints). And at the broadest level, the content is unclear because it is both a series of facts and assertions and, implicitly, a question requiring an answer.

The message is also somewhat unclear as to *sender,* even as that dimension has been redefined. Will starts by giving what seems to be public knowledge (about the dinner and the meeting afterwards), although we may wonder how he knows about McGovern's private invitation. The somewhat catty comment about quiche seems to be the reporter's own. He then identifies some opinions as Hart's and Jackson's, but the last statement, a strong announcement, is unclear as to source. Is it the opinion of these two candidates that McGovern will have to deal with their substantial differences? What about Mondale, the third candidate? Or is it McGovern's opinion, because he issued the invitation? Or is it the reporter's own analysis of McGovern's dilemma?

The message is relatively clear as to *receiver.* It is addressed to McGovern, with direct eye contact and content that is at least arguably appropriate to

McGovern's role as senior statesman of his party. However, the information about the dinner is presented as if it is news to McGovern, without a prefatory "**As you KNOW.**"

The message is highly equivocal on the *context* dimension. It is in no sense responsive to McGovern's previous speaking turn, which focused on whether he was in or out of the mainstream of his party. We do not know if Will has accepted McGovern's assertion and is moving on to a new question or if he has rejected it and is challenging it with new evidence. Thus, although articulately and urbanely delivered, the message is, on examination, quite ambiguous.

Conflicts for Reporters

Having proposed that the reporter's communication in political interviews is often as equivocal as the politician's, we will hasten to add that the cause is the same. A reporter is subject to many pressures that create avoidance conflicts, some of which are directly comparable to the pressures on the politician. We identified at least six sources of conflict for interviewers:

There are demands on his or her own *own performance*. Reporting and interviewing are, after all, highly competitive jobs, and the personal cost of not doing well may be as heavy as for the politician who makes a mistake. For example, even when the issues at hand are thin and uninteresting, the interviewer must avoid boring the audience. Even though every conceivable angle may have already been covered, the reporter must "find a different angle." While avoiding dull material and seeking novelty, the reporter must not "go too far," into offensive or silly directions—or by pursuing the equivocating politician aggressively. And it is going to be particularly difficult to find something new (and "newsworthy") if the politician's best strategy is to avoid mistakes by saying as little that is new as possible. The reporter must exploit those very policy problems that will make the politician equivocate.

The *time limits* that the interviewer imposes on the politician also fall on the interviewer. The reporter's news clip must be brief to be selected for broadcast. Even during interview programs, when more time is available, the interviewer is constantly aware that many topics must be covered. There is pressure to avoid getting "bogged down" while, at the same time, not appearing superficial or cursory. As a result, rapid topic-switching is often hidden behind obscure connections to the previous question or answer.

The reporter, too, may have *confidential sources*. He or she may introduce information obtained from a source that cannot be made public ("**a highly**

placed source" is very equivocal on the Sender dimension). Presenting enough details to formulate a question while withholding enough information to maintain confidentiality is a difficult balancing act.

Inevitably, the reporter too is sometimes *unprepared* for the interview, lacking adequate background information on some of the issues involved. He or she must then avoid details that would reveal this lack of knowledge while at the same time conducting an "in-depth" informative interview. Being unprepared, in a broader sense, can also mean (for both politician and reporter) being too immersed in details to be able to discuss the issue clearly and free of jargon. Reporters and politicians develop through daily immersion in the issues of the campaign and through their off-camera interaction with each other, phrases that are unintelligible to the average listener and therefore unclear in content.

Interpersonal conflict can threaten the reporter as well. If the politician, for example, insults the reporter (or his or her questions), the reporter must remain professional. This means avoiding any comment on the insult, maintaining respectful address while not implying agreement, and avoiding escalation into a personal dispute.

Finally, there is the special problem presented by the *politician's equivocation*. Reporters told us frequently that, when the politician has not answered their question, they have only unpalatable alternatives. Commenting explicitly on the equivocation (as Thomas did to Zeigler, Chapter 1) risks interpersonal conflict. In any case, such a comment is itself a change of topic, and the conversation may shift to whether the politician did or did not answer the question. Simply repeating the question can appear either aggressive or dense. Rephrasing the question or asking an entirely new question disrupts the continuity of speaking turns. There may be no unequivocal response to an equivocation in these circumstances.

The Dyad in an Interview

We have tried to suggest the multiplicity of pressures on both politicians and reporters when they deal with each other in a political interview. These pressures, including the ones they put on each other, create many-faceted avoidance conflicts for both. Our conclusion from this analysis is that we should abandon descriptions that are monadic and judgmental and move instead toward a dyadic, discourse-focused approach. Interviews are dialogues and should be treated as such, as a sequential creation of two partners.

This is congruent with the position of a group of conversation analysts (Greatbatch, 1988; Heritage, 1985; Heritage, Clayman, & Zimmerman,

1988) who have recently conducted a systematic examination of news interviews. Although they were not interested in equivocation in particular, their general formulations are quite relevant. They assumed that television interviews are a social event with special constraints, in which interviewers and interviewees follow strict rules in formulating their speaking turns. According to Greatbatch (1988), the television interview is both a cooperative event and one in which the parameters of conversation are relatively inflexible. Because of institutional demands on the reporter and on the interviewee, the conversation between them is task-oriented—directed toward producing "talk for an overhearing audience" (Heritage, 1985). Thus, the interviewers and interviewees typically use extremely long, relatively unconnected speaking turns. Interviewers accomplish this by maintaining the position of questioner, for example, by: (1) stating opinions indirectly and not commenting on the interviewee's previous responses; (2) avoiding "backchannel" comments such as "**Mhm**"; and (3) speaking only in turn and not interrupting the interviewee. Interviewees phrase their speaking turns as answers by: (1) not questioning the interviewer; (2) only speaking after the interviewer has finished his or her question; and yet (3) often responding minimally to the interviewer's question. At a more strategic level, the reporter's role is to set the agenda for the interview. He or she can control the topic of discussion by changing it, pursuing a vague answer, or ending the interview. The interviewee usually follows the set agenda but can resist it by responding to supplemental information in the interviewer's previous turn or by shifting to an "unsolicited topic" (Heritage et al., 1988).

We would add to this dyadic view of an interview the special nature of the political interview, which is that the participants continually place each other in avoidance-avoidance (or even multiple-avoidance) conflicts. For example, the reporter asks about a controversial issue; the politician equivocates to avoid losing voter support; the reporter can then change topic or press the politician to answer; the politician will evade the topic again; and so forth. The "cause" of equivocation is systemic, it is in the situation that each person creates for the other.

The following excerpt is from an interview we observed while traveling with a local news reporter during the 1984 Canadian federal election; our analysis is based on discussions with both participants after the interview. (Certain details that would identify the participants have been changed or omitted.)

For the reporter, this interview was part of a series to be conducted with candidates for the major parties in several important ridings (electoral districts) of the province. Excerpts from each interview would be used for a daily news segment that sought to cover the federal election, constituency by constituency. Thus, what the reporter needed in each interview was an excerpt that could be used to distinguish this particular politician from the other candidates in his or her electoral district. The interview was equally important to the candidate in this case, as it would be broadcast on a news show that was highly popular in his area. Given that he had so far only limited exposure in some parts of his district, his performances could affect voters' opinions.

Reporter: [1.6 sec.] (Unless noted otherwise the reporter speaks in a pleasant yet assertive tone of voice:) **Are you ready YET?**

Cameraman: [0.4 sec.] (Gutturally:) **Yehn.**

Reporter: [2.3 sec.] (Initially quickly and then more slowly:) **What are the most IMPORTANT issues in your CAMPAIGN?**

Politician: [1.3 sec.] (Confidentially:) **The ECONOMY and jobs is a . . . is the . . . issue that REALLY is CONCERNING** (spoken more softly, with a didactic tone:) **the majority of people. UNEMPLOYMENT is pretty high in this area, and uh there's NEGLIGIBLE amount of work for YOUNG people. So the PUBLIC is taking a PARTICULAR interest in what the PARTIES have to say about— how they— propose to solve those problems.**

Reporter: [1.5 sec.] **ARE there ANY REAL LOCAL ISSUES HERE? Anything that relates to [name of district]?**

Politician: [2.1 sec.] (As if relieved:) **NOTHING has developed SO FAR.** (Didactically:) **Ahhm . . . OF COURSE in [this district] we have ahh a heavy military COMPONENT, so THAT is an ISSUE that is ahh** (almost mumbling) **PERHAPS not quite as interesting ELSEWHERE in other ridings. As we have [names some military functions and employment]. So our POSITION on the MILITARY and the . . . our INTENTION to increase the STRENGTH and to FIND some money— in to ADDITION TO what the [opposing party]— have promised— I think is . . . is ATTRACTIVE certainly to some.**

Reporter: [0.8 sec.] (Quickly and slightly slurred:) **WHAT do you THINK YOU can DO?** (Matter-of-factly:) **Ah uh everyone I've been talking to is saying that JOBS ARE THE ISSUE. What-what do you think you can DO ABOUT— the UNEMPLOYMENT if you are ELECTED?**

Politician: [1.9 sec.] (In a didactic tone:) **Well, I-I'm one CANDIDATE ONE member of PARLIAMENT. It ahhh OBVIOUSLY has to be a GOVERNMENT DECISION— with how to deal with things. THERE is NO way that I can PROMISE to throw MONEY at a pet project HERE.** (Haltingly:) **WE are COMMITTED to ah a major— ATTACK on the ILLS of the FOREST INDUSTRY, and that has a BEARING on our riding.** (More quickly, as if an aside:) **CERTAINLY in the [name] area we have SMALL MILLS that are virtually DEFUNCT, because of the state of the MARKET.** (Very slowly, deliberately, and haltingly:) **We have a VERY LARGE community of sports FISHERMEN. And and they're all very keenly aware of the needs to resurrect our— FISH STOCK. And again ahh part of our POLICY of ahh of is a major program is to get THAT squared away. . . . Tourism um-ah is one of our major industries HERE and and . . . the CRUMBLING— fishing opportunities** (very quickly) **you know are a GRAVE concern for a great many people. WE are directly involved in TOURISM and that's one of the main attractions of COMING HERE is that you can get into the [name] INLET and off the [name] waterfront and CATCH FISH under— NICE CONDITIONS . . . attractive scenery. Its-ah its-ah REAL SELLING point when you are WELCOMING people to the AREA. Um-ah its VERY IMPORTANT to AFFECT the whole economy of British Columbia with— SALMON STOCK— be replenished.**

Reporter: [1.5 sec.] (Stacatto:) **HOW do you think you're gonna FARE in the election? THIS always has been a [his party] stronghold. Do you think THAT you're gonna come up AHH with as MUCH an advantage over the other parties, OR do you feel that it is gonna be a THREE WAY RACE, OR how do you feel at this point?**

Politician: [1.1 sec.] (Didactically:) **Well as a first time CANDIDATE I can't PRESUME that my predecessors SUPPORT is going to ACCRUE to me just because I threw my HAT into the RING. I'VE got to go out and earn it. I'm doing a— SUBSTANTIAL amount of door KNOCKING so I'm going to work HARD until the last minute. I'm CAUTIOUSLY optimistic, because we do have a bit of track record of electing [his party] here. And uh we've lost the riding ONCE in the last forty years, and uh I'd sure SOONER— RUN for the first time in that circumstance than in a place where we'd only won it ONCE in forty years. But I'm taking NOTHING for granted.**

Reporter: [0.9 sec.] (Conversationally:) **Okay thanks. Can we just get you to stay here for a while?**

The reporter's first question does not place the politician in an avoidance conflict. Unemployment was the most important issue at both the federal and local level, and the politician's response to this open-ended, "motherhood issue" question is, except for the errors of spontaneous speech, unequivocal.

However, his reply put the reporter in a conflict. The politician's reply was too banal to be suitable for broadcast. Restating the question would probably only result in another formulaic answer. Nor could the reporter ask about issues more specific to the riding, as he had had only 10 minutes to prepare for the interview, did not live in the area, and had not yet talked to other politicians in the riding. Nor could he change the topic, because the news feature was supposed to be focussed on the various politicians' positions on local issues. The reporter's next question is moderately equivocal. It changes the topic slightly, to a more personal and somewhat abrasive tack. Also, **"everyone I've been talking to"** is a vague source for the sender of the message. The question skillfully stayed on the topic and avoided offering specifics while at the same time pressing the interviewee to be specific.

This second question, however, put the politician in an avoidance conflict. As a nonincumbent and first-time candidate, he could not credibly promise economic development that he was, personally, powerless to secure, yet he could not admit the solution was beyond him. His solution was to change topics markedly, to a discussion of economic issues in the riding.

Now the reporter was in an even more difficult situation. The answer just given was not suitable for the clip he needed because it was too long, did not answer the question, and contained some obscure if not illogical connections between various industries in the area. It would be hard to follow up on these specific issues because, first, the candidate had been quite obscure and, second, the reporter had no background on them. He could not repeat or rephrase a question that had at least apparently been answered at length, without appearing to badger the interviewee. And he could not comment on how unsatisfactory the answer was without insulting him. It is not surprising, then, that he changed topic completely, leaving all of the bad options and still seeking a new topic that would be usable. Note that this speaking turn consisted of an assertion plus three different questions, two of which could be seen as observations or opinions from unknown sources (i.e., having an advantage or being in a three-way race).

The candidate is now caught in another conflict: He cannot say he will win easily nor can he appear to lack confidence. His "Yes but no" reply does not answer the question(s), skips from topic to topic, and gives several different personal opinions. This was, however, the excerpt that was ultimately used in the program, as the best of the available possibilities.

We do not mean in this analysis to belittle the two participants. If anything, we would question the wisdom of sending reporters out to find gems with little time to prepare, and we would question the meaningfulness of the superficial series of questions asked for assessing the qualifications of any candidate. Our point is that, once they begin, their dance cannot take any meaningful form.

Consider, finally, an example originally given in Chapter 1 as an example of a politician's equivocation. When we also examine the interviewer's question, we can see the dyadic nature of the process:

Frost: (Pleasantly, gesturing frequently toward Bush:) **But the— OBVI-OUSLY, with seven DAYS to go in the CAMPAIGN, ah ... it would be ... UNREALISTIC to expect you to say ANYTHING, that was-ah announcing a new candidate** (laughing and faster:) **for Vice-President or anything like that. But you WOULD have to AGREE, wouldn't you, that Lloyd BENSON has more GRAVITAS than Dan Quayle?**

Bush: [1.0 sec.] (Looking at Frost with little facial expression; earnestly:) **I studied LATIN** (looks away and down) **for about eight years, but— refresh my MEMORY** (looks back) **as what GRAVITAS means.**

This does not imply that we accept — much less approve of — political equivocation. In insisting that such equivocation is situational, not personal, we have still not said that it is acceptable. Obviously, lack of clarity in political communication interferes with the electoral process. Voters cannot obtain the information they need to make their own decisions. Practiced widely enough, equivocation can make voters cynical and thereby further undermine the process. Equivocation is in this sense to be condemned. Understanding does not mean approval; understanding may even lead to change.

SUMMARY

Our final empirical studies were conducted in the field. First, we created conflict and nonconflict conditions for delegates at an important political convention and found that our theory held outside the lab as well. Then we turned to non-experimental methods and studied communication in the political interview, specifically focussing on equivocation by both interactants — reporters and politicians — in this setting. We propose a dyadic theory, in which both parties create for each other the conflicts that perpetuate equivocation.

NOTES

1. Boorstein's work (1961/1985) is still a classic analysis of the broader pressures on modern newsmakers, many of which shape the specific conflicts we will describe.

2. Unfortunately, we have only the transcript of this excerpt and cannot indicate the nonverbal aspects of the messages.

10

Overview and Implications

By equivocation we mean nonstraightforward communication, including messages that are ambiguous, indirect, contradictory, or evasive. The goal of the ten-year project reported here was to focus more carefully and respectfully on such communication than has been done previously — to bring "poor" communication to center-stage as a commonplace yet important phenomenon, not to be dismissed, glossed, or denounced. The dominant models of communication have been prescriptive and judgmental, focusing on too-narrow definitions of accuracy and efficiency, and stressing "communication skills," "clarity," and "communicative competence." In the extreme case, ambiguity is vilified:

> Interpreting messages is a dirty business. From the simplest greeting to the most complex rationalization, messages are inherently ambiguous and sometimes intentionally misleading. (Hewes, Graham, Doelger, & Pavitt, 1985, p. 299)

Equivocation is not the deliberately deceitful "dirty old man" of communication. It is subtle, often commendable, and entirely understandable, if only the observer will expand his or her analysis to include the communicative situation. When seen in context, not making sense does makes sense. To the extent that we have been successful in "rehabilitating" equivocation, readers will begin both to notice the equivocation around them and also to inquire as to its cause and function when it occurs. In our experience, real living messages do not fit prescriptive and judgmental models; they are more subtle, more skillful, and more interesting.

MEASUREMENT

The next step, after noticing instead of dismissing equivocation, is an operational definition that leads to standardized and reliable measurement.

We developed such a method, which measures the degree of equivocation in relatively brief written, spoken, or face-to-face messages by assessing their impact on the receiver (Chapter 2 and Appendix A). That is, we ask lay judges to tell us how clear the message is to them in four different respects:

1. How clear is this message, in terms of just what is being said?
2. To what extent is this message the speaker's own opinion?
3. To what extent is the message addressed to the other person in the situation?
4. To what extent is this a direct answer to the (implicit or explicit) question?

These four elements of communication—Content, Sender, Receiver, and Context—serve as our filter for identifying equivocation in messages, with very high reliability and replicability.

Because there has previously been no standard or fully explicated method, experts typically identify and characterize ambiguity in their own ways (see Stohl & Redding, 1987, pp. 483-490). These definitions are more literary than scientific; we doubt they can be replicated with high reliability. One of our strongest hopes is that other researchers will adopt our scaling method so that we can all begin to speak the same language.

Using this method does *not* require agreement with our situational theory of equivocation or even with the "four elements" principle. For example, rules theorists could still pursue the cognitive rules that generate ambiguous messages, but they would be reassured that we all agree about whether and to what degree a given message is in fact ambiguous. It may even be that other researchers will find a more parsimonious and elegant way of characterizing why and how messages are equivocal, but to validate their proposal they will need a measure of which messages are equivocal and to what degree. Our scaling method offers an "arms-length," objective assessment of the amount and kind of equivocation that pragmatically exist in a message and as such can be used in a wide variety of different research programs. And, while we do not regret the hours spent with judges examining messages, we would be equally pleased if someone develops a better, quicker method that has the same properties as our painstaking procedure.

THEORY

Our theory (Chapter 3) treats the sender's communicative situation at a given moment as a "field," with the possible messages treated as different paths, each of which may have positive or negative consequences. When all clear and direct messages would lead to negative consequences, the individual is said to be in an avoidance-avoidance conflict, which can be resolved by equivocation. Equivocation is a means of "leaving the field," or at least avoiding the negative consequences of unequivocal communication. *The cause of equivocation is a communicative avoidance-avoidance conflict.* We have explicitly rejected individual differences as a cause of equivocation and have also argued that cognitive or "rules" theories can describe but not predict equivocation.

We tested this theory experimentally, first with very simple and constrained formats and then with increasingly complex and spontaneous experiments (Chapters 4 through 7). Using a forced-choice among prepared alternatives, we established that an avoidance-avoidance conflict is the necessary and sufficient condition for eliciting equivocation. Then we asked people to give their own replies, in conflict or nonconflict conditions, in writing, on the telephone, or face-to-face. Their messages were scaled by our judges, and in every experiment the replies people gave in the conflict condition were significantly more equivocal than those from the nonconflict condition. In two repeated-measure experiments, we reversed experimental condition for the same subjects and showed that their communication changed according to experimental condition, that is, there was strong evidence for situational effects rather than individual differences.

One variation on our basic design included a comparison of equivocation with falsification, for which an objective procedure to measure the truthfulness of a message was developed. We showed empirically that equivocations are not false, but are unclear truths and that neither equivocal nor false messages manifest nonverbal leakage. That is, we did not find discrepancies between verbal and nonverbal aspects of a message: Equivocal messages are vague both verbally and nonverbally, and false messages are equally deceptive verbally and nonverbally. These findings support our integrated-message model rather than a separate "channel" view of nonverbal communication.

Finally, we did preliminary work extending our theory to children (Chapter 8) and to political communication (Chapter 9). Over the lifetime of the project, we conducted a total of 19 different experiments using 14 different scenarios and several hundred subjects. All confirmed that equivocation is the predictable and intriguing consequence of a communicative avoidance-avoidance conflict.

We would like to emphasize here the broader theoretical implications of this research, particularly that communication can be seen as emanating from *situations* rather than individuals. In traditional psychological theories, behavior is explained by the inferred mental processes or characteristics of the behaving individual, for example, by cognitions, motivations, emotions,

Figure 10.1.

or personality traits. Indeed, the behavior itself is often of interest solely or primarily because of its usefulness in revealing the nature of these individual processes. Social psychological theories are no exception: Social behavior is commonly viewed as the medium from which we are able to infer the psychological processes that are presumed to cause the behavior, and these processes (such as social cognitions, attitudes, and motivations) are of primary interest. The same theoretical paradigm extends to other social and behavioral sciences, including the fields of communication, linguistics, and discourse analysis, where communicative behaviors are also usually explained by reference to "underlying" (i.e, mental) processes. Thus, there is a widely shared assumption that the explanation of behavior lies within the person and that our explanatory models and theories must, in effect, be maps of the mind.

This assumption is an unfortunate and infelicitous one for researchers whose true interest is communicative behavior, because it implies that we cannot study communication for its own sake and in its own context. Indeed, the social or communicative aspects of behavior are often explicitly called *secondary* or *surface* phenomena. We propose that such assumptions are a matter of choice and of data. That is, it should be as legitimate to ignore intrapsychic explanations as to ignore situational ones — unless there are data addressed to these differences. Here, we have primarily ignored intrapsychic explanations in order to develop a situational theory, in which communicative behaviors are generated by communicative contexts. We have shown that the communicative parameters of a situation are sufficient to produce clarity or equivocation; that individual differences have little or no effect; and that it is not necessary to have a cognitive or motivational model to predict equivocation. This does not mean that people lack cognitions, motivations, personalities, and so forth, or that these mental processes are not interesting in their own right. It simply means that it is not mandatory to delve into them to understand communicative behaviors. Indeed, such a focus may be counterproductive, leading us away from studying communication itself.

The contrast between traditional approaches and ours is most stark when we consider deceptive communication (Chapter 7). Previous researchers have not treated deception as discourse, that is, they have not focused on the messages themselves. Instead, attention has been given to why people deceive, how well others can detect deception, and how deception might "give itself away." The verbal aspects have been treated as noncommunication (because untrue), and the nonverbal aspects have been treated as inadvertent clues or "leakage" — again, as noncommunication. Yet deception is a speech event, a communicative act. Only when a message exists does deception exist. We have shown that, when such messages are examined, they do not fit the traditional deception model.

One important expansion of our theory would be into the sequential, systemic level of communication. As noted in Chapter 9, the simple two-step, question-answer unit we have studied can be extended to a series of exchanges. What does the asker reply to an equivocal response? Diane Rotter conducted some pilot work, using equivocations obtained in our research as replies to subjects in hypothetical situations. It seemed that there might be two kinds of responses to equivocation: further equivocation (getting off the topic) or metacommunication (asking what was meant). Thus, it is possible to move from our current sender-receiver model to the dyad (or group) in multiple exchanges.

Black (1988) studied longer sequential exchanges, treating the conversation itself as the unit of analysis. He showed that statement-by-statement coherence (which can be equated with our Context dimension) fluctuates regularly over the course of the conversation, in a way that maintains overall coherence. That is, discontinuities between adjacent statements do occur, but they are held to the minimum possible for overall coherence of the conversation.

APPLICATIONS

Our research strategy may seem to some readers to have been excessively cautious, as we virtually crawled from forced-choice to written, to spoken, to visual messages (all in the lab), and only then to the outside world. More adventurous researchers would undoubtedly have leaped immediately into naturally occurring, verbal and nonverbal messages. Yet our journey did not seem to us too slow or too safe. We remain impressed by the complexity of communication and by the limits of our knowledge of it. Working gradually not only forestalled large-scale failures but also let us appreciate the subtleties.

In the last two chapters (8 and 9), we let go a bit and went into unfamiliar areas. While these findings are necessarily more tentative than those based on our main research, they were encouraging, in that our theory seems, with further work, extensible to new areas of research (e.g., language and social development) and of application (e.g., political communication). We are confident that there are many other areas of extension and application as well.

Other researchers have already applied this theory to an important work setting. Cunningham and Wilcox (1984) pointed out that, in a hospital setting, when a physician gives a nurse a wrong order that would be a harmful to the patient, an avoidance-avoidance conflict is created:

> [The] two undesirable and seemingly contradictory alternatives are compliance or noncompliance with the order. If the former is done, the patient's welfare is risked. If the latter is done, the relationship with the physician, and perhaps future effective patient care, is risked. (p. 765)

As Stein (1967) had pointed out, this creates a communicative situation fraught with penalties and results in an institutionalized "doctor-nurse game" of avoiding direct communication:

> when [the nurse's] good sense tells her a recommendation would be helpful to [the doctor] she is not allowed to communicate directly nor is she allowed not to communicate it. The way out of the bind is to use the doctor-nurse game and communicate . . . without appearing to do so. (p. 703)

"Saying something without really saying it" or "saying nothing while saying something" are of course classic descriptions of equivocation.

Cunningham and Wilcox (1984) asked a large sample of nurses how they would respond to such a bind, for example:

> An experienced attending physician has left a written order which you are expected to carry out for one of your patients. You feel certain that the order will have seriously harmful consequences for the patient. You know of an alternate order which would eliminate this serious harm and be beneficial to the patient. This physician has been negative about your making recommendations in the past, and you would tend to expect a negative response if you made a recommendation. (adapted from pp. 767-768)

In their questionnaire, the researchers varied whether there would be serious harm to the patient (as above) or only slight discomfort. They also varied the physician's status, either experienced (as above) or a first-year resident, and whether previous recommendations had been received negatively (as above) or positively.

In addition to asking for the way they would handle the problem in general, the questionnaire offered a choice of possible specific messages, ranging from highly indirect to direct:

1. **Doctor, I'm not sure I understand this order. Would you clarify it for me?**
2. **Doctor, I'm concerned about possible negative effects with this order. Could you explain the order to me?**
3. **Doctor, I'm concerned about X and Y effects with this order. Would some other order eliminate these effects?**
4. **Doctor, I recommend a change to order Z. In my experience it has eliminated the X and Y effects.** (p. 769)

Although these messages were not scaled by our method, we agree that they probably approximate a continuum from equivocation to directness. The fourth is particularly clear and specific in content and gives a stronger personal opinion than, for example, asking a question. If we can imagine the implicit question is **"What do you think of this order?,"** then the fourth is also the most direct reply.

The results showed a strong tendency to avoid the two extreme messages (1 and 4 above) and to choose one of the two middle messages. Open-ended survey questions revealed the nurses' preference for more direct messages at a *later* time, if the physician did not change the order after the first message.

Figure 10.2.

Of the factors varied, one had a particularly interesting effect. When the consequence for the patient was serious harm (rather than slight discomfort), the nurse was *less* likely to be direct. Our interpretation of this finding is that, while the risk of harm increased the pressure to avoid letting the order stand, it also increased the cost of direct confrontation, because the nurse would be, in effect, exposing a graver error on the part of the physician. They could afford to be more direct when the error could be treated as a minor oversight.

Another potential area of application is equivocation in organizational communication, for example, in business settings. As noted in Chapter 1, Eisenberg (1984) and Stohl and Redding (1987) have emphasized the likelihood and function of indirect or ambiguous communication in organizational settings. For example, Eisenberg (1984, pp. 230-235) proposed the following functions of what he called *strategic ambiguity* in formal organizations: promoting unified diversity, that is, handling the inevitable tensions between the individual and the aggregate; facilitating organizational change, both at the central and interpersonal levels, by leaving room for people to "fill in" rather than being specific; and preserving privileged positions, for example, by "deniability." Because organizations keep track of their communication (e.g., memos, reports, etc.), the data exist to explore these hypotheses.

Finally, we suggest there is a wide range of other interesting communicative settings where equivocation could be studied: ordinary conversation, including "small talk"; formal diplomatic communication; legal and other negotiation processes; professional evaluations and recommendations; formal etiquette; marital and family interaction; psychotherapy; advertising; interviewing; literary and rhetorical analysis. Whenever the situation is not straightforward and whenever exactly what people say is of interest, our theory of equivocation will be relevant.

We hope that other researchers will expand the studies reported here in new directions, both theoretical and applied. What we have tried to contribute is a solidly based set of techniques and findings on which such extensions can be built.

Appendix A

Training Judges to Scale
Messages for Equivocation

Written with the assistance of John Connors

PREPARATION	270
Equipment	270
Videotape Stimuli	271
Endpoints	272
Dimension 1	272
Dimension 2	272
Dimension 3	273
Dimension 4	274
Videotapes for Training Sessions	275
Session I Messages (Four dimensions)	275
Session II Messages (Dimensions 1 and 2)	276
Session III Messages (Dimensions 3 and 4)	279
Session IV Messages (Four dimensions)	281
Session V and VI Messages (Real messages)	283
Session VII Messages (Reliability)	284
PROCEDURE	288
Recruiting Judges	288
Preparing the Room	290
Script	290
Session I (Introduction)	290
Session II (Dimensions 1 and 2)	298
Session III (Dimensions 3 and 4)	303
Session IV (All four dimensions)	308
Sessions V and VI (Real messages)	311
Session VII (Reliability)	312
Real Messages (From experiments)	313
IPSATIZING AND CALCULATING RELIABILITIES	314

In the following, we describe the procedures for scaling face-to-face, videotaped messages. Videotaped messages are the most complex, and we have found that judges can move "down" from them to scaling spoken or written messages but not easily "up" from written messages. (If you anticipate working only with written or spoken messages, you could train judges in that specific medium. Where there are important differences from the videotaped-message procedure, these will be noted below.)

PREPARATION

Equipment

You will need a VCR and monitor that provide very good resolution and sound quality. The same equipment (plus a camera, of course) can be used for making training videotapes and recording experimental messages. A useful but optional device for scaling videotaped messages is an Auto-Search, a fairly expensive remote control with which the experimenter can move directly to any message on the videotape. (For spoken messages, an audiotape recorder with good sound quality is required. Written messages are simply retyped onto small cards, with an arrow at the center to indicate the exact placement; the cards are placed directly on the scaling tape.)

The videotape onto which messages are copied for scaling should be of high quality (and short length) so that, when messages are played over and over for judges, the signal is not degraded. In all of our video work, we put originals on longer videotapes and then copy onto shorter ones; we play the originals (very carefully!) only when making copies. Copying requires access to a second VCR and the appropriate cable hook-ups.

Our scaling was done on a standard office desk (60.5 × 101.5cm); any table of approximately this size would do as well. (Because the scale values will be ipsatized, the length of the desk need not be exactly the same as ours.) We drew four equally spaced lines running the full length of the desk, where four clean strips of masking tape would be placed before each session to represent the four dimensions; several rolls of masking tape (3 to 4 cm wide) are needed for these strips. Small numbered cards (approximately 3 × 7 cm) represent the messages on the masking tape. These should be plasticized or laminated for frequent handling, or you might use numbered tokens of some kind. In addition to its number, each card or token should have an arrow in the middle, pointing up, to indicate exactly where the message is being placed. Finally, you need a metric tape measure.

Videotape Stimuli

Once the judges are trained, you will simply copy the experimental messages (in random order) onto a scaling videotape. For training, however, you need a videotape containing endpoints for the four dimensions and several videotapes with training messages.

It is not necessary — and may not be practical — for you to obtain copies of our training videotapes, although we are glad to try to provide them or to help you make your own if you contact us. Making your own videotapes is a good way to get a first-hand understanding of the four dimensions of equivocation. It can also be fun, especially if you have friends and colleagues with some "ham" in them. In this section, we will describe our video training messages, emphasizing the properties we wanted them to have. These properties are more important than the other details of the message. That is, you need not recreate the message slavishly, as long as the main points that each message illustrates are captured.

Some practical hints, before you become a producer: If possible, use the same studio or setting in which you plan to gather experimental messages, and keep this setting plain so it does not introduce unintended contextual differences. Try to get as many different people as possible on your videotapes, and avoid using the experimenter(s) who will be playing them for judges. We do not think that the gender of the speaker matters and have simply tried to balance the numbers of male and female speakers. Be ready with what you want each actor to say and do, but also let individuals improvise some variations as well, if they wish. Have each message enacted by several people, then select the best to edit into your final videotape. Always have the back of another person (the receiver) across from the speaker, without blocking a full camera view of the speaker.

The descriptions of messages, below, use the transcription system set out in Chapter 6, as well as the following conventions: The speaker can be assumed to be looking at the other person unless otherwise indicated. The response can be assumed to begin without hesitation unless otherwise indicated. If a particular gesture or facial expression is important, it will be specified; if it is only important that a lot (or none) occur, then that will be indicated, and the actors can improvise their own. Tone of voice will always be indicated, but speed and fluency can be assumed to be normal unless otherwise indicated.

Finally, it is useful to make up a separate videotape showing the numbers 1 to 20, each held for a few seconds. This can be used during copying and editing to insert an on-tape identification number before each message.

ENDPOINT EXAMPLES

Dimension 1 (Content)

There are four endpoints illustrating the extremes of each dimension, two at each end. The first of two left-hand endpoints (very clear messages) for Dimension 1 is:

> *Female:* (Looks down, then back up at the other person while rubbing the back of her neck; then, still holding her hand on her neck, looking and sounding in some pain:) **I have a STIFF neck** (sighs slightly as she finishes, and looks back down).

The facial expression, tone of voice, and neck-rubbing all match what she is saying, and she speaks clearly and concisely. The other completely clear message is:

> *Female:* (Eyes down briefly at first, then looks up at the other person, puts her index finger to her mouth and, with an almost stern facial expression, goes:) **SHHH!**

Even without any other words, the meaning of this message should be perfectly unambiguous.

Because they are intended to be meaningless, the two right-hand endpoints seem bizarre, but the speaker should in no way convey that he or she is just joking. They should be enacted "straight" (as should all of the messages). The first is completely nonverbal:

> *Female:* (Smiling; shrugs, laughs, and then swings her head around in a bizarre fashion.)

The other message illustrating what we mean by extreme unclarity is:

> *Female:* (Looking slightly down, with eyes darting a bit; hands folded in lap, spoken distinctly and in a tone completely without commitment:) **I THINK I'm going GLOVE, impossibly**.

The speaker's manner should not be too strange, and the words should not be given any inflection that might suggest a meaning.

Dimension 2 (Sender)

The first left-hand endpoint is clearly the speaker's own opinion:

Male: (Squinting slightly, unsmiling; sounding very "stuffed up," with a distinct though not exaggerated emphasis on the first personal pronoun:) **I think I have the FLU.**

The "nonverbal" endpoint is as follows:

Male: (First takes a drink from a coffee mug, then shakes his head with a "disgust" expression on his face, and says, with feeling:) **YUCK!**

It should be clear that, from his first-hand experience, the speaker thinks the coffee is bad.

At the other end, the two messages that are clearly not the speaker's opinion are:

Male: (Reading from a book held close to his face and tracing the words with his finger; said as if merely reporting what he has read, with no indication of agreement or disagreement:) **Henry FORD SAYS, "History is BUNK."**

and

Male: (Looking slightly confused; hesitates slightly before saying, in a subdued, neutral tone:) **ONE DOCTOR says I'm OKAY. The OTHER ONE says I need SURGERY.**

Dimension 3 (Receiver)

The first left-hand endpoint depends entirely on nonverbal actions:

Female: (Leans toward and looks directly at the person sitting across from her, smiling and nodding, as if very involved in a conversation with the other person.)

It should be clear that she is smiling and nodding to the other person, not in general or to herself. The second endpoint uses a name (which is identified by the experimenter as the receiver's) plus appropriate nonverbal actions:

Male: (Smiles, looks at the other person, and in an ordinary tone of voice:) **FINE, thanks, JENNIFER.**

One right-hand endpoint is completely nonverbal; it conveys by orientation that the person being addressed is off-screen:

Male: (Looking to his right, not at the person across from him; points off-screen with raised finger, scowls, and shakes his head.)

The other right-hand endpoint uses a whimsical device to address someone who is definitely not the person across from the speaker:

> *Female:* (turns her face away from the other person to talk to her own hand, which she moves as if it were a hand puppet addressing her; when it stops "talking," she replies in a chirpy tone of voice:) **HI!**

Dimension 4 (Context)

For this dimension, the situation and question are given as follows: The other person and the speaker have met in a seminar room before class, and the other person has asked the speaker, "**HOW are YOU?**" This question must be on the videotape, so enact the question anew with each endpoint, as a pair, ensuring that the manner in which the question is asked stays constant. Unless otherwise indicated, the answer is given with normal quickness, that is, with no noticeable hesitation. The left-hand endpoints (completely responsive to the question) are:

> *Other:* **HOW are YOU?**
>
> *Female:* (Smiling; in a polite and friendly tone of voice:) **I'm FINE**.

and

> *Other:* **HOW are YOU??**
>
> *Female:* (Says nothing but makes an "OK" sign with her hand and smiles broadly.)

One right-hand endpoint is verbally unresponsive and nonverbally inappropriate:

> *Other:* **HOW are YOU?**
>
> *Female:* (With a severe facial expression; leans forward and pounds her fist on the arm of the chair to stress her first word; in a firm tone:) **NO!** (Shaking her head:) **I DON'T think it's going to RAIN!**

The other right-hand endpoint is completely nonverbal, but it obviously answers a different question (such as, "**What TIME is it?**").

Other: **HOW are YOU?**

Female: (Hesitates slightly, then looks down at wrist watch; sighs; looks back at the other person with a somewhat exasperated expression and holds up three fingers.)

Written or spoken messages. If the judges are to be trained only for spoken or written messages, then different endpoints are required. The purely non-verbal ones cannot and need not be used; these are primarily to encourage judges who will be scaling videotaped messages to focus on the nonverbal as well as verbal aspects of a message. For written messages, you can use the endpoints given in Figure 2.3. These can also be used for spoken-message training, if the general guidelines for their paralinguistic aspects given above are applied. For example, the person saying **"I have the FLU"** should sound miserable, and **"I THINK I'm going GLOVE. Impossibly"** should be said without feeling or meaning.

VIDEOTAPES FOR TRAINING SESSIONS

Session I Messages

In the first session, in addition to the endpoints there are four messages for the judge to scale for his or her first practice. One message is scaled after each dimension is introduced; at the end of the session, the first one is scaled on all four dimensions.

Message 1, to be scaled by the judge on Dimension 1, is not perfectly clear:

Male: (Waits a moment before speaking; has a melancholy facial expression and a grim tone of voice:) **Yeah, it's a pretty DARK DAY out TODAY.**

In this message, the words, facial expression, and tone of voice are consistent with each other, but the word **"DARK"** is ambiguous because it is not clear whether it is intended literally or metaphorically. The message is neither as clear or as unclear as the endpoints for this dimension and belongs somewhere in between.

Message 2 is also intended for somewhere in the middle (of Dimension 2):

Male: (Reading with interest from a book he is holding with both hands, propped up on his crossed knee; in an enthralled tone of voice:) **One touch of NATURE, makes the WHOLE World KIN ... Shakespeare.** (Then looks up and smiles as if very pleased.)

Although someone else's words are being given, it is obvious by his manner that the speaker agrees with the sentiment.

Sample Message 3 is close to or at the left-hand endpoint of Dimension 3, as it is clearly addressing the person opposite:

> *Female:* (Leans forward; looks, smiles, and points at the other person while stroking a pointed index finger with the other index finger, i.e., a "naughty, naughty!" gesture.)

Message 4, to be scaled on Dimension 4, is not a direct answer to the question. However, an answer to the question can be inferred from it, so it is not on the far right either.

> *Other:* **HOW are YOU?**
>
> *Female:* (Smiles, snaps her finger, shakes her head, and says, saucily:) **IT'S the END of TERM!**

Session II Messages

Session II focuses on the first two dimensions (Content and Sender), each of which has its own set of training messages. There is a third set to be scaled on both dimensions at the end of the session. The endpoints will also be replayed, so it is convenient to copy them onto this videotape as well.

The first five messages illustrate variation in clarity of content and the reasons for the clarity or unclarity. In Message 1, it is the second phrase that detracts from the clarity of the first:

> *Female:* (At the start of the message, raises both hands from the arms of the chair till palms are spread outward, facing up, and are used to emphasize her first stressed words; said enthusiastically:) **I feel SO GOOD**, (then suddenly candid and without enthusiasm, as arms drop back to chair:) **I DON'T believe it**.

Message 2 is quite clear:

> *Female:* (While speaking, she gestures with every phrase, e.g., gestures toward the other person, points at her own nose, and holds "parts" of the words in her fingers; speaks in a didactic, even pedantic, tone and manner:) **The word RHINITIS means an INFLAMATION of the NOSE. Because "RHINE" — that root RHINE, is the GREEK term for nose, and "ITIS" always means an inflamation**. (Then in a rhythmic inflection and cadence:) **So RHINITIS**

means an INFLAMATION of the NOSE (ends by folding hands together on lap and nodding with a self-satisfied smile).

Message 3 illustrates the inherent ambiguity of sarcasm:

Male: (With a sneering facial expression and heavy irony in his voice:) **I LOVE gardening**. (Rolls his eyes, snorts and laughs, and gestures toward the other person. Then looks back and says, even more scornfully:) **Getting DIRTY — it's GREAT.**

Message 4 is clear in its main theme (except for repeating one name), but the aside about Ontario and the manner of speaking toward the end introduce some ambiguity:

Female: (With exaggerated counting on fingers throughout; begins in a fast, matter-of-fact tone:) **The TEN provinces of CANADA are BC, Alberta, Manitoba, SASKATCHEWAN,** (then sarcastically:) **the CENTER of the universe — ONTARIO,** (quickly:) **then there's QUEBEC,** (now smirking and with an increasingly mocking and disparaging tone:) **NEWFOUNDLAND, NEW BRUNSWICK, Prince EDWARD Island, and — Newfoundland.**

Message 5 introduces an indirect phrasing (**"LESS SUCCESSFUL than we'd HOPED"**) and a stark incongruity between the negative words and the upbeat manner of speaking:

Female: (With a brittle smile and head bobbing throughout; shrugs shoulders up at first, then says in a bright, high pitch, as if reporting very good news:) **Well it-was — It was LESS SUCCESSFUL than we'd HOPED.**

In Message 1 for Dimension 2, the speaker gives her own opinion (and not someone else's). Her manner, although unusual for what she is saying, is serious and sincere:

Female: (Nodding slightly throughout and with a pleasant but determined facial expression; in a calm, neutral tone:) **I HATE that shirt.**

In contrast, Message 2 uses an impersonal phrasing and is said with no personal conviction, so it is not clear whether she agrees or disagrees:

Female: (Flips palm upward at start; speaks quickly and in an off-hand manner:) **One LIKES to THINK so.**

Message 3 gives someone else's opinion, but the speaker obviously agrees with it:

> *Female:* (Nodding slightly throughout; said earnestly and confidently:) **JERRY'S convinced me that REAL ESTATE'S the ONLY thing to BUY.**

The content of Message 4 is wrong, but the speaker clearly believes it:

> *Female:* (While settling down in chair and putting both hands on crossed knee; as if stating a simple fact:) **Ahm . . . EDMONTON is the CAPITAL of CANADA.**

Message 5 introduces another source of ambiguity, which the judge will have to sort out:

> *Female:* (Looks down at and places hand on stomach; then looks up at the other person, grimaces, and says in a somewhat embarrassed and solemn manner:) **My STOMACH SAYS I'm HUNGRY.**

The last three messages are to be rated on Dimension 1, then on Dimension 2. Message 6 is both unclear in content and undecided as to the speaker's opinion:

> *Female:* (Moves eyes away and around as if thinking; frowning with wrinkled brow; slight head nodding and shaking throughout; doubtfully:) **WELL** — (then firmly:) **may-MAY-be.**

Message 7 is clear in content and sincerely offered, even though it is very odd indeed:

> *Male:* (With a sincere face and "explanatory" tone:) **I'm a FRISBITERIAN** (nods). **That is, I BELIEVE** (gestures toward other person) **that WHEN — I DIE, my SOUL'll go up on the ROOF — and it'll NEVER come down.** (Nods.)

The phrasing of Message 8 undermines its clarity of content somewhat, but the speaker does convey that she believes the other will "**NEVER GUESS**".

> *Female:* (Gestures with both hands on emphasized words; smiling; in an excited and happy tone, with each word articulated distinctly:) **NEVER! You'll NEVER GUESS what HAPPENED!**

Session III Messages

This session explores Dimensions 3 and 4 (Receiver and Context). There is a set of messages for each dimension (but none for both dimensions, because the session is already quite a long one).

For the first set, to be scaled on Dimension 3, the receiver is identified for the judge as male, a fellow student, good friend, and classmate of the speaker. In Message 1, eye contact is minimal, and the message is very general—it could be addressed to almost anyone:

> *Male:* (Looking at his fingernails throughout; with no facial expression; in a guarded, subdued tone of voice.) **IT was a FAIR weekend.** (Then looks up at the other person.)

Both the content of the answer and the fact that the speaker is looking directly at the other person make Message 2 more likely to be addressed to a classmate:

> *Male:* (Looks down briefly, then up to the other person; playing with his fingernails but not looking at them; with a worried facial expression and tone of voice:) **What did YOU write for question number THREE on the MIDTERM?**

Message 3 is similar except for the way it is asked, which makes it much more appropriate to a professor-student relationship than two classmates:

> *Female:* (Nodding throughout; in a formal, almost patronizing manner:) **Well— WHAT WAS** (gestures toward the other) **your ANSWER for question number THREE on the midterm?**

The content and manner of Message 4 make it suitable for a friend and fellow student—but not a male, because "Suzy Creamcheese" is a local clothing store for young women:

> *Female:* (Initially smiling, with an animated facial expression, fast and enthusiastic:) **LET'S** (raises both hands from lap and gestures quickly toward the other person) **go DOWNTOWN after CLASS. There's a BIG** (same gesture again) **sale ON at Suzy Creamcheese.**

In contrast, Message 5 is more likely to be addressed to a male friend:

Male: (Initially looking at the other person, then glances away briefly and back for the rest of the message; gestures frequently; with rising enthusiasm:) **I was READING in the PAPER yesterday — the Expos are only THREE GAMES out of first place.**

The last message, 6, is more *about* the other person than *to* him:

Female: (Looks upward and to the side; gestures in the same direction with open palm; in an exasperated, rather loud voice:) **WHY does he PESTER me with this?** (Then looks at the other person.)

All of the messages to be scaled on Dimension 4 are in answer to the question, "**HOW are YOU?**," which should be on the videotape with each. Message 1 answers the question and adds some extra, though relevant, information:

Other: **HOW are YOU?"**

Female: (With a somber facial expression; shaking head at first; said quickly, mumbled, and with little inflection:) **I'm not WELL. I SHOULDN'T** (stops shaking head) **'ve gone JOGGING in that AWFUL weather.**

Message 2 does not answer the question directly, but an answer can be inferred from it:

Other: **HOW are YOU?**

Female: (The speaker grabs the arms of the chair and pushes herself forward, toward the other person; smiling throughout; quickly and somewhat shrilly:) **I THINK I'm WINNING!!** (Leans back and puts her hands in lap.)

Message 3 does not precisely match the question asked:

Other: **HOW are YOU?**

Female: (Looking serious and nodding slightly throughout; fidgeting with hands on lap; briefly shifts eyes away from the other person at the start; very seriously:) **"Tsk — it's MUCH BETTER** (nods down) **TODAY.**

Message 4 contains no information in answer to the question:

Other: **HOW are YOU?**

Male: (A long pause before answering; staring intensely at the other person; in a soft but challenging tone:) **How are YOU?**

In Message 5, additional information is given before the question is answered, so it is not at the very left, with the endpoint:

Other: **HOW are YOU?**

Female: (Leans forward at the start; smiling throughout; in an amiable and sincere tone:) **How SWEET of you to ASK!** (Leans back slowly.) **I'M FINE!**

The information in Message 6 answers the question, but the delay and irrelevant actions make it, altogether, less than a direct answer:

Other: **HOW are YOU?**

Male: (A 5-second delay before answering, during which he removes his glasses, examines them while frowning, and puts them back on; then, quickly and sullenly:) **I'm FINE.** (Purses lips.)

Session IV Messages

These and all future messages are to be scaled on all four dimensions; first, the entire set is scaled on the Content dimension; they are replayed for scaling on the Sender and then the Receiver dimension. Finally, the same messages are played with their corresponding question for scaling on the Context dimension. So there should be two copies of each message on the videotape: the first is just the message itself (for the first three dimensions), the second comes with its preceding question. Because we use an Auto-Search, we can save editing time by stacking them on the videotape in pairs in which the odd-numbered segments are the messages alone and the even-numbered segments are the same message plus question. If you locate messages without an Auto-Search, you may prefer to put, first, one set of all the messages alone, then (in the same order) all of the second version, each with the question.

In this session, the other person is a good friend who has invited the speaker to dinner, and all five messages are in response to the question, **"What kind of FOOD do you LIKE?"** The relevant aspects of each message for each dimension are discussed in more detail in the Procedure section for this session, which should be studied before the messages are enacted.

Message 1 is:

Male: (With an intense look; quickly, as if to correct an impression:) **I like SHRIMPS,** (then, more slowly, with head shaking and one-sided grimace:) **but they DON'T like ME.**

The second phrase of Message 1 creates ambiguity on the first two dimensions. The words and direct eye contact make it appropriate for the specified receiver. It is also a good answer to the question, although extra information is added.

Message 2 is:

> *Male:* (During a long pause, he looks toward the right and then shifts his body to the right; then, thoughtfully and quietly:) **The capital of CANADA is OTTAWA.** (Looks at other person and nods slowly.)

The solemn tone given this innocuous statement may keep it from being perfectly clear. The lack of conviction may raise some question about whether the speaker agrees. The words are inappropriate for the receiver in this case, and the speaker does not make eye contact while talking. The message is virtually a right-hand endpoint on Dimension 4.

Message 3 is:

> *Female:* (While nodding; quickly and pleasantly:) **My FAMILY loves pic-aladoes.**

The content of this message has two potentially unclear aspects, the unfamiliar food name and an emphasis on the word "FAMILY." This same emphasis creates ambiguity about what the speaker's own opinion is. It also makes the message somewhat inappropriate for a receiver who has invited only the speaker to dinner, but this may be offset by the eye contact and the appropriateness of the general subject matter. The message is at least indirectly related to the question, but how closely depends on how the judge resolved the speaker's opinion — does her family include her?

Message 4 is:

> *Male:* (Pauses while taking a puff from a cigarette, then exhales loudly; throughout the message he is bobbing his head while looking at and counting on his fingers; said as if listing and with rising intonation at the end of each phrase:) **I like— MEXICAN FOOD. I like— GREEK FOOD.** (Conversationally:) **I like— SPANISH food. All SCANDINAVIAN food. . . . And I even LIKE . . . East INDIAN and Malaysian food.**

The content of this message is straightforward and clear, and it is obviously the speaker's own opinion. The words are appropriate for the receiver, but there is no eye contact. Still, this is a good answer to the question asked.

The last message, 5, is:

> *Male:* (Nodding head slightly throughout, with an earnest expression, quickly, pleasantly, but not very enthusiastically:) **I REALLY like cooking MEXICAN food.**

This message is clear enough to be at or near the left-hand endpoint. However, the lack of enthusiasm may affect its placement on Dimension 2 somewhat. The words are not appropriate for a dinner guest to say to his host, although he looks straight at the receiver. From the words, we might infer that he also likes eating Mexican food, but he has not answered directly.

Sessions V and VI Messages

The first four sessions consist of messages written and acted by the researchers and are designed to highlight particular aspects of the dimensions. Because of this, they tend to be simple and often weird or exaggerated. Sessions V and VI use messages produced by "real people," in conditions similar to those that will ultimately be scaled. These sessions give the judges a chance to apply their learning to spontaneous discourse. Recreating our messages would not produce such discourse, so rather than describing the messages we used, we will discuss some considerations for creating your own.

The messages we used for these two sessions were collected during pilot studies for the experiments described in Chapter 6. We used face-to-face versions of the Employee Reference and Bizarre Gift scenarios, in both conflict and nonconflict conditions. If your scaling needs are like ours, you can conduct similar pilot tests to obtain your own "real" messages. (This would also provide practice with the experimental procedures.) For example, adapt the instructions for any of the experimental situations in this book that you are *not* going to use for your own studies; it is essential that the training messages be completely different from those scaled later. You would need only six to eight messages in each scenario (one for each session), with equal numbers from conflict and nonconflict conditions. Edit them into a videotape in random order, with no indication that they were elicited in different conditions. (As mentioned above, the messages should be edited in twice, once alone and then along with the question asked.)

We found that even the short messages given by participants in our experiments were more subtle and difficult than the training messages. You can expect at least the following differences: The messages may be longer, with more potential for internal inconsistency. They may be cryptic, with incomplete sentences, imprecise or vague terms, and more "fillers" such as "**uh**" and "**ah.**" Eye contact may be odd or erratic. There will probably be wider variations in volume, inflection, and clarity of speech. Some messages will be smooth and eloquent, some will be almost incomprehensible. (It is handy for the experimenter to have a transcript of the words to read out in case the judge cannot understand something. However, the judge should scale the videotaped message, not the transcribed words.) Finally, the ways in which a question can be "not answered" are more subtle than in previous practice messages.

Exactly what you need for these phasing-in sessions depends on your particular scaling goals. Probably only one "real message" session was needed for our purposes, rather than the two we used. If the messages for which you are training judges are much longer or more complex than ours, you could need more than two such sessions. Factors that require increased practice include not only longer messages or larger message sets (both of which could be increased gradually) but also messages obtained in three or more different experimental conditions, such as our Experiment 15. In order to decide what messages you need for these sessions, make a careful analysis of the differences between the training messages and the messages you want to have scaled. Then obtain practice messages with these properties, phasing in the new aspects slowly.

Session VII Messages

This session will assess the judges' reliability. We use enacted messages one last time, in order to ensure an uncurtailed range on all four dimensions and to test the judges on basic principles. For Dimension 2, the judge will be told that the speaker is a librarian. For Dimension 3, the other person is Mr. McDonald, a patron of the library. For Dimension 4, the question is added, **"Do you HAVE any BOOKS on CATS?"**
Message 1 is:

Male: (Hesitates slightly before beginning; unsmiling and looking directly at the other person throughout; inclines his head forward and down on each emphasized word; looking and sounding slightly confused:) **BIG ones — or ... LITTLE ones?**

This message lacks clear content; out of context, we have no idea what he's talking about. It also sounds confused and uncertain and gives neither a personal opinion nor an opinion typical of librarians. Aside from the continuous eye contact, the message is neutral as to receiver; nothing indicates that it is addressing Mr. McDonald, a patron of the library. Finally, it postpones (rather than answers) the question asked.
Message 2 is:

Male: (Looking interested; quickly and pleasantly:) **OH** (raises eyebrows) **do you own a CAT Mr. McDonald?**

The content is straightforward and clear, but no opinion is voiced that might be the speaker's. It is directly addressed to Mr. McDonald, but it does not answer his question.

Message 3 is:

> *Male:* (While speaking, looks quickly to the side twice, as if thinking, but otherwise looking directly at the other person; sounding slightly doubtful:) **YEAH. I THINK there are some NEW ones on AFRICA.**

The answer makes sense, but it is not clear what the "**ones**" are, and the speaker's doubtfulness also takes away some clarity. This lack of conviction and unsureness obviously affect the message's position on Dimension 2. The eye contact brings it toward the left on Dimension 3; also, the content (but not the delivery) could be appropriate for a library patron. Finally, it answers a question about books on Africa, not on cats.

Message 4 is:

> *Female:* (Nodding frequently; arms straight down at sides, with no movement or gestures; sounding professional but a bit mechanical:) **The head LIBRAR-IAN says the library has TWENTY books on cats, both DOMESTIC AND wild cats.**

The message itself is quite straightforward and clear in content. However, it attributes the opinion expressed to someone else, so we do not know the speaker's own opinion. The content and delivery are appropriate for the receiver, although perhaps somewhat too formal. It is a good answer to the question asked, except for bringing the head librarian into it.

Message 5 is:

> *Male:* (Bobbing head throughout; enthusiastically:) **Oh YES,** (then matter-of-factly, sounding memorized:) **SPEAKING of cats— we have a LARGE selection of books dealing with HOUSEHOLD PETS.**

The first and second parts of the message are incongruent in that there is no logical progression from "**SPEAKING of cats**" to "**HOUSEHOLD PETS.**" For Dimension 2, there is no uncertainty in the way the message is delivered, and it is appropriate for a librarian. Both the eye contact and content make it appropriate for the receiver. It answers the question ("**YES**"), but then shifts obliquely to the broader category of "**HOUSEHOLD PETS.**"

Message 6 (an English translation of a Scottish family motto) is strange and menacing:

> *Male:* (Head turned to the side but looking at other person; stern, almost sneering facial expression; after a 2-second pause, says distinctly and forcefully:) **TOUCH** (raises one eyebrow) **not the CAT, but the GLOVE** (raises eyebrow).

The content will be meaningless to most people, and nothing in the words seems to go with the severe facial expression and tone of voice. No particular opinion is expressed. The eye contact addresses the other person, but the content is not appropriate to the relationship. The word "**CAT**" alone is not enough to make it an answer to the question asked.

Message 7 is lengthy (and modeled after a real one, in Experiment 10):

> *Female:* (Formal expression, with exaggerated articulation of the mouth; prissy, almost scolding tone:) **COULD WE BE more** (eyebrows raised quickly) **SPECIFIC about WHAT it IS we WANT. WHEN ONE asks for INFOR-MATION, ONE should TRY to give as much DETAIL** (eyebrows raised quickly) **as ONE POSSIBLY can. It's DIFFICULT for US to give the best SERVICE if the PUBLIC DOESN'T do their PART.**

There are no contradictions or ambiguities in content, but the use of "**WE**" and "**US**" makes it vague on Dimension 2. Both the direct eye contact and the officious tone make it appropriate for the receiver on Dimension 3, unless the judge feels it is a bit too officious. It does not answer the question much better than answering with a question would.

Message 8 is:

> *Female:* (Smiling falsely throughout; in a condescending tone, as if addressing a small child:) **Well, DEAR, we have some NICE LITTLE pamphlets in our CHILDREN'S section.**

"**NICE LITTLE pamphlets**" is not very precise, but otherwise the message is fairly clear. "**We**" and "**our**" create ambiguity about the speaker's own opinion. The tone, phrasing, and content ("**DEAR**" and "**CHILDREN'S section**") make the message inappropriate for the receiver. It answers a somewhat different question than the one asked (which was about books, not "**NICE LITTLE pamphlets**").

Message 9 is:

> *Male:* (Head tilted to one side; stern expression; said forcefully, almost hos-tilely:) **Ah — that's NOT in my DEPARTMENT.** (Tilts head to the other side and, in a more neutral tone:) **You'll HAVE to try ELSEWHERE madam.**

The content of the message is direct and internally consistent. The assertiveness makes it likely to be the speaker's own opinion. Both **"madam"** and the unfriendly tone are inappropriate for the receiver. The question is responded to but not answered directly.

In Message 10, the speaker seems preoccupied with something else and unsure of herself:

> *Female:* (Concerned, unsmiling expression throughout; pauses slightly, then says timidly:) **AAHMM . . . WELL sir ahm . . . I'll HAVE to look.** (Looks away.) **. . . But . . . not TODAY. Ah, too BUSY.** (Looks back at other person and shakes head.) **Come BACK . . . mmm-YEAH. Come BACK tomorrow.**

The uncertainty, puzzlement, and broken phrases make the message quite unclear in content. The unsureness in words and manner also affect its position on Dimension 2. There is little eye contact, and the manner and words are inappropriate for the relationship to the receiver. There is no direct answer to the question asked.

Message 11 borrows from a Kliban cat cartoon:

> *Female:* (Smiling broadly throughout; with exaggerated gestures and body movement, all in time with the words—almost dancing in her chair; exclaims:) **OH CATS!** (Then sings the rest:) **LOVE to EAT them MOUSIES.** (Turns to the side, puts hand to mouth, opens and closes pinched fingers—imitating a cat eating a mouse.) **BITE their LITTLE heads!** (Ends by laughing.)

The content is out of the ordinary, even if the judge recognizes its source, and the manner of delivery is extremely odd. It does carry some conviction, although it is not very "librarianlike." The pattern of eye contact and unsuitability of the message make it unlikely to be addressed to the other person, and it does not answer the question at all.

Alternative reliability messages. If you are going to be working only with spoken messages, Mr. McDonald could telephone the library with his question, and you could make audiotaped versions of the above messages. Most of the visual nonverbal information can be shifted into paralinguistic form (e.g., sounding uncertain, formal, or stern). The major difference would be on the Receiver dimension, where the absence of eye contact clues would necessarily increase the influence of the content of the message. If desired, tone of voice could be used to produce contradictions in a few messages between the content and the manner in which it is said, in terms of the Receiver dimension.

Our set of written reliability messages is easy to reproduce. The writer (for Dimension 2) is Professor Parker. The recipient is Dean Davis. The Dean has written a memo asking Professor Parker for a written evaluation of a student, and his question is "**Was John Jones a good student?**" The messages are:

1. To whom it may concern: I don't know.
2. It's not that I don't want to exclude not doing it, but I don't know, Mr. Minton.
3. Dear Dean Davis:
   Antidisestablishmentarianism is very manful.
   (signed) Professor Parker
4. The general consensus on the new building is that it was a waste of money.
5. John Jones, kin of graboon, was a very nugacious student.
6. I can't remember.
7. Very interesting.
8. It depends on what you mean by "good," Dean.
9. He might be brilliant. He might be an idiot.
10. I have to go along with the majority opinion and say he was lazy. But he could be bored.
11. Professor McDonald thought he was an average student.
12. I'm always happy to recommend him to my friends.
13. You men might as well know he was the worst student I've ever had.
14. I'm convinced that he will never do.

If your scaling needs are very different, you may have to develop your own reliability messages, using the following principles: First, examine in detail both the messages described here and our qualitative analyses of real messages (in Chapters 5 through 7) and create these differences in your messages. Second, be sure to produce variance on each dimension by including messages near both endpoints and in the middle of the dimension. Third, distribute this variation so that the positions of messages are uncorrelated across dimensions. As much as possible, each message should be on the high side on one dimension, lowish on another, and in the middle on yet another.

PROCEDURE

Recruiting Judges

The judges for our experiments were university students, male and female. We found that English and Linguistics students were usually the best judges because they focused on the syntax and semantics of the messages. Psychology students, on the other hand, often read too much into the messages, so we avoided using them.

Judges were initially recruited by canvassing classes on campus. The researcher explained that we needed volunteers to help us rate messages obtained in our communication experiments. What they would be doing is examining short videotaped messages very carefully, using guidelines we would teach them. They were told that this would take about an hour or so a week for the term (or the whole year, depending on our needs) and that we would pay $5.00 per hour (our 1985 rate). The recruiter did not mention the name or purpose of the project — not at this or any other time while the judges were still scaling messages. It was simply the "scaling project" or "communication study." The researcher asked members of the class to fill out volunteer forms if they were interested in being contacted about helping us. The forms requested the volunteer's name, gender, phone number, and the times he or she would be available. It was emphasized that filling out the form did not commit them to being in the study, it only meant that they were interested in being contacted.

After 15 to 20 names were collected, the volunteers were contacted by telephone. The researcher introduced himself or herself and asked if the volunteer were still interested in the possibility of participating in our communication study. He or she went on to repeat that this involved watching and rating some videotaped messages and that it would take about an hour per week for whatever number of sessions we were planning at the time, although they were free to drop out of the study at any time. They were reminded that they would be paid for their participation. If the volunteer was still willing, an appointment was arranged at a mutually agreeable time. (Judges were always seen individually.)

We usually started by training about 10 to 12 judges, as some would usually drop out, chiefly because of their schedules. (Rarely, a judge would ignore our training and make up idiosyncratic procedures, and it was necessary to phase him or her out tactfully.) The goal was to have at least eight judges, in order to assure high reliability. If the judge did not show up at the arranged time, he or she would be called to find out what had happened. If the judge was still interested, another appointment would be arranged. If the judge did not show up for the second appointment, there was no attempt to book a third.

When the judges had finished the series of scalings we needed (which could be between four and eight months), they were given a complete explanation of the project, along with reprints of articles if they wished. Until then, however, they were told nothing about the project, its hypotheses, or even that the messages were elicited under different experimental conditions.

Preparing the Room

Before the judge arrived for a session, the room was prepared and equipment was checked to ensure everything was working properly. All the materials needed (instructions, videotapes, etc.) were placed in the room before starting the session.

Four strips of masking tape were laid out along the length of the desk, about 12 cm apart. A pencil mark was put on the tape where it met the left-hand edge of the desk. This served as the reference point from which measurements were made later. There was also a pencil mark indicating for the judge the exact middle of the tape. Finally, the experimenter wrote, by hand, a brief, concrete description of the dimension being scaled on each piece of masking tape. These read, in order from the top of the desk,

What is being said
Speaker's own opinion
Addressing the other person
Direct answer

The experimenter always referred to the dimensions simply as Dimension 1, 2, 3, or 4. We did not want to bias the judges with our terms for the dimensions, and in any case our terms are abstract while we wanted the judges to be concrete.

Script

The following is a step-by-step transcription of the instructions used by the experimenters. It includes the script (in boldface) of what was said to the judges, as well as the other procedures used in the sessions. Some ad-libbing was always necessary, depending on questions that were asked or misunderstandings that arose. A good way to learn how to be an experimenter is first to be a judge yourself. For example, two people can take turns being experimenter and judge. For further practice, the person playing the judge can be easy or difficult.

SESSION I

The goals of the first session are to introduce the judges to the scaling procedure and the dimensions (without overwhelming them) and to begin to develop a working relationship. Especially because the very label "psychologist" often makes people nervous, we made every attempt to ensure that the judges felt comfortable and relaxed, especially when they came for the first session. For example, we usually asked the judge to come to the experimenter's office, and they walked together to the room set up for scaling; this created a natural opportunity to chat and joke on the way. Remember that the role of judges in this procedure is *not* that of formal experimental subjects; they are closer to being technically specialized research assistants. So, other than keeping the judge "blind" to the purpose of the project, the experimenter should treat the judge as a peer. The judges, on their side, usually treat the scaling as a job which they take seriously.

The experimenter takes an active role in the early training sessions, explaining dimensions and suggesting ways that messages can differ from each other along the various dimensions. Still, he or she should give the judge a lot of praise and encouragement during this period. As the judge becomes more knowledgeable about what is involved and develops his or her own approach, the experimenter should shift to a less active role, becoming more and more just an attentive listener to the judge's reasons for placing a message where he or she did. That is, the experimenter's role changes from being a teacher to being an assistant who simply confirms that the judge (who is now the expert) is using correct and consistent criteria for scaling each dimension. This begins even in the first session, when the judge places his or her first few messages: Within very wide limits, the experimenter should accept any placement as long as the judge gives clear and consistent reasons. After all, these are matters of opinion, not fact, and what we ultimately want is a decoder's perspective on the messages. If the experimenter seems to have the "right answer," then the judge will probably treat the sessions as a guessing game (or, worse, as a test) and try to figure out what the experimenter thinks instead of making his or her own judgments. We learned early on that our own first impressions of messages would often be corrected by the judges. Because of their single-minded, intense focus and their freedom from pre-conceived ideas, they frequently saw aspects of messages that we had missed.

Once settled in the room, with the judge at the desk facing the monitor and the experimenter off to one side, the introduction begins:

> This is a scaling project, and we'd like you to rate different messages on four scales or dimensions. We want to know YOUR opinion of these messages, and we hope you'll find it quite interesting.

> In this first session, we just want you to learn what the dimensions are and how the procedure works. Please ask any questions that you think of as we go through the session. What you will be scaling are videotaped messages. They are represented by these little cards.

Explain that the number on the card is the number of the message that is being scaled. Point out the arrow in the middle, which is to indicate precisely where the message is being placed on the scale.

> **There are four dimensions or characteristics of the message we'd like you to scale. Each tape on the desk is one of these dimensions. Okay? What we're going to do today is show you some examples of endpoints of the four dimensions. By endpoints, we mean messages that would be placed at the ends of each dimension.** (Point to the ends of the tape.)
>
> **After that, we'll ask you to scale one message on each dimension. Each message will hold still on the TV screen for a second or so; the message starts once the still picture is over.** [Note: This is caused by our editing technique and may not be true of yours.]
>
> *Dimension 1*
>
> **Let's look at the first dimension, then, the one at the top of the table, "What is being said." Here you scale how CLEAR the message is. By "perfectly clear," we mean unambiguous messages that have only one meaning.**

Give the judge the sheet (reproduced in Figure 2.2) that summarizes the endpoints of each dimension, and ask him or her to read about Dimension 1.

> **Now I'm going to show you two examples of perfectly clear messages.**

Show the two left-hand endpoint examples. In the first, the speaker is rubbing her neck and saying "I have a STIFF neck." Explain to the judge that this is a perfectly clear message because it has no ambiguity: Her facial expressions and tone of voice match what she says, and she speaks clearly and concisely. In the second endpoint, the speaker puts her index finger to her mouth and says "SHHH!" Again, point out to the judge that the message contains no ambiguity. It is perfectly clear, even though no words were spoken, and therefore can also be placed at the endpoint of the scale, on the judge's left.

> **Messages that are less clear are scaled more to the right. How far to the right depends on the message. Can you think of any ways to change "I have a STIFF neck" so that it would be less clear?**

This technique is used to start the judges talking about the messages and to get them to think about the scaling criteria, so it is important to be positive about anything they contribute. (This is also a first check that they understand what we are doing—some very general questions may arise at this point.)

Great! Now I'll play two examples of perfectly UNCLEAR messages.

In the first right-hand endpoint, the speaker is moving her head in a bizarre fashion. Discuss the example with the judge, pointing out that nothing is said, and no clue is given as to the meaning of the movements. Therefore, the message is as unclear as a message can get (at least for the purposes of this project). The second endpoint is another speaker saying **"I THINK I'm going GLOVE, impossibly."** Explain to the judge that, although nothing about her actions is too strange, verbally the message makes no sense, so it too is scaled at the right-hand endpoint of this dimension. Point out that:

> **You may be able to think of some bizarre situations where these messages could make some sense, but for our purposes these will be defined as completely unclear.**
>
> **Now I'll show you the message we'd like you to scale. Place it where you think it belongs and tell me why you think it belongs there. In other words, we want you to think out loud.**

In Message 1, the speaker is saying **"Yeah, it's a pretty DARK DAY out TODAY."** We expect judges to place this somewhere near the middle. Although the speaker's melancholy facial expression and tone of voice correspond to what he says, it is not considered perfectly clear because of the ambiguity of the word **"DARK"**: Is the day literally dark, or is he using a metaphor? If the judge does not notice this, point it out casually, because this is a training session and you want to remain positive about the judge's efforts. Be pretty flexible with the placements at this point; as long as this message is not rated as completely clear or completely unclear, accept the judge's rating.

If the message is placed at an endpoint, ask the judge why he or she put it there. A typical reason might be **"It's CLEAR that he's DEPRESSED."** This would be a good opportunity to talk about making inferences: Remind the judge that the speaker did not *say* that he was depressed and that for this dimension the judge should consider only the actual message rather than any inferences about what lies behind it. It would have been clearer to say explicitly **"I feel DEPRESSED."** If the judge has to make inferences in order to understand what is being said, then the message cannot be seen as perfectly clear and therefore must go somewhere to the right of the "perfectly clear" endpoint. However, it is up to the judge to decide how unclear the message is. It is important to be reassuring and encouraging, so the judges will develop their own approaches. *The reason we use several judges is to capture the variety of interpretations receivers may make. If there were only one way to view a message, we could do it ourselves.*

Dimension 2

Refer to the definitions of this dimension on the judge's sheet, and summarize:

Dimension 2 is "to what extent is the message the speaker's own opinion?" Here are two examples of endpoints that are definitely the speaker's own opinion.

The first example shows the speaker saying "**I think I have the FLU.**" Point out that by stressing "**I think,**" he is definitely stating his own opinion and nobody else's. In the second endpoint, the speaker takes a drink from a mug, makes an unpleasant face, and says "**YUCK!**" Explain that the speaker's reaction is a direct result of a taste sensation that the speaker had, so the message is rated as definitely his own opinion and is placed at the extreme left end of this dimension.

Now, at the other end of the scale, here are two examples of the speaker expressing someone ELSE'S opinion; we have no idea what the speaker's opinion is.

Show the two messages that are definitely not the speaker's own opinion: In the first, the speaker is reading a book, and without looking up from the book, he says "**Henry FORD SAYS 'History is BUNK',**" while following along in the book with his finger. Referring to the definition of this endpoint on the judge's sheet (Figure 2.2), point out that he is just reading someone else's words, not giving his own opinion at all. In the second example, the speaker is saying "**ONE DOCTOR says I'm OKAY. The OTHER ONE says I need SURGERY.**" Make sure the judge notices that, here too, nothing the speaker says or does indicates his own opinion or even his degree of agreement with the doctors, so the message is definitely not his own opinion.

Next show the judge the message that he is to scale on this dimension. In Message 2, a man reads enthusiastically from a book, "**One touch of NATURE makes the WHOLE world KIN . . . Shakespeare,**" then looks up and smiles. Again ask the judge to place the message where he or she thinks it belongs and to explain why. This message is sometimes difficult to rate because the person is reading, as in the endpoint example, yet he seems to agree with what he is reading. It will probably fall somewhere in the middle, perhaps somewhere slightly left of center. It is important to ensure that the judge realizes why this message cannot go on either endpoint: Although someone else's opinion is being expressed (not "his personal opinion" as the left-hand endpoint), we also know the speaker shares this opinion (by his manner and especially the smile). You might discuss how this makes the message different from the "**Henry FORD**" endpoint.

Dimension 3

Again refer to the definitions on the sheet and say:

Dimension 3 is "to what extent is the message addressed to the other person in the situation?" In the examples I'm going to show you, the other person in the situation is always the head in the lower portion of the screen.

In the first left-hand endpoint, nothing is said; instead, it shows the speaker smiling, nodding, and leaning toward the person in the lower portion of the screen. Before the second endpoint, tell the judge that the person in the foreground is a fellow student named Jennifer. The other person smiles and says "**FINE, thanks, JENNIFER.**" Point out to the judge that, even though in the first message we do not know the other person's name, it is still obvious that the speaker is addressing her, so both of these messages belong at the left-hand endpoint of the dimension.

Now at the other end of the scale, I'll show you two examples of the speaker addressing someone else.

The first example shows the speaker looking offscreen, pointing, scowling, and shaking his head. At no point does he look at the other person. The second endpoint example shows the speaker turning away from the other person to talk to her own hand. Clearly, neither of these two messages were addressed to the other person, so both would be placed at the end of the scale on the judge's right.

Now I'll show you a message that we'd like you to scale on this dimension. Put the card where you think the message belongs, then tell me why you put it there.

In Message 3, the speaker leans forward, looks at, and smiles at the other person while stroking her finger, which is pointed at the other person, in a nonverbal gesture of "naughty, naughty." This message will probably be scaled at or close to the endpoint on the judge's left. As usual, it is important to make sure that the judge gives a reason for the placement. Possible reasons could be that the speaker is looking directly at the other person, she's leaning forward, pointing, and so forth.

Dimension 4

Dimension 4 measures to what extent the message is a direct answer to the question asked. For this dimension, we'll always tell you the situation or context in which a question was asked, then we'll tell you what the question is.

For this session, the situation and question are: Jennifer and the speaker meet in a seminar room before class, and Jennifer asks the speaker "HOW are YOU?" These first two examples will be direct answers to the question "HOW are YOU?"

In the first endpoint, in reply to Jennifer's question the speaker answers **"I'm FINE"** without hesitation. In the next, the speaker says nothing but makes an "OK" sign with her hand and smiles broadly. In both messages we know exactly how the speaker is. Their replies were perfect answers to the question asked, so these messages go to the judge's left-hand end of the scale.

The next example is at the other end of the scale. The response seems totally unrelated to the question.

In the first example, in reply to the question **"HOW are YOU?"** the speaker says, shaking her head and banging her fist for emphasis, **"NO! I DON'T think it's going to RAIN!"** Obviously this is completely unrelated to the question, so it belongs at the endpoint on the judge's right. The other message is completely nonverbal, but the woman seems to be giving the other person the time of day, which is "way off" the question **"HOW are YOU?"**

I'll show you the last message I'd like you to scale. Tell me where you think it belongs and why. Again the situation is: Jennifer and the speaker meet in a seminar room before class. Jennifer asks the speaker "HOW are YOU?"

In Message 4, the speaker smiles and says happily, **"IT'S the END of TERM!"** Judges tend to rate this message differently from each other: It is not a direct answer, but an answer can easily be inferred from it. Accept the judge's placement as long as there is a reason given for it and it is not placed at either of the endpoints. The message is not a direct answer to the question, but it is not totally unrelated either.

> Okay, that's all there is to the scaling procedure. Before we end this session, though, I'd like to point out that a message scaled to the left on one dimension does not necessarily get scaled to the left on another dimension. Let's take the first message you scaled and go through all four dimensions with it to see the difference.

Go back to Message 1 ("a pretty **DARK DAY**"):

> Where do you think this message should be scaled on Dimension 2? Dimension 3? Dimension 4?

Again, be flexible and encouraging at this point. The goal is to have the judge talk confidently about his or her placements and not look to the experimenter for the "correct answer."

This message usually winds up pretty far on the left on Dimension 2 (because it is the speaker's opinion, and probably nobody else's, that the day is dark) and also on the left on Dimension 3 (because the speaker is looking at and addressing the person in the foreground) but somewhere to the right of center on Dimension 4 (because the message is not a good answer to the question, "**HOW are YOU?**," although an answer of sorts can be inferred from it).

As emphasized repeatedly above, in the first session, it is better to be lenient with the judges' placements than to intimidate them with a lot of details. Remember, the purposes of this session are (1) to familiarize the judges with the dimensions, the physical layout, and procedural details and (2) to establish that we want *their* opinions, not our own. Information about the dimensions will be built up gradually over the next few sessions. So, for instance, if the judge places the last message on the far right on Dimension 4, accept it for now; the intricacies come later. However, if a judge places it on the far left end of this dimension, it usually indicates that the judge has confused this with another dimension or does not understand the criterion for a direct answer. If this is the case, a typical reason the judge might give would be, "**He ANSWERED without HESITATION, so it was DIRECT.**" In this case, review the information on the summary sheet with the judge.

This is the end of the first session. Always finish the session by telling the judge that he or she did very well, and emphasize that feeling a bit confused at this point is normal and expected. Pay the judge for the session, and ask whether he or she would like to continue. If so, arrange another time for the next session.

When preparing the room before the judge arrives, put masking tape on the desk only for the first two dimensions, because the purpose of this session is to deal with Dimensions 1 and 2 in more detail.

From now on, record all of the judge's placements in pencil on the tape by making a pencil mark and writing the number of the message on the tape where the arrow on the card falls. After the session, put the number of the session and the judge's initials on each tape.

Dimension 1

Begin by explaining that:

For this session we will just deal with the first two dimensions, so that we can concentrate on them a little more closely. In Dimension 1, the main property of the message we want you to look at is the content – that is, just what is being said, or how clear the message is.

For this dimension, the message is to be judged on its own, with no inferences about context. That is, for now, DON'T consider who the people are, why they are talking, in what situation, or anything like that – you'll get to worry about those things later. For now, look at the message as if you happened to see it while changing channels on TV – as if it just flicked by with no context. The question is: how clear is it, on its own?

(If the judge is scaling written messages, the analogy could be **"as if you found this written on a note lying on a table."** If the messages are spoken, **"as if you overheard a snatch of telephone conversation."**)

In this sesson the judge gets the full summary sheet (see Figure 2.3) including the "rules of thumb," which will be dealt with shortly.

Now, could you re-read the definition for Dimension 1 on the sheet, please.

After the judge has refreshed his or her memory of Dimension 1, play the four endpoint examples for this dimension.

Of course, few messages will be that extreme. Most are somewhere in between, and that's what we'll concentrate on today. Notice that on your summary sheet there are now "rules of thumb" under each definition. These

rules are useful to keep in mind when you're scaling messages that fall IN BETWEEN the endpoints.

There are several ways a message can be unclear. For example, you may notice that the STRUCTURE or SYNTAX may be unclear. This could be things like mismatched words, peculiar phrasing, inarticulateness (hesitation or repetition), changes of topic within the message, and other things like that. Out-of-place emphasis (that is, which word is stressed) or gestures can also make a message unclear. Can you think of any examples of these?

Again, this question is intended to keep the session from becoming a lecture by the experimenter to the judge. If the judge cannot think of any examples, ask him or her to vary the left-hand endpoints so that they would be less clear.

Related to this is the unclarity produced by CONTRADICTIONS, that is, by saying two or more incompatible things, or saying something in an unexpected or incongruent way, for example, saying "I am VERY ill" in a cheerful voice. Another way that messages can be unclear is that they are simply AMBIGUOUS: the facial expression, the words, or whatever just don't convey a precise meaning. These are just some examples of reasons a message might be less than perfectly clear. Can you think of specific examples of any of these?

As we go along, you'll develop your own rules for looking at messages. We can't predict all the factors that may be important. The examples I have given you here are just to get you started thinking about exactly what makes a message clear or unclear.

The important thing here is your OVERALL IMPRESSION of the message—how it strikes you, how well you can understand what it means. So you'll be paying attention to the details and the reasons that a message isn't clear, but in the end we're interested in the whole message, not the parts.

Now I'm going to show you some examples of messages that vary in clarity on Dimension 1, for you to start with. I will play them all through once first, then one at a time for you to scale.

Before we start—some practical details. If you feel that a message belongs at an endpoint, put the edge of the card, not the arrow, to the edge of the table. Otherwise the card just falls off the desk.

(This means that the actual endpoints are about 4 cm from each end. Because the scores will be ipsatized, the raw scale values do not matter.)

Try to make distinctions among messages, however slight they may be. That is, if possible, try NOT to stack a lot of them in one place unless you really

believe they are IDENTICAL in clarity. You can overlap cards, if you like, in order to make small distinctions.

This may raise the tricky question of absolute versus relative scaling. Ideally, we wanted the judges to scale each message independently of the others, but it is often impossible for the judges (or us) to completely disregard the placement of other, similar messages. If the question does come up, deal with it by telling the judge to try to scale the message independently of the others first, then to use its relation to other messages on the scale as a check.

Now play the five messages to be scaled on Dimension 1. The first one shows the subject smiling and saying **"I feel SO GOOD, I DON'T believe it."** We expect this message to fall somewhere left of center. We know what the speaker is talking about, but most judges find the **"I DON'T believe it"**part a bit peculiar — they wanted to know *why* she doesn't believe it. If the judge puts this message on the left endpoint, ask if there is any way the message could be made clearer (for example, if the speaker had simply said **"I feel GREAT!"** This kind of questioning is one way to suggest a correction while still letting the judge find his or her own answer.

The next message shows the speaker saying **"The word RHINITIS means an INFLAMATION of the NOSE,"** etc. The message is basically clear. There are no ambiguities or repetitions, her speech is fairly smooth, and her facial expressions are appropriate. This message illustrates that, even though its subject matter may seem strange when taken out of context, a message can still be clear.

The next message is not so clear. After the speaker says **"I LOVE gardening,"** he rolls his eyes, snorts, and laughs derisively; then he adds **"Getting DIRTY — it's GREAT."** Because we're not sure how he really feels about gardening, the message on the whole is unclear. A word of caution: The judge may say, **"It's CLEAR that he's being SARCASTIC"** and rate the message as clear. If this happens, point out that sarcasm is necessarily an ambivalent way of speaking and that if the speaker in fact hates gardening, it would have been much clearer simply to have said **"I HATE gardening."**

A similar issue arises in the next message, in which the speaker gives us the ten provinces of Canada. It is not clear what is meant by **"the CENTER of the universe — ONTARIO."** (We might suspect a Westerner's sarcasm, but this would be a big inference.) For some reason, she also uses a mocking tone of voice when she lists the maritime provinces, and she lists Newfoundland twice. The message is understandable but certainly not completely clear.

The last message for the judge to rate on Dimension 1 is an example of incongruency between what is actually said and the facial expression and tone of voice with which it is said. The speaker says, **"It was LESS**

SUCCESSFUL than we'd HOPED," with a smile and a cheery voice. Together, these create ambiguity. Also, "**LESS SUCCESSFUL than we'd HOPED**" is in itself a vague and indirect description.

Mark the judge's placements on the tape, gather up the cards, give them back to the judge, and proceed with Dimension 2.

Dimension 2

Okay, let's look at Dimension 2. I'll play the endpoint examples for you first.

After playing the endpoints, continue:

> **As in Dimension 1 there will be messages that will fall somewhere in between these endpoints. For instance, a GROUP opinion may be expressed, but the speaker's agreement or disagreement may be indicated by how it's said — for example, if it's said with conviction, it would mean that the speaker agrees with what he is saying.**
>
> **In some messages, there will appear to be no opinion expressed. However, you will have to decide whether there is any agreement or disagreement with the message. For example, the speaker could say "The earth is ROUND?" (say this for the judge in a questioning voice), and you must decide, by the speaker's tone of voice, facial expression, or whatever, to what extent the message was the speaker's own opinion.**
>
> **As we look at the examples for Dimension 2, you'll see other ways that a speaker's opinion can be expressed or not.**

Play the judge the five messages to be rated on Dimension 2. Message 1 shows the speaker saying "**I HATE that shirt.**" The speaker says it seriously, and because there is no way that anyone else's opinion is being expressed, the message should be placed at or near the left endpoint. (The judge may feel that the speaker could have spoken with more conviction, in which case the message would move slightly to the right.)

Message 2 shows the speaker saying "**One LIKES to THINK so**" in a matter-of-fact sort of tone. "**ONE**" refers to an undefined group, and "liking" to think something is different from actually thinking it. Finally, the absence of conviction in the speaker's tone gives no clue as to her agreement or disagreement with the message. So while she has hinted at an opinion, we do not know what her opinion is, and the message falls somewhere in the middle.

Message 3 shows the speaker saying "**JERRY'S convinced me that REAL ESTATE'S the ONLY thing to BUY.**" The speaker is expressing someone else's opinion, but because of her apparent conviction as well as literal words ("**JERRY'S convinced me**"), it is clear that she agrees with his opinion. Therefore, the message would be placed somewhere to the left of center.

In Message 4, the speaker says "**Ahm . . . EDMONTON is the CAPITAL of CANADA**" as if it were common knowledge. It is clear that she believes what she is saying, wrong as it may be, so the message belongs near the left end of the scale.

Message 5 shows the speaker looking down to her stomach and putting her hand on it, as if it had just "growled." She then makes an embarrassed face and says "**My STOMACH SAYS I'm HUNGRY.**" Judges vary in how they deal with this message. If they consider the subject's stomach to be an inseparable part of her, they scale the message to the left, considering it synonymous with "**I'M hungry.**" If they believe that by saying "**My STOM-ACH SAYS,**" the speaker is treating her stomach as something separate from herself, they put the message nearer the middle. Accept any reason the judge may give as long as the reason and the placement correspond. However, it is a good idea to point out the other interpretation, just to show that two possibilities exist and neither is wrong.

> Now I'll show you the three messages that I'd like you to scale on BOTH Dimensions 1 and 2. I'll play them all through to begin with, then one at a time so you can rate them. Rate all of them first on Dimension 1, then we'll run through them again so you can rate them on Dimension 2.

Play the three messages through, then one at a time, so the judge can rate them on Dimension 1. The first of the three (Message 6) shows the speaker looking confused. With a puzzled frown and a slow nod of the head, she says "**WELL may-MAY-be.**" We have no idea what she's talking about, so the message falls at or near the right-hand endpoint on Dimension 1. In Message 7, the speaker explains his "**FRISBITERIAN**" beliefs, completely seriously. This message illustrates the point that a message can be clear even though it may seem off-the-wall and unlikely to be true. There are no ambiguities, and we know exactly what he's talking about, absurd as it is. The last Message, 8, shows the speaker saying "**NEVER! You'll NEVER GUESS what HAPPENED.**" Starting a sentence with "**NEVER**" pushes the message away from the left endpoint, but in the end we have some idea what the speaker is talking about. Although there isn't much to go on, we expect this one to end up somewhere slightly left of center on Dimension 1.

Then play the same messages, one at a time, for scaling on Dimension 2. We expect Message 6 ("**may-MAY-be**") to fall near the middle because, whatever it is that the speaker is talking about, she appears to have no opinion on it; she seems undecided. In contrast, the speaker of the "**FRISBITERIAN**" message (7) seems earnest and prefaces what he says with "**I BELIEVE.**" It is obvious that this is his own opinion, so it should be rated at or near the left-hand endpoint of Dimension 2. Finally, it seems apparent that the speaker of Message 8 believes that the other person will never guess what happened, so we expect this to fall near the left end of Dimension 2.

Okay, that's the end of this session. You did great. Any questions?

Remember to be encouraging with the judge. Pay him or her for Session II, and arrange a time for the next session. After the judge has left, label the masking tapes, remove them from the desk, and carefully put them aside for measurement. (We usually hang them on walls, which gives our offices an unusual decor.)

SESSION III

Just as Session II focused on Dimensions 1 and 2, Session III focuses on Dimensions 3 and 4 in detail. Prepare the lab as usual, but only the last two strips of tape are needed for this session. Remember to mark the place on the tape where it meets the edge of the desk on the judge's left as well as the center point.

Today, we will be concentrating on Dimensions 3 and 4. Before we start, do you have any questions about the last session?

Dimension 3

Okay, we'll start with Dimension 3 first.

Give the judge the summary sheet with the rules of thumb on it (Figure 2.3).

So could you read the definition for Dimension 3 please, then we'll look at the endpoint examples.

Play the four endpoint examples for this dimension.

The first two examples were messages that were obviously addressed to the other person. In the first, the speaker looks directly at the other person and even leans towards him. In the second example, the other person's name is Jennifer, and the speaker addresses her by name.

In the last two examples, one speaker does not address the person across from him, and the other speaker talks to her hand.

Notice on the sheet that we've added a rule of thumb to help you scale messages on this dimension. This is that "the key issue here is whether the speaker is addressing the other person POINT-BLANK. If so, then the message goes on the far left. If not, then it goes somewhere to the right — you decide where."

I can give you some examples of aspects of the message that may help you decide where to place it on this dimension. First, the name or title of the person can be used to make a decision. If you know the other person's name is Jennifer, and the speaker calls her "Fred" or "Sir", then he obviously isn't addressing the other person.

Often, however, people don't use a name when they address someone. So another clue is whether the speaker looks at the other person or looks somewhere else. This is often a subtle matter of degree. The other person's head will always be visible on the screen, so you can judge whether the speaker seems to be addressing that person or not.

Another clue you can use is what is being said and how it is said. If the other person is a close friend, you would not expect the speaker to talk very formally or stiffly. So for a message to go on the far left, you must be able to tell, by what the speaker says and how he says it, that the other person in the picture is who we tell you it is (assuming, of course, that the speaker is looking at the other person throughout the message). As with the first two dimensions, you'll develop your own rules, and don't be afraid to make subtle distinctions between messages.

Now we'll scale some messages on this dimension. For all these messages, the other person in the situation is a good friend of the speaker; he is also a fellow (male) student in the same class as the speaker. So to be scaled on the far left, you must be able to tell that the person being addressed is a male, a fellow student, and a friend and classmate of the speaker.

Play all the messages through once, then one at a time for the judge to rate on Dimension 3. In Message 1, the speaker is examining his nails while saying "IT was a FAIR weekend." Then he looks up directly at the other person. Because he looks at the other person for so little of the message, and because what is said and how he says it are appropriate for a conversation with nearly anybody, the message belongs somewhere to the right of center.

The next message (2) shows the speaker asking the other person, "What did YOU write for question number THREE on the MIDTERM?" Although nothing is said to indicate that the person being addressed is male, the words and manner make it likely that the speaker is a friend and a fellow classmate of that person. In addition, the speaker looks directly at the other person, so this one is rated somewhere quite low (to the left) on the scale.

In Message 3, the speaker asks "**Well— WHAT WAS your ANSWER for question number THREE on the midterm?**" and is looking straight at the other person the whole time. Obviously, this message is similar to the previous one, except that the speaker's manner has changed. The phrasing and delivery imply a demand rather than a simple request, suggesting that the speaker may be the instructor rather than a classmate of the other person. For this reason, the message should fall somewhere further to the right than the one before it.

Message 4 is also scaled to the right on this dimension. The speaker suggests, enthusiastically, that they go after class to a big sale at "**Suzy Creamcheese**," a local women's clothing store. This suggests that the other person is a classmate, probably a friend, but almost certainly not male.

In Message 5, the speaker reports the standing of the "**Expos**" baseball team. He is looking at the person in the foreground most of the time. The subject matter is appropriate for a male and a friend and not inappropriate for a classmate. Therefore, the message should be placed somewhere to the left of center.

The last message to be scaled on Dimension 3 in this session (6) shows the speaker looking above her and to the right and saying, loudly, "**WHY does he PESTER me with this?**" Then she looks at the person in the foreground. The message seems addressed to someone else. In fact, both the orientation and the third-person pronoun suggest that the speaker is talking *about* rather than *to* the person across from her. Therefore, this one is scaled far up to the right on this dimension.

Dimension 4

Now we'll go to Dimension 4, which is "to what extent is the message a direct answer to the question asked?" Could you read the definition of Dimension 4 on your sheet again, please, then I'll show you the endpoints for this dimension again. You'll notice that the question in this case is always "HOW are YOU?" (Play the two left-hand endpoints for Dimension 4.) From both of these, we know exactly how the person is. That is, the question "HOW are YOU?" has been answered directly. (Play the two right-hand endpoints for Dimension 4.) From these two messages, we have NO answer to how the person is; that question has not been answered at all. In fact, each answers a DIFFERENT question. Can you think of a question to which each of these would be a good answer? (These would be something like "You DO think it's going to RAIN, don't you?" *and* "What TIME is it?") This will be the most

useful rule-of-thumb for this dimension, as you can see on your sheet: Does the message fit TIGHTLY to the question asked, or does it fit a DIFFERENT question better? So some guidelines for Dimension 4 are, first of all, try to match the answer with the question. If it is a very close fit, then put the message on the left. If there is some slight difference, then it moves to the right.

Another point to consider is that a message may answer the question and then add extra information not directly relevant to the question, so it answers another question in addition. Therefore, it would not go on the far left. If the extra information is first, before the question is answered, the message is even less responsive, so it would go farther to the right. Another way of "not answering directly" may be not picking up the usual rhythm of question and answer in conversation.

A useful guide for discriminating between messages that fall somewhere in the middle is the amount of inference needed. That is, sometimes you can INFER an answer to the question from a message that is overtly saying something else. You may recall from the first session the example "HOW are YOU" answered by "IT'S the END of TERM!" So although the message answers something like "What PART of the ACADEMIC YEAR is it?", we can easily infer "I'm feeling GOOD, because it's the END of TERM." So when you can infer an answer to the question, that message would not go on the far right. But because it doesn't answer the question directly, it doesn't go on the far left either. In other words, you can start developing a continuum – from direct answers here on the left to "sort of" answers just left of center to "not really an answer" just to the right of center to "no answer at all" down here at the far right – based on the kind of things we've talked about. If you can think of any other things that make a message less responsive, you should take those into account too.

Okay, are there any questions?

Now we'll look at six more messages that I'd like you to scale on Dimension 4. I'll run them through once for you, then one at a time so you can rate them. The question asked in all of these is still "HOW are YOU?"

After playing all the messages through, return to Message 1, which shows the speaker replying, without hesitation, "I'm not WELL. I SHOULDN'T 've gone JOGGING in that AWFUL weather." By telling us why she doesn't feel well, she answers another question in addition to "HOW are YOU?" so we expect the message to move a bit to the right. Because the additional information is related to the question, it stays near the left endpoint. Again, accept any good reason and placement that are consistent with each other.

In Message 2, the speaker replies immediately and enthusiastically, "I THINK I'm WINNING!" Although this would be a better answer to a question such as "HOW do you think you're DOING in the COMPETITION?," it is easy to infer from her answer how she is. We expect this to fall somewhere to the left of the center.

Message 3 has the speaker answering, without hesitation, "**How SWEET of you to ASK. I'M FINE!**" Had she simply said, "**I'M FINE**," the message would have gone to the left endpoint, but any additional information moves the message to the right, and because the additional information comes *before* the direct answer, it should go a bit farther right. However, the message as a whole is definitely still directly related to the question, so we expect it to be placed well left of center.

In Message 4, there is not only a pause before replying, the reply is a question itself: "**How are YOU?**" It is difficult to infer any kind of answer from this, so most judges put this message at or near the right endpoint. A few judges said we could infer that the speaker was having a very bad day, on the basis of his expression and tone of voice, so they moved the message down a bit from the far end.

Message 5 shows the speaker nodding and saying "**It's MUCH BETTER TODAY.**" Again, this would be a better reply to another question, such as "**How's that ANKLE you twisted YESTERDAY?**" But because we can infer an answer to "**HOW are YOU?**," the message should not go to the extreme right. It usually ends up somewhere in the middle.

In Message 6, after the question has been asked, the speaker takes off his glasses, examines them, and finally says "**I'm FINE.**" Although the answer itself is an appropriate reply to the question, both the pause and the seemingly unrelated actions with his glasses make the reply indirect. This one is usually placed towards the middle.

Congratulate the judge on finishing this set, pay him or her, and later mark on the tape where the messages were placed, as well as the session number and the judge's initials. These first three sessions have given the judge all the information needed to rate any message he or she may come across. There are no further instructions on the scaling procedure itself, just more practice. We hope that the judge has gotten into the habit of scaling the message, then giving a reason for it, and from now on will be doing most of the talking. As this happens, the experimenter's job gradually changes from being an instructor to being a coach to being just an assistant. While it will remain the experimenter's job to listen carefully to the judge's reasoning, this is principally to ensure that the judge does not confuse the dimensions or forget the criteria for them. *The fact that you do not agree with a judge's rating is not a reason to question it*, as long as his or her reasoning is valid. (If you were the ultimate authority, there would be no reason to train and use judges.) Finally, remember to remain encouraging; the messages will become more difficult both in number and in kind.

SESSION IV

From this session on, the full scaling procedure will be used, that is, all messages will be scaled on all four dimensions. As noted above, this means there are two versions of each message on the tape: the first is the message alone, for scaling on Dimensions 1 to 3; the second includes the preceding question and should not be played until Dimension 4.

> **Okay, in the first three sessions, we covered what the four dimensions are, and you scaled messages on each of them separately. However, from now on we'll be looking at MORE MESSAGES and scaling all of them on ALL FOUR of the dimensions. So we'll run through the messages once, then one at a time so you can rate them on Dimension 1. Why don't you read the rules of thumb for this dimension again and then I'll play you the messages. There are five of them this time.**

(Keep in mind, without mentioning it, that this means 20 different decisions.) After playing all of the messages through for the judge,

> **Okay? Now I'll play them one at a time. Remember, for Dimension 1 you're judging how clear the message is, without worrying about whose opinion it is, or who it's addressed to, or anything like that.**

Go back and play each message for the judge to scale on Dimension 1. In Message 1 ("**I like SHRIMPS, but they DON'T like ME**"), the meaning of "**like**" in the second part is ambiguous. We assume it means that shrimps give him indigestion, but it could mean, literally, that they do not like him (to eat or as a person). Because we have to infer the first meaning, the message cannot be at the far left.

Message 2, "**The capital of CANADA is OTTAWA,**" is basically clear except that the serious manner in which it is said is unusual, given the innocuous content. Therefore we expect it to move slightly to the right but to remain near the left endpoint.

In Message 3, the judge should notice two sources of ambiguity: If, as we expect, the judge does not know what *picaladoes* are (a Mexican pastry stuffed with sweet meat), the message would move to the right. The judge should not simply assume that someone else knows what this word means. Also, there is a slight but unexpected stress on "FAMILY." Because this implies a contrast with those (unspecified) people who do *not* like picaladoes, the message moves to the right. On balance, though, this message is still more clear than unclear, so we expect it to be scaled somewhere left of center.

In the next message, 4, the speaker simply lists the foods that he likes, with virtually no ambiguities. Similarly, the meaning of Message 5 ("**I REALLY like cooking MEXICAN food**") is very clear, and it should be scaled at or near the left-hand endpoint.

When all of the messages have been scaled on Dimension 1, mark the placements with the message number on the masking tape, then collect the cards and proceed with Dimension 2. The placement of "**SHRIMPS**" (Message 1) on this dimension depends on the judge's interpretation of it. The main possibility is that is the speaker's opinion both that he likes shrimp and that they give him indigestion, in which case the message would fall at or near the left endpoint. The other, literal possibility is that he is expressing his own opinion when he tells us that he likes shrimp but someone else's (namely, the shrimps') when he says "**but they DON'T like ME.**" In this case, the message would fall somewhere in the middle. Remember, one interpretation is not more correct than the other; what is important is that the judge has a plausible reason for his or her decision.

Message 2 probably goes near the middle because, although the speaker lacks conviction, he might agree that "**The capital of CANADA is OTTAWA.**" That is, nothing indicates that he is definitely *not* expressing his own opinion.

Message 3 could go one of two ways. If the judge feels that the speaker is including herself in her family when she says "**My FAMILY loves picaladoes,**" then the message would go to the left of center on this dimension — but not at the end, as it would have been more clearly the speaker's opinion if she had said "**I love picaladoes.**" The second possibility is that the judge hears the emphasis as meaning that the speaker is contrasting her family with someone else, possibly herself. In that case, she has only given someone else's opinion, and we have no direct idea how she herself feels about picaladoes, so the message would fall at the right endpoint.

We expect to find Message 4 placed at or near the left-hand endpoint of this dimension. The speaker refers to himself directly ("**I like**") and nods as he lists his favorite foods. What he says is obviously his own opinion.

We can tell from the words in Message 5 ("**I REALLY like**") that this is the speaker's opinion, so it should be rated well to the left on Dimension 2. The only aspect that might move this message to the right is the speaker's lack of enthusiasm in both tone of voice and facial expression. Leave it to the judge to decide whether these are important factors.

Once again, mark the judge's placements on the tape and collect the cards. Before scaling on Dimension 3, tell the judge:

> **The situation for this session is: the speaker is a good friend of the other person, who has just invited him (or her) to dinner.**

We expect to find Message 1 ("**SHRIMPS**") scaled far to the left-hand end of Dimension 3. The speaker looks directly at the other person, and the subject matter of the conversation is appropriate for the situation. On the other hand, Message 2 ("**OTTAWA**") should end up at the opposite end of the scale. The speaker does not look at the other person at all, and what he says is not at all appropriate for the situation or his relationship with the other person (a good friend who has just asked him to dinner). We expect to find Message 3 ("**picaladoes**") scaled somewhere to the left of center on this dimension because the speaker looks directly at the other person as she is speaking, and because the subject matter (food) is appropriate for the situation. However, the message is not completely appropriate because the receiver is inviting the speaker, not her family, to dinner. The content of Message 4 (listing foods he likes) is appropriate for the situation and the receiver, but the speaker looks at his hands through the whole message and never once looks at the other person. These two factors work against each other, and the message usually ends up somewhere in the middle. The last message ("**cooking**") should be scaled to the left of center on this dimension because, although the speaker looks directly at the other person throughout the message, what he says is not completely appropriate for the situation: A person who is invited to dinner would be expected to comment on what he likes to eat rather than what he likes to cook.

For Dimension 4, tell the judge:

> **For this dimension the situation and speaker remain the same, but you will hear the question, which is: "What kind of FOOD do you LIKE?"**

Remember to switch to the question-plus-message segments for this dimension.

Message 1 would be a perfect answer to the question *if* the speaker had stopped after he said "**I like SHRIMPS.**" By adding "**but they DON'T like ME,**" he is adding information that is not directly related to the question, which moves the message to the right on the scale—let the judge decide how far.

The next message (2) belongs at the extreme right-hand side of this dimension. No answer whatsoever to "**What kind of FOOD do you LIKE?**" can be inferred from his naming the capital city of Canada.

The placement of Message 3 depends on how the judge interprets the phrase "**my FAMILY.**" If he or she assumes that the speaker is including herself with her family, then we can infer that she also likes picaladoes, and the message belongs somewhere to the left of center. It would still not go at the end, because it would have been more direct to answer "**I like pic-aladoes.**" If the judge assumes that the speaker is excluding herself from her family, then we have no idea what kind of food she likes and no answer to the question asked. Therefore the message would move to the right of center, but not to the endpoint, because the message is at least related to the question (unlike "**The capital of CANADA**" reply).

On the other hand, Message 4 is a very direct answer to the question. No irrelevant information is given, and the reply fits the question perfectly. The only thing that detracts from the directness is the pause between the question and the reply, but we still expect to find this placed well to the left of center on Dimension 4.

In Message 5, the speaker is answering an altogether different question than the one asked when he tells us he likes *cooking* Mexican food. Still, his reply is tangentially related to the question. We can infer that if he likes cooking Mexican food, he probably likes eating it as well, but because this is quite a large inference, the message moves to the right. Again, let the judge decide how far.

This is the end of the fourth session. Reemphasize for the judge the independence of the dimensions by taking a message such as "**I REALLY like cooking MEXICAN food**" and pointing out its different placements on the four dimensions.

By this time the judge should be getting comfortable with the scaling procedure. Point this out and congratulate the judge on his or her performance. Later, mark and collect the tapes for scoring.

SESSIONS V AND VI

As indicated earlier, how you adapt and use these "phasing in" sessions depends on your particular scaling needs. You will probably wish to call the judges' attention to the new aspects of messages you are introducing. In any case, be sure to write out the information to be given to the judges, for example, before Dimensions 3 and 4. Have a transcript of the messages if they are difficult to hear, and always have a summary scaling sheet available for the judge to refer to.

Here are the instructions we used:

> This session will be the same as the last one in that the scaling procedure is the same; but the other person and the situation are different, and we have eight messages for you this time instead of five. Also, you might find that some of the messages are hard to hear, but that is because the speaker said them indistinctly or in a low voice. You should take this into account when scaling them, though, because if I were to mumble something, it would affect the clarity of what I'd said. These messages will be more like "real-life" messages than the ones you've seen so far, but you're getting pretty good at scaling now, and you seem comfortable with the procedure, so you should have no problems. However, if you do have problems with any of these, or if you have any questions about scaling in general, be sure to tell me so we can discuss it. Okay? Good. Here's the summary sheet for you to refer to if you need it. As before, I'll play the messages through for you, then one at a time for you to scale.

You're on your own, supervising the judges for these messages, as we cannot know what they will be. While helping the judges attend to new details, be sure not to tell them what to do. The judges are fully informed about the dimensions now, and they only need practice, not instruction. Let each develop his or her own standards for these more complex messages, based on what has been learned in previous sessions.

SESSION VII

The last training session is for assessing reliability and uses scripted messages one last time, in order to ensure a standard set with full variance on each dimension. These are messages that test the judge's ability to apply the guidelines learned in previous sessions — good reliability indicates that a group of judges knows the system and is "ready to go." From now on, reliability should be assessed for each scaling session. If your experimental messages are trickier than these, then you will want to know how well the judges do with them. Keep in mind, though, that reliability coefficients are greatly affected by variance. The first place to check if the intraclass R's are low is the standard deviation for the messages on that dimension.

Obviously, the judge is on his or her own for this session. While each judge should continue the habit of explaining aloud the reasons for each placement, the experimenter should be very careful not to direct the decisions in any way. We told judges they would have 11 enacted messages and that this was a reliability session, so the experimenter would not be "interfering" as much, but the judge should continue to explain his or her reasons for placements. Only if the judge makes an obvious error (e.g., mishearing a message) should the experimenter interfere. This session was much like future sessions in our research, because of the number of messages and the time it took. (Because this is the first time the judge will have this many messages, the session can be a long one. If necessary, take a break after the first two dimensions.)

In previous sessions, the speaker's role or identity was not relevant to scaling the messages on Dimension 2; the speaker could be any ordinary person. Here, because of the situation and the messages, the speaker's occupation may be relevant. The following background should be given before the judge scales on Dimension 2:

The speaker in this session is a librarian.

(Another instance in which information about the speaker was relevant to Dimension 2 was Experiment 19 in Chapter 9, where the speakers were delegates at a political convention talking to an interviewer.)

For Dimension 3, the receiver should be identified:

The other person in the situation is Mr. McDonald, a patron of the library.

Finally, before beginning on Dimension 4, the judge will need to know that:

This takes place in the reading room of a library. Mr. McDonald turns to the librarian and asks "Do you have any books on cats?" So you will be rating how good an answer the message is to "Do you have any books on cats?"

Real Messages (from Experiments)

From now on, your procedures depend on your particular use of this method. If it is like ours, you will edit about 12 or 14 messages into a tape in random order, with no indication of experimental condition. (If you have more, you can divide them into two sessions, as we did with Experiment 15.) They should be played through two or three times at first to familiarize the judge with so many messages. It is helpful to the experimenter to have a transcript of the words of each message, in case the judge has difficulty making it out. Write out the information to be given the juges before Dimensions 3 and 4 (and 2, if appropriate). Have a copy of the summary scaling sheet available so that the judge can refer to it easily.

By now, the judges know the routine well, and the relationship with the experimenter is quite informal. The main problems the experimenter will have are quirky criteria occasionally creeping in, for example:

Dimension 1: putting all messages with pronouns to the right, instead of considering the whole message;

Dimension 2: focusing on the degree to which an opinion is present, rather than what the speaker's opinion is;

Dimension 3: attending only to eye contact and no other clues;

Dimension 4: being unduly influenced by the clarity of the message on Dimension 1.

Or, a judge may say that there are big differences among a set of messages but not spread them out on the scale. All of these can be handled by discussion or gentle reminders. We usually had more than one experimenter working at a time, and they met early in the scaling of a new set of messages to discuss problems that came up and solutions they had found.

What about experimenter bias? We're not impressed with the reputed ubiquity of the problem. First, it is difficult for the experimenter to have the necessary information to be able to influence the judge: He or she would have to memorize the messages by number and experimental condition and also be able to ipsatize raw scores mentally, on the spot. Moreover, this would have to be done consistently across judges so that the averaged scores would be affected and the reliability would be high. Second, our judges have been firm and independent people, quite prepared to be mavericks and to ignore the experimenter. If the training is successful, yours will be too, and you will learn a great deal about the particulars of communication from them.

IPSATIZING AND CALCULATING RELIABILITIES

The masking tapes for each session are measured with a metric tape measure, yielding centimeter placements by each judge for each message on each dimension — the raw scores. As explained in Chapter 2, ipsatizing is a very simple procedure: Take one of the tapes; it has the cm values for all of the messages that one judge scaled on one of the dimensions in one session.

Calculate the mean and standard deviation of this set of raw scores, and then transform each of them, X, into a standard score:

$$\frac{X - M}{S}$$

It is easy to write a routine for a programmable calculator or a microcomputer to do this transformation and store the results for further manipulation.

We always do these calculations twice, by two entirely different procedures. The properties of standard scores also provide a good check, because a judge's ipsatized message values for each dimension should add to zero, within rounding errors.

The average of these ipsatized values (across judges, on one dimension) is the final value of that message on that dimension (see Figure 2.4). So you start out with a matrix of raw scores for N judges by M messages by 4 dimensions and end up with one averaged ipsatized value for each of the M messages on each of 4 dimensions. These can be further summarized by adding the ipsatized scores for a message across the dimensions, yielding a single (Sum) score for each of M messages.

Remember that, with good reliability, these averaged ipsatized scores will remain standard scores with a mean of 0 and a standard deviation of 1. (For the Sum, the mean remains 0, and the standard deviation is 4.) Any division of a set of standard scores into equal halves will produce two means that add to 0, so if you have two experimental conditions with equal n, the two means will "reflect" each other (e.g., 1.23 and −1.23) within rounding errors. This is not true for unequal n's or more than two experimental conditions.

The formula we use for the intraclass reliability coefficient (R) is taken from Winer (1962, pp. 124-128). Essentially, this is

$$R = 1 - \frac{\text{mean squares due to judges}}{\text{mean squares due to messages}}$$

As this formula shows, a high R comes from low variance among judges compared to high variance among messages. That is, we expect the judges to agree and the messages to differ.

In the above formula, the mean squares due to judges is the sum of squares due to judges divided by its degrees of freedom, which is the number of messages times one less than the number of judges. The mean squares due to messages is the sum of squares due to messages divided by one less than the number of messages.

You can get the required sums of squares from any analysis of variance program and then enter them in the final formula. The trick is to find out what they are calling the figures you want. For example, Winer is describing reliability in the measurement of people, whereas we are measuring messages. So where his formulas refer to between or within *people*, you should read between or within *messages*. In other programs, we have found that the sum of squares due to judges may be called "error" sum of squares and the sum of squares due to messages may be called the "treatment" sum of squares.

As Ebel (1951) made clear, R is not the average of bivariate r's (Pearson product-moment correlations) *between* judges, which would be appropriate only if you used judges as individuals. Rather, it assumes you will always use the judges as a group, as we did. Should you train a second set of judges later, you can check their agreement with the first set by correlating the averaged ipsatized scores from the two reliability sessions, using bivariate r.

Finally, a well known way to increase reliability is to increase the number of items, which in this case means the number of judges. Before going to the trouble of training more judges, you can get a statistical estimate of how much effect more judges would have. Alternatively, you may want to know how much having fewer judges would hurt you. In either case, the formula (adapted from Nunnally, 1970, p. 557) is

$$r' = \frac{kr}{1 + (k - 1)r}$$

where r is the reliability you actually obtained with the present number of judges and k is the factor by which you wish to increase or decrease the number of judges. So if you are thinking of doubling the number of judges, $k = 2$. If you are thinking of cutting the number in half, $k = .5$.

Appendix B

Statistical Data

SUMMARY CORRELATIONS FOR EACH FORMAT

Experiment 6: Class Presentation (written; N = 20)

CORRELATIONS BETWEEN DIMENSIONS AND NUMBER OF WORDS

	Content	Sender	Receiver	Context	Sum
Content					
Sender	$.67^*$				
Receiver	$.81^*$	$.51^*$			
Context	$-.11$	$-.18^*$	$-.09$		
No. of Words	$-.68^*$	$-.38^*$	$-.87^*$	$.18$	$-.66^*$

Experiment 7: Member of Parliament (written; N = 14)

CORRELATIONS BETWEEN DIMENSIONS AND NUMBER OF WORDS

	Content	Sender	Receiver	Context	Sum
Content					
Sender	$.54^*$				
Receiver	$.44$	$.12$			
Context	$.40$	$.27$	$-.01$		
No. of Words	$-.29$	$-.08$	$-.35$	$.11$	$-.20$

AUTHORS' NOTE: * indicates $p < .05$. For correlations, this is a two-tailed test; for the *t*-tests on latencies, this is a one-tailed test. The N = the number of messages; the messages of subjects in back-to-back experiments are assumed to be independent.

Experiment 8: Bizarre Gift (written; N = 18)

CORRELATIONS BETWEEN DIMENSIONS AND NUMBER OF WORDS

	Content	Sender	Receiver	Context	Sum
Content					
Sender	.29				
Receiver	.34	.43*			
Context	.20*	.44*	.09*		
No. of Words	-.46*	-.06	-.45*	.15	-.26

Experiment 9: Car Ad (written; N = 18)

CORRELATIONS BETWEEN DIMENSIONS AND NUMBER OF WORDS

	Content	Sender	Receiver	Context	Sum
Content					
Sender	-.07*				
Receiver	.42*	-.03			
Context	.60*	.17*	.33		
No. of Words	-.01	-.53*	.18	-.35	-.26

Experiment 10: Class Presentation (spoken; N = 12)

CORRELATIONS BETWEEN DIMENSIONS AND NUMBER OF WORDS

	Content	Sender	Receiver	Context	Sum
Content					
Sender	.74*				
Receiver	.35*	.31*			
Context	.67*	.74*	-.11		
No. of Words	.01	.43	-.14	.60*	.30

LATENCIES TO FIRST UTTERANCE AND FIRST WORD

	Utterance	Word
Nonconflict mean =	0.8	1.4
Conflict mean =	1.1	1.9
t =	1.48	2.38*

Experiment 14A: Car for Sale (face-to-face; N = 12)

CORRELATIONS BETWEEN DIMENSIONS AND NUMBER OF WORDS

	Content	Sender	Receiver	Context	Sum
Content					
Sender	.34				
Receiver	.12*	.62*			
Context	.54*	.75*	-.71*		
No. of Words	.26	.62*	-.75*	.84*	.44

LATENCIES TO FIRST UTTERANCE AND FIRST WORD

	Utterance	Word
Nonconflict mean =	0.5	0.6
Conflict mean =	0.8	1.0
t =	1.80	1.55

Experiment 14B: Class Presentation (face-to-face; N = 12)

CORRELATIONS BETWEEN DIMENSIONS AND NUMBER OF WORDS

	Content	Sender	Receiver	Context	Sum
Content					
Sender	.65*				
Receiver	.63*	.67*			
Context	.55*	.86*	.86*		
No. of Words	-.19	-.09	.41	.20	.09

LATENCIES TO FIRST UTTERANCE AND FIRST WORD

	Utterance	Word
Nonconflict mean =	0.6	0.6
Conflict mean =	1.8	2.4
t =	2.71*	3.34*

Experiment 15: The Local Musical (face-to-face; N = 18)

CORRELATIONS BETWEEN DIMENSIONS AND NUMBER OF WORDS

	Content	Sender	Receiver	Context	Sum
Content					
Sender	.64*				
Receiver	.19*	-.44*			
Context	.93*	.56*	.21		
No. of Words	.31	-.18	.02	.50*	.28

LATENCIES TO FIRST UTTERANCE AND FIRST WORD

	Utterance	Word
Nonconflict-true mean =	0.6	0.6
Conflict mean =	1.8	2.4
Nonconflict-false mean =	1.0	1.7

	Utterance	Word
$F_{(2, 15)}$ =	8.54*	10.90*
t: NC-T vs. C =	3.35[a]	3.56[a]
t: NC-T vs. NC-F =	2.22[a]	2.92[a]
t: C vs. NC-F =	1.66	1.46

[a] $p < .05$ one-tailed, adjusted for alpha inflation

Experiment 18A: Hairdo (spoken; N = 12 children)

CORRELATIONS BETWEEN DIMENSIONS AND NUMBER OF WORDS

	Content	Sender	Receiver	Context	Sum
Content					
Sender	.90*				
Receiver	.80*	.78*			
Context	.76*	.56*	.68*		
No. of words	.03	-.05	.14	.20	.11

LATENCIES TO FIRST UTTERANCE AND FIRST WORD

	Utterance	Word
Nonconflict mean =	1.1	1.1
Conflict mean =	2.2	2.2
t =	2.13*	2.13*

Experiment 18B: Gift (spoken; N = 12 children)

CORRELATIONS BETWEEN DIMENSIONS AND NUMBER OF WORDS

	Content	Sender	Receiver	Context	Sum
Content					
Sender	.78*				
Receiver	.78*	.75*			
Context	.50*	.79*	.57*		
No. of Words	-.49	-.53*	-.37	-.01	-.39

LATENCIES TO FIRST UTTERANCE AND FIRST WORD

	Utterance	Word
Nonconflict mean =	0.9	0.9
Conflict mean =	1.0	1.0
t =	0.74	0.74

Experiment 19: Liberal Leadership Convention (spoken; N = 12)

CORRELATIONS BETWEEN DIMENSIONS AND NUMBER OF WORDS

	Content	Sender	Receiver	Context	Sum
Content					
Sender	.46				
Receiver	.24	.46			
Context	.19	.07	-.45		
No. of Words	.34	.07	-.32	.94*	.53*

LATENCIES TO FIRST UTTERANCE AND FIRST WORD

	Utterance	Word
Nonconflict mean =	0.7	0.8
Conflict mean =	1.2	1.7
t =	2.36*	2.00*

Summary Correlations for Each Format

WRITTEN MESSAGES:
CORRELATIONS BETWEEN DIMENSIONS AND NUMBER OF WORDS (N = 70)

	Content	Sender	Receiver	Context	Sum
Content					
Sender	.40*				
Receiver	.52*	.29*			
Context	.27*	.07*	.10*		
No. of Words	.33*	−.25*	−.36*	.03	−.30*

SPOKEN MESSAGES:
CORRELATIONS BETWEEN DIMENSIONS AND NUMBER OF WORDS (N = 96)[a]

	Content	Sender	Receiver	Context	Sum
Content					
Sender	.47*				
Receiver	.64*	.32*			
Context	.58*	.52*	.18*		
No. of Words	.03	.11	−.19*	.39*	.12

[a] The messages of participants in back-to-back experiments are assumed to be independent.

FACE-TO-FACE MESSAGES:
CORRELATIONS BETWEEN DIMENSIONS AND NUMBER OF WORDS (N = 42)[a]

	Content	Sender	Receiver	Context	Sum
Content					
Sender	.48*				
Receiver	.21*	.12*			
Context	.71*	.61*	.20		
No. of Words	.19	.06	−.13	.41*	.25

[a] The messages of participants in back-to-back experiments are assumed to be independent.

Experiment 11A: Bizarre Gift (spoken; N = 12)

CORRELATIONS BETWEEN DIMENSIONS AND NUMBER OF WORDS

	Content	Sender	Receiver	Context	Sum
Content					
Sender	.62*				
Receiver	.90*	.61*			
Context	.52*	.90*	.56*		
No. of Words	-.61*	-.04	-.52*	.24	-.25

LATENCIES TO FIRST UTTERANCE AND FIRST WORD

	Utterance	Word
Nonconflict mean =	0.4	0.5
Conflict mean =	0.8	1.3
t =	1.32	3.43*

Experiment 11B: Meat Market (spoken; N = 12)

CORRELATIONS BETWEEN DIMENSIONS AND NUMBER OF WORDS

	Content	Sender	Receiver	Context	Sum
Content					
Sender	.30*				
Receiver	.62*	-.28*			
Context	.75*	.69*	.28		
No. of Words	.04	.22	-.28	.32	.11

LATENCIES TO FIRST UTTERANCE AND FIRST WORD

	Utterance	Word
Nonconflict mean =	0.8	1.0
Conflict mean =	0.9	2.1
t =	0.26	1.43

Experiment 12:   Employee Reference (spoken; N =12)

CORRELATIONS BETWEEN DIMENSIONS AND NUMBER OF WORDS

	Content	Sender	Receiver	Context	Sum
Content					
Sender	.21				
Receiver	.78*	.14			
Context	.59*	.19	.12		
No. of Words	-.26	.48	-.39	.17	.00

LATENCIES TO FIRST UTTERANCE AND FIRST WORD

	Utterance	Word
Nonconflict mean =	0.8	1.4
Conflict mean =	0.9	2.0
t =	0.28	1.60

Experiment 13:   Car for Sale (spoken; N = 12)

CORRELATIONS BETWEEN DIMENSIONS AND NUMBER OF WORDS

	Content	Sender	Receiver	Context	Sum
Content					
Sender	-.36				
Receiver	.55*	-.53*			
Context	.59*	.22	-.12		
No. of Words	.26	.01	-.49	.49	.19

LATENCIES TO FIRST UTTERANCE AND FIRST WORD

	Utterance	Word
Nonconflict mean =	0.6	0.7
Conflict mean =	1.0	1.7
t =	1.71	4.88*

References

Ackerman, B. P. (1982). Contextual information and utterance interpretation: The ability of children and adults to interpret utterances. *Child Development, 53,* 1075-1083.

Austen, J. (1982). *Sense and sensibility.* (2nd ed.). Oxford: Oxford University Press. (Originally published 1811.)

Austin, J. L. (1969). *On pretending.* In *Philosophical Papers.* Oxford: Oxford University Press.

Barker, R. G. (1942). An experimental study of the resolution of conflict by children: Time elapsing and amount of vicarious trial-and-error behavior occurring. In Q. MacNemar & M. A. Merrill (Eds.), *Studies in personality.* New York: McGraw-Hill.

Bates, E. (1976). *Language and context: The acquisition of pragmatics.* New York: Academic Press.

Bateson, G., Jackson, D. D., Haley, J., & Weakland, J. (1956). Toward a theory of schizophrenia. *Behavioral Science, 1,* 251-264.

Bavelas, J. B. (1978). *Personality: Current theory and research.* Monterey, CA: Brooks/Cole.

Bavelas, J. B. (1983). Situations that lead to disqualification. *Human Communication Research, 9,* 130-145.

Bavelas, J. B. (1984). On "naturalistic" family research. *Family Process, 23,* 337-341.

Bavelas, J. B., & Chovil, N. (1986). How people disqualify: Experimental studies of spontaneous written disqualification. *Communication Monographs, 53,* 70-74.

Bavelas, J. B., & Smith, B. J. (1982). A method for scaling verbal disqualification. *Human Communication Research, 8,* 214-227.

Bavelas, J. B., Black, A., Bryson, L., & Mullett, J. (1988). Political equivocation: A situational explanation. *Journal of Language and Social Psychology, 7,* 137-145.

Bavelas, J. B., Black, A., Chovil, N., & Mullett, J. (in press). Truths, lies, and equivocations: The effects of conflicting goals on discourse. *Journal of Language and Social Psychology.*

Beavin, J. (1970). *Interpersonal judgment and performance control.* Unpublished doctoral dissertation, Stanford University.

Black, A. (1988). The syntax of conversational coherence. *Discourse Processes, 11,* 433-455.

Boorstein, D. J. (1985). *The image: A guide to pseudo-events in America.* New York: Antheneum. (Originally published 1961.)

Bowers, J. W., Elliott, N. D., & Desmond, R. J. (1977). Exploiting pragmatic rules: Devious messages. *Human Communication Research, 3,* 235-242.

Brown, P., & Levinson, S. (1978). Universals in language usage. In E. N. Goody (Ed.), *Questions and politeness: Strategies in social interaction.* Cambridge: Cambridge University Press.

Bugenthal, D., Kaswan, J., & Love, L. (1970). Perception of contradictory meanings conveyed by verbal and nonverbal channels. *Journal of Personality and Social Psychology, 16,* 647-655.

Carrell, P. (1981). Children's understanding of indirect requests: Comparing child and adult comprehension. *Journal of Child Language, 8,* 329-345.

Chovil, N. (1989). *Communicative functions of facial displays in conversation.* Unpublished doctoral dissertation, University of Victoria.

Clark, H. H., & Lucy, P. (1975). Understanding what is meant by what is said: A study in conversationally conveyed requests. *Journal of Verbal Learning and Verbal Behavior, 14,* 56-72.

Coulthard, M. (1977). *An introduction to discourse analysis.* London: Longham Group.

Cunningham, M. A., & Wilcox, J. R. (1984). When an M.D. gives an R.N. a harmful order: Modifying a bind. In R. N. Bostrom & B. H. Westley (Eds.), *Communication yearbook, Vol. 8.* Beverly Hills: Sage.

Depaulo, B. M., & Rosenthal, R. (1979). Telling lies. *Journal of Personality and Social Psychology, 37,* 1713-1722.

Ebel, R. L. (1951). Estimation of the reliability of ratings. *Psychometrika, 16,* 407-424.

Eisenberg, E. M. (1984). Ambiguity as strategy in organizational communication. *Communication Monographs, 51,* 227-242.

Ekman, P. (1985). *Telling lies,* New York: Berkley Books.

Ekman, P., & Friesen, W. V. (1969). Nonverbal leakage and clues to deception. *Psychiatry, 32,* 88-106.

Ekman, P., & Friesen, W. V. (1974). Detecting deception from the body and face. *Journal of Personality and Social Psychology, 29,* 288-298.

Freud, S. (1959). Fragment of an analysis of a case of hysteria. *Collected papers, Vol. 3.* New York: Basic Books. (Originally published 1905.)

Goss, B., & Williams, M. L. (1973). The effects of equivocation on perceived source credibility. *Central States Speech Journal, 24,* 162-167.

Graber, D. A. (1976). *Verbal behavior and politics.* Urbana: University of Illinois Press.

Greatbatch, D. (1988). A turn-taking system for British news interviews. *Language and Society, 17,* 401-430.

Green, M. G. (1979). The developmental relation between cognitive stage and comprehension of speaker uncertainty. *Child Development, 50,* 666-674.

Grice, H. P. (1975). Logic and conversations. In P. Cole & J. L. Morgan (Eds.), *Syntax and semantics, Vol. 3.* New York: Academic Press.

Haley, J. (1958). An interactional explanation of hypnosis. *American Journal of Clinical Hypnosis, 1,* 41-57.

Haley, J. (1959a). An interactional description of schizophrenia. *Psychiatry, 22,* 321-332.

Haley, J. (1959b). The family of the schizophrenic: A model system. *Journal of Nervous and Mental Diseases, 129,* 357-374.

Haley, J. (1961). Control in brief psychotherapy. *Archives of General Psychiatry, 4,* 139-153.

Heritage, J. (1985). Analyzing news interviews: Aspects of talk for an overhearing audience. In T. A. van Dijk (Ed.), *Handbook of discourse analysis.* New York: Academic Press.

Heritage, J. C., Clayman, S., & Zimmerman, D. H. (1988). Discourse and media analysis: The micro-structure of mass media messages. In R. P. Hawkins, J. M. Wiemann, & S. Pingree (Eds.), *Advancing communication science: Merging mass and interpersonal processes.* Newbury Park: Sage.

Hirsh-Pasek, K., Gleitman, L. R., & Gleitman, H. (1978). What did the brain say to the mind? A study of detection and report of ambiguity by young children. In A. Sinclair, R. J. Jarvella, & W.J.M. Levelt (Eds.), *The child's conception of language.* Berlin: Springer-Verlag.

Hopper, R., & Bell, R. A. (1984). Broadening the deception construct. *Quarterly Journal of Speech, 70,* 288-302.

Hyman, R. (1989). The psychology of deception. In M. R. Rosenzweig & L. W. Porter (Eds.), *Annual Review of Psychology, 40,* 133-154.

Jackson, D. D. (1959). Family interaction, family homeostasis and some implications for conjoint family psychotherapy. In J. H. Masserman (Ed.), *Individual and familial dynamics* (pp. 122-141). New York: Grune & Stratton.

Jackson, D. D. (1961a). Family therapy in the family of the schizophrenic. In M. I. Stein (Ed.), *Contemporary psychotherapies* (pp. 272-287). New York: Glencoe.

Jackson, D. D. (1961b). Interactional psychotherapy. In M. I. Stein (Ed.), *Contemporary psychotherapies* (pp. 256-271). New York: Glencoe.

Jackson, D. D. (1962). Psychoanalytic education and the communication processes. In J. Masserman (Ed.), *Science and psychoanalysis*. New York: Grune & Stratton.

Jackson, D. D. (Ed.). (1968). *Human Communication, Volumes 1 & 2.* Palo Alto, CA: Science and Behavior Books.

Jackson, D. D., & Watzlawick, P. (1963). The acute psychosis as a manifestation of growth experience. *American Psychological Association of Research Reports, 16*, 83-94.

Jackson, D. D., & Weakland, J. (1961). Conjoint family therapy: Some considerations on theory, technique, and results. *Psychiatry, 24* (Suppl. to No. 2), 30-45.

Jackson, D. D., Riskin, J. V., & Satir, V. M. (1961). A method of analysis of a family interview. *Archives of General Psychiatry, 5*, 321-339.

Keith, W. M. (1984). *Varieties of deception.* Paper presented at annual meeting of Speech Communication Association, Chicago.

Kess, J. F., & Hoppe, R. A. (1981). *Ambiguity in psycholinguistics.* Amsterdam: John Benjamins.

Knapp, M. L., & Comadena, M. E. (1979). Telling it like it isn't: A review of theory and research on deceptive communications. *Human Communication Research, 5*, 270-285.

Kraut, R. E. (1978). Verbal and nonverbal cues in the perception of lying. *Journal of Personality and Social Psychology, 36*, 380-391.

Lee, E. S. (1977). *A test of two minimax models for predicting the scaling of partitions of stimulus sets.* Unpublished doctoral dissertation, University of Victoria.

Levine, M. V. (1974). Geometric interpretations of some psychophysical results. In D. H. Krantz, R. C. Atkinson, R. D. Luce, & P. Suppes (Eds.), *Contemporary developments in mathematical psychology, Vol. 2. Measurement, psychophysics, and neural information processing* (pp. 203-208). San Francisco: W. H. Freeman.

Lewin, K. (1938). The conceptual representation and measurement of psychological forces. *Contributions to Psychological Theory, 1* (4, Serial No. 4).

MacGregor, J. N. (1975). *Two tests of a coded-element model of perceptual processing.* Unpublished master's thesis, University of Victoria.

McNeill, D. (1985). So you think gestures are nonverbal? *Psychological Review, 92*, 350-371.

Mehrabian, A., & Ferris, S. R. (1967). Inference of attitudes from nonverbal communication. *Journal of Consulting Psychology, 31*, 248-252.

Miller, G. R., & Burgoon, J. K. (1981). Factors affecting assessments of witness credibility. In N. L. Kerr & R. M. Bray (Eds.), *The psychology of the courtroom.* New York: Academic Press.

Miller, G. R. (1983). Telling it like it isn't and not telling it like it is: Some thoughts on deceptive communication. In J. Sisco (Ed.), *The Jensen lectures: Contemporary communication studies* (pp. 91-116). Tampa: University of South Florida Press.

Nofsinger, R. E., Jr. (1974). *Conversational interaction in informal settings: Answering questions indirectly.* Paper presented at the convention of the Speech Communication Association, Chicago.

Nofsinger, R. E., Jr. (1976). On answering questions indirectly: Some rules in the grammar of doing conversation. *Human Communication Research, 2*, 172-181.

Nunnally, J. C., Jr. (1970). *Introduction to psychological measurement.* New York: McGraw-Hill.

Pascale, R. T., & Athos, A. G. (1981). *The art of Japanese management.* New York: Simon & Schuster.

Randolph, T. (1968). An apology for his false prediction that his Aunt Lane would be delivered of a son. In W. C. Hazlitt (Ed.), *Poetical and dramatic works of Thomas Randolph (Vol. II)*. New York: Benjamin Blom. (Originally published 1875.)

Robinson, E. J., & Robinson, W. P. (1978a). The roles of egocentrism and of weakness in comparing children's explanations of communication failure. *Journal of Experimental Child Psychology, 26*, 147-160.

Robinson, E. J., & Robinson, W. P. (1978b). The relationship between children's explanations of communication failure and their ability to deliberately give bad messages. *British Journal of Social and Clinical Psychology, 11*, 189-208.

Robinson, E. J., & Robinson, W. P. (1981). Ways of reacting to communication failure in relation to the development of the child's understanding about verbal communication. *European Journal of Social Psychology, 11*, 189-208.

Robinson, E. J., & Robinson, W. P. (1983). Communication and metacommunication: Quality of children's instructions in relation to judgments about the adequacy of instructions and the locus of responsibility for communication failure. *Journal of Experimental Child Psychology, 36*, 306-320.

Schaefer, B. A. (1979). *A quantification of symmetry and stability in goodness of form perception*. Unpublished master's thesis, University of Victoria.

Schegloff, E. A., & Sacks, H. (1973). Opening up closings. *Semiotica, 8*, 289-327.

Searle, J. R. (1975). Indirect speech acts. In P. Cole & J. L. Morgan (Eds.), *Syntax and semantics, 3*. New York: Academic Press.

Shorter Oxford English Dictionary, The (3rd ed.). (1970). Oxford: Clarendon Press.

Sluzki, C. E., Beavin, J., Tarnopolsky, A., & Verón, E. (1967). Transactional disqualification: Research on the double bind. *Archives of General Psychiatry, 16*, 494-504.

Smith, B. J. (1979). *Perception of organization in an isotropic stimulus*. Unpublished master's thesis, University of Victoria.

Spero, R. (1980). *The duping of the American voter: Dishonesty and deception in presidential television advertising*. New York: Lippincott & Crowell.

Spradley, J. P. (1982). *Participant observation*. New York: Holt, Rinehart, & Winston.

Stevens, S. S. (1966). On the operation known as judgment. *American Scientist, 54*, 385-401.

Stein, L. I. (1967). The doctor-nurse game. *Archives of General Psychiatry, 16*, 699-703.

Stohl, C., & Redding, W. C. (1987). Messages and message exchange processes. In F. M. Jablin, L. L. Putnam, K. H. Roberts, & L. W. Porter (Eds.), *Handbook of organizational communication*. Newbury Park: Sage.

Tager-Flusberg, H. (1989). Putting words together: Morphology and syntax in the preschool years. In J. B. Gleason (Ed.), *The development of language (2nd ed.)*. Columbus, Ohio: Merrill.

Tupper, M. F. (1854). Of discretion. In *Proverbial philosophy*. London: Thomas Hatchard.

Turner, K. E., Edgley, C., & Olmstead, G. (1975). Information control in conversations: Honesty is not always the best policy. *Kansas Journal of Sociology, 11*, 69-89.

Walters, R. (1974). What did Ziegler say, and when did he say it? *Columbia Journalism Review, 13*, 30-37.

Washburne, C. (1969). Retortmanship: How to avoid answering questions. *Etc, 26*, 69-75.

Watzlawick, P. (1963). A review of the double bind. *Family Process, 2*, 132-153.

Watzlawick, P. (1964). *An anthology of human communication: Text and tape*. Palo Alto: Science and Behavior Books.

Watzlawick, P., Beavin, J., & Jackson, D. D. (1967). *Pragmatics of human communication: A study of interactional patterns, pathologies, and paradoxes*. New York: W. W. Norton.

Watzlawick, P., & Weakland, J. H. (1977). *The interactional view*. New York: W. W. Norton.

Weakland, J. H. (1962). Family therapy as a research arena. *Family Process, 1*, 63-68.

Weakland, J. H. (1967). Communication and behavior: An introduction. *American Behavioral Scientist, 10, (8)* 1-4.

Weakland, J. H., & Fry, W. F., Jr. (1962). Letters of mothers of schizophrenics. *American Journal of Orthopsychiatry, 32*, 604-623.

Weblin, J. E. (1962). Communication and schizophrenic behavior. *Family Process, 1*, 5-14.

Wiener, M. & Mehrabian, A. (1968). *Language within language: Immediacy, a channel in verbal communication.* New York: Appleton-Century Crofts.

Williams, M. L., & Goss, B. (1975). Equivocation: Character insurance. *Human Communication Research, 1*, 265-270.

Wilmot, W. W. (1980). Metacommunication: A re-examination and extension. In D. Nimmo (Ed.), *Communication Yearbook Vol. 4.* New Brunswick, NJ: Transaction-ICA.

Winer, B. J. (1962). *Statistical principles in experimental design (1st ed.).* New York: McGraw-Hill.

Zuckerman, M., DeFrank, R. S., Hall, J. A., Larrance, D. T., & Rosenthal, R. (1979). Facial and vocal cues of deception and honesty. *Journal of Experimental Social Psychology, 15*, 378-396.

Zuckerman, M., DePaulo, B. M., & Rosenthal, R. (1981). Verbal and nonverbal communication of deception. In L. Berkowitz (Ed.), *Advances in experimental social psychology, vol 14* (pp. 1-59). New York: Academic Press.

Name Index

Ackerman, B. P., 210-11
Athos, A. G., 22
Austen, J., 17-18, 34
Austin, J. L., 173

Barker, R. G., 55, 168
Bates, E., 215-217
Bateson, G., 16, 19, 126
Bavelas, J. B., 32, 55, 55, 65, 67, 97, 126, 180, 236
Beavin (Bavelas), J., 20, 21, 39-30, 35, 36, 54-55
Bell, R. A., 173
Bellugi, U., 231
Black, A., 126, 180, 236, 264-65
Boorstein, D. J., 245n, 259
Bowers, J. W., 25-26, 30, 62
Brown, P., 26-27, 30, 62
Bryson, L., 236
Bugenthal, D., 126
Burgoon, J. K., 171

Carrell, P., 212-13
Chovil, N., 97, 126, 176, 180
Clark, H. H., 213
Clayman, S., 254, 255
Comadena, M. E., 171, 172-73
Coulthard, M., 13
Cunningham, M. A., 265-67

DeFrank, R. S., 180
Desmond, R. J., 25-26, 30, 62
DePaulo, B. M., 171, 172, 177, 180
Doelger, J., 260

Ebel, R. L., 48, 316
Edgley, C., 58, 176
Eisenberg, E. M., 22, 268
Ekman, P., 171, 172, 173, 180, 182, 192, 235

Elliott, N. D., 25-26, 30, 62

Ferris, S. R., 126
Freud, S., 171
Friesen, W. V., 171, 180, 192
Fry, W. F., Jr., 17, 20

Gleitman, H., 209-10
Gleitman, L. R., 209-10
Goss, B., 21-22, 246
Graber, D. A., 235
Graham, M. L., 260
Greatbatch, D., 254-55
Green, M. Gg., 211-12
Grice, H. P., 22-23, 24

Haley, J., 16, 19, 20, 32-34, 126
Hall, J. A., 180
Hazlitt, W. C., 170
Heritage, J., 247, 254, 255
Hewes, D. E., 260
Hirsh-Pak, K., 209-10
Hoppe, R. A., 21n, 28
Hopper, R., 173
Hyman, R., 170n, 207

Jackson, D. D., 19, 20, 21, 35, 54-55, 126

Kaswan, J., 126
Keith, W. M., 173
Kess, J. F., 21n, 28
Knapp, M. L., 171, 172-73
Kraut, R. E., 180

Larrance, D. T., 180
Lee, E. S., 36

Levine, M. V., 36
Levinson, S., 26-27, 30, 62
Lewin, K., 55-57, 60, 163, 168
Love, L., 126
Lucy, P., 213

MacGregor, J. N., 36
McNeill, D., 127, 175-76
Mehrabian, A., 30, 126
Miller, G. R., 171, 172, 182
Mullett, J., 126, 180, 236

Nofsinger, R. E., Jr., 24, 25, 30, 35
Nunnally, J. C., Jr., 316

Olmstead, G., 58, 1766

Pascale, R. T., 22
Pavitt, C., 260

Randolph, T., 170
Redding, W. C., 261, 268
Riskin, J. V., 20
Robinson, E. J., 214-15
Robinson, W. P., 214-15
Rosenthal, R., 171, 172, 177, 180

Sacks, H., 35
Satir, V. M., 20

Schaefer, B. A., 36
Schegloff, E. A., 35
Searle, J. R., 23-24, 174
Sluzki, C. E., 20, 29-30, 35
Smith, B. J., 32, 36
Spero, R., 235
Spradley, J. P., 245
Stein, L. I., 265
Stevens, S. S., 36
Stohl, C., 261, 268

Tager-Flusberg, H., 231
Tarnopolsky, A., 20, 29-30, 35
Tupper, M. F., 168
Turner, K. E., 58, 176

Verón, E., 20, 29-30, 35

Walters, R., 25-26
Washburne, C., 18
Watzlawick, P., 11-12, 19, 20, 21, 25, 54-55
Weakland, J. H., 17, 19, 20, 126
Weblin, J. E., 20
Wiener, M., 30
Wilcox, J. R., 265-67
Williams, M. L., 21-22, 246
Wilmot, W. W., 31
Winer, B. J., 46, 48, 99, 315-16

Zimmerman, D. H., 254-44
Zuckerman, M., 171, 172, 177, 180

Subject Index

Ambiguous language, 21n, 28, 260, 261; children's use and understanding of, 209-17, 233; in instructions, 214-15; strategic (deliberate) ambiguity, 21-22, 215, 268

Application scenario, 88-92, 92-96

Approach-approach conflict (*see* Conflict)

Aristotle, 21

Artifacts in equivocation values, possible, 124-25

Audiotaped messages (*see* Spoken messages)

Avoidance-avoidance conflict (*see* Conflict)

"Back-to-back" experiments, 134-43, 156-67, 222-31, 262

Behaviorist theory, 63

Boldface, in transcriptions, 129

Bush, George, 15-16, 247-48, 259

Capitals, in transcriptions, 129

Car Ad (Car for Sale) scenario, 59; face-to-face, 156-62, 188-89; spoken, 150-55, 187-88; written, 118-124, 124-25, 184-85

Causal inferences, 65, 85

Cause and effect, 65

Children: ambiguous language, understanding of, 209-17; ambiguous language, use of, 208, 215-17; equivocation by, 208, 218-33; experience with conflict situations, 232

Chretien, Jean, 236-43

Class Presentation scenario: face-to-face, 162-67, 188-89; forced choice, 68-78, 80-81, 81-85, 219-21, 232; spoken, 129-34, 185-86; written, 99-105, 124-25, 183-85

Cognitive (or mental) processes, 262-64; as cause of equivocation, 27, 62, 66; in children's understanding of sarcasm, 210-11

Coherence (of conversation), 264-65

Conflict: approach-approach, 56-57, 85-96; avoidance-avoidance, 57-58, 66, 261-62 (as necessary cause of equivocation, 80-96, 235-36, 261-62; children's experience of, 232; communicative, kinds of, 57-59, 68, 69, 87, 88, 92, 93, 99-100, 106, 112, 118, 129, 134, 139, 144-45, 150-51, 157, 162, 194, 222, 223, 235, 236-37, 246-49, 253-54, 257-59; in colloquial language, 60-61; reciprocal, 255; response latency in [*see* Latency of response]); situations, 56

Consequences, of messages, 56-60, 261

Comma, in transcription, 129

Communication, as object of study, 27-28, 264

Content analysis, 29-31; criticism of, 30-31

Content (dimension of equivocation): applied to reporters' communication, 250, 252; correlation with number of words, 124-25, **Appendix B**; correlation with other dimensions, 125, **Appendix B**; definition and measurement, 32-35, 39, 40, 41-42, 47-48; endpoints for, 40, 42, 272, **Appendix A**; qualitative aspects of, 59, 69, 73, 101-04, 106-07, 112-13, 119-22, 130-31, 135, 140, 148-49, 151-54, 157, 205, 226-27, 239, 246, 250, 252; significant quantitative effect in, 109, 115, 121, 137, 143, 153, 160, 167, 202, 229; training judges to scale, **Appendix A**

Context (dimension of equivocation): applied to reporters' communication, 251-52; as coherence, 264-65; correlation with number of words, 124-135, **Appendix B**; correlation with other dimensions, 125, **Appendix B**; definition and measurement, 32-35, 39, 41, 42-43, 48; endpoints for, 41, 42; qualitative aspects of, 59, 73-74, 104-05, 110-11, 117-18, 123-24, 131-34, 138, 141, 148, 149, 155, 161, 163, 205-06, 227, 30, 243, 250-51, 253, 258; significant quantitative effects in, 103, 109, 115, 121, 133, 137, 143, 147, 153, 160, 167, 202, 229; training judges to scale, **Appendix A**

Conversation analysts, 254-55

Conversational maxims (Grice's), 23
Correlational research (*see* Research methods)
Cultural assumption, 22

Dash, in transcription, 129
Deception: as discourse, 171-80, 264; as speech act, 172, 264; as truthfulness-falsity dimension, 175 (*see also* Truthfulness-falsity); clues, 171, 175, 179, 189, 206; definition, 170n, 172-75, 206-07 (by noninformational criteria, 172-75, 206-07); dimensions of, 175, 206-07; eliciting, 193-205; situation of, 176, 193; versus equivocation, 170, 177-79, 180-206, 207, 262
Deception research: assumptions in, 177-80; implications for, 206-07
Decoding: versus detection, 181
Deniability, 14, 176
Detection of deception, 170-71, 180-81, 264
"Devious" messages, 25-26
Dimensions of equivocation, 32-35; correlation among, 125, **Appendix B**; operational definitions, 39-44; training judges to scale, 38-44, **Appendix A**; (*see also* Content; Receiver; Sender; Sum)
Discourse analysis, 171-76, 263
Disqualification, 20-21, 28, 30, 32, 126; definition, 21
Distance-from-the-truth: as property of messages, 175; measurement of, 183, 184-89
Double bind, 19
Double-blind procedure, 112
Dyadic interaction between reporters and politicians, 234, 245-59

Employee Reference scenario: forced choice, 69-77; spoken, 141-49, 186-87
Endpoints for scaling, 39; face-to-face (videotaped), 40-41, **Appendix A**; spoken (audiotaped) or written, 42, **Appendix A**
Equipment needed for scaling equivocation, **Appendix A**
Equivocation: alternative theories of, 61-63, 74, 264; as avoidance, 54, 57-60, 66, 261-62; as error, 61, 77, 96; as incongruence or disqualification, 20-21; as indirect speech act, 174; as solution, 60, 261-62; by children, 208, 218-33; by politicians (*see* Politicians); by reporters (*see* Reporters); definition: (conceptual, 34; dictionary, 13; operational, 34, 53, 261); effect on audience, 22, 246, 264; first use of term, 21; four dimensions of, 32-35 (*see also* Content, Context, Sender, Receiver, Sum); in colloquial language, 60-61; measurement of (*see* Measurement of equivocation); naturally occurring, 234-35, 245-59; overview, *Chapter 10*; reply to, 264; settings for studying, 265-68 (*see also* Conflict, avoidance-avoidance, kinds of); situational theory of (*see* Situational antecedents of equivocation); value judgements about, 26, 61-62, 259, 260; versus deception (*see* Deception versus equivocation)
Equivocation values (*see* Measurement of equivocation; Ipsatized scores; Reliability; Redundancy; Artifacts, possible; Content; Sender; Receiver; Context; Sum)
Equivocator: as cause of equivocation, 61-62, 141 (*see also* Individual differences)
Ethnographic research, 245
Exemplification (*see* Research methods)
Experimental research (*see* Research methods)
Experimenter: effect of, 62, 112, 157; relationship to judge (scaling equivocation), 37-38, **Appendix A**
Expert measurement, 29-31

Face-to-face messages, experiments eliciting, 66, 156-67, 192-207, 262; not limited to speech, 176; scaling: (endpoints, 40-41, **Appendix A**; equipment for, 156, **Appendix A**; reliability of, 50, 52, 160, 167, 201; reliability test messages, **Appendix A**)
False messages (*see also* Deception): as option, 58-59, 68-69; measurement, 181-83; occurrence of, 148, 179, 183-92, 192-206; qualitative aspects of, 205-06; versus equivocation (*see* Deception versus equivocation)
Family communication, 16, 17, 18, 20, 64, 268

Field: communicative, 56, 261; psychological, 55

Field study, 236-45; (*see also* Research methods)

Forced choice method, **Chapter 4**, 218-222, 262; procedure, 67-68, 76; rationale, 67

Frost, David, 15-16, 259

Generalizability, of findings, 65-66, 77, 98, 99

Gift scenario: awful gift, 58-59 (forced-choice, 68-77, 77-80, 80-85, 218-219; spoken [children], 223-26); bizarre gift: (written, 112-18, 124-25; spoken, 134-35)

Goal gradient, 56

Hamlet, 33

Hart, Gary, 236

Henry II, 14, 34

Humor, children's understanding of, 209-10

Hyphen, in transcription, 129

Hypothetical situations, criticisms of, 74-75, 77

Iago, 13-14, 17, 33

"Illogic" of natural communication, 22, 23-24, 27

Incongruence, 20-21, 32-34; of verbal and nonverbal, 126-27, 155, 231 (*see also* Leakage, nonverbal)

Indirect replies, 24-26

Indirect requests, children's understanding of, 212-13

Indirect speech acts, 22-27; equivocation as, 174

Individual differences, 65; and equivocation, 61-62, 66, 74, 134; evidence against, 77, 96, 140, 162, 262, 264

Integrated message model, 127, 162, 169, 175-76, 179-80, 262; test of (versus nonverbal leakage), 190-92, 203-04, 207; (*see also* Incongruence)

Interviews, news, 254-55; (*see also* Political interviews)

Ipsatized scores: calculation, 46, **Appendix A**; interpretation, 47-48; properties, 47, 100, **Appendix A**; rationale, 44-46

Judges (of equivocation): characteristics, 37, **Appendix A**; recruiting, **Appendix A**; relationship to experimenter, 37-38, **Appendix A**; reliability (*see* Reliability of equivocation measure); role, 44, **Appendix A**; versus raters of truthfulness, 181

Laboratory research (*see* Research methods)

Latency of response, 128; effects of experimental condition, 168, **Appendix B**; interpretation, 167-68

Lay (nonexpert) receivers, 31; raters, 181

Leakage, nonverbal, 171, 175, 179-80, 189, 190-92, 192-204, 206, 207, 231, 262; tests for, 190-92, 192-204

Leaving the field, 57, 66, 262

Liberal Leadership field study, 236-45

"Lie" (as term), 58, 172-75, 176, 177; (*see also* Deception; False messages)

"Lies of omission," 182, 206; equivocation as, 189-90

Local Musical scenario, 192-206

Logic: formal, 22, 27, 28; of natural language, 22-25, 27, 28

Magnitude estimation, 36-37, 181

Meaning of messages, quantitative measure of, 183

Measurement of equivocation: assumptions behind, 34-35; attempted "short form," 49-53; by lay receivers, 31; full details, **Chapter 2**, **Appendix A**; on continuum, 31; operational definition, 34, 63, 261; quantification (ipsatizing), 44-48, **Appendix A**; relationship to avoidance theory, 31, 59-60; requirements for, 30-31; scaling procedure, 37-44, **Appendix A**; summary, 260-61; (*see also* Reliability of equivocation measure)

Meat Market scenario, 139-43, 186

Member of Parliament scenario, 106-111, 124-25, 207, 235

Message length, 124-25, **Appendix B**

Messages: as paths or options, 56, 261; forced-choice (in tables, with equivocation values), 70-72, 84, 89, 94; reliability sets, **Appendix A**; subjects' (transcribed in

tables, with equivocation values), 102-03, 108-09, 114-15, 120-21, 132-33, 136-37, 142-43, 146-47, 152-53, 158-60, 164-67, 196-201, 224-25, 228-29, 240-42; training and practice, **Appendix A**
Metacommunication, 264
Metalinguistic ability, in children, 210, 215, 216
Metatheoretical assumptions, 63, 262-64
Methods (*see* Research methods)
Mr. R's reply, 11-12; analysis of, 12-13, 20, 33, 61-62; situation of, 13, 54, 57
Mondale, Walter, 246
Mudd, Roger, 236

N, larger versus small, 80, 99, 238, 244
"Naturalistic" research, 65
New Hairdo scenario, 222-23, 232
New Look scenario, 93-96
News interviews, 254-55; (*see also* political interviews)
Non-immediacy, 30
Nonverbal aspects of communication, 31, 66, 98, 126-27, 156-57, 161, 230-31, 262; as "channels," 175, 179-80, 262; leakage in (*see* Leakage, nonverbal); separation from verbal, 175-76; transcription conventions for, 128-29
Nurses, equivocation by, 265, 67

Organizational communication, 22, 267-68
Othello, 13

Palo Alto Group, 19-21, 27, 28, 30, 54, 55, 64
Paralinguistic aspects of messages (*see* Spoken messages)
Paths: consequences of, 56, 261-62; messages as, 56, 261-62
Period (or dots), in transcription, 129
Physician, effect on nurses' communication, 265-67
Politeness in language, 26-27, 30; development of, 215-17, 233
Political communication, 15-16, 25-26, 59, **Chapter 9**
Political interviews, 245-59

Political reporters (*see* Reporters)
Politicians: conflict situations of, 246-49, 255-59; equivocation by, 235, 236-45, 246-49, 254, 256-59
Pretending, deception as, 173

Qualitative analysis of messages: face-to-face, 157-61, 162-63, 205-06, 251-53, 256-58; spoken, 130-34, 135-38, 140-41, 148-49, 151-55, 226-31, 239-43; written by experimenter, 73-74; written by subjects, 100-04, 106-11, 112-18, 119-24
Quarles, Norma, 247-48
Quiz scenario, 92-96

Rather, Dan, 246
Receiver (dimension of equivocation): applied to reporters' communication, 250, 252; correlation with number of words, 124-25, **Appendix B**; correlation with other dimensions, 125, **Appendix B**; definition and measurement, 3-35, 39, 41-42, 42-43, 48; endpoints for, 40-42, **Appendix A**; qualitative aspects of, 73-74, 104, 110, 116, 123, 131, 135-38, 140-41, 148, 149, 155, 161, 163, 205, 229, 243, 250-51, 252; significant quantitative effects on, 121, 137, 167, 202, 229; training judges to scale, **Appendix A**
Redundancy, in four dimensions of equivocation, 125, **Appendix B**
"Relationship lie," 58, 176
Reliability: bivariate correlation, 48, **Appendix A**; intraclass correlation, 48, **Appendix A**; of equivocation measure: (calculation, 48, **Appendix A**; coefficients, 49-52, 103, 109, 115, 121, 133, 137, 143, 147, 153, 160, 167, 201, 225, 229, 242; messages for testing, **Appendix A**; session for testing, **Appendix A**)
Replication (*see* Varied replication)
Report scenario, 87-92, 92-96
Reporters (news), 254-55
Reporters (political), 234, 235, 245; conflicts for, 253-54, 255-58; equivocation by, 250-53, 255-58

Research methods: choice among, 64-66; comparisons of, 64-65, 243-45; correlational, 64-65; creation of conditions, 64-65; ethnographic, 245; exemplification, 64-65; experimental, 64-66; field study, 64, 234, 243-45; laboratory, 64-66, 234-35, 244-45; "naturalistic," 65; selection of cases, 64-65

Research strategy for studying equivocation, 64-66, 97-98, 126-27, 156, 234-35, 244-45, 262, 265

Role-playing, criticism of, 75, 77

Rule-based approaches, 22, 27, 28, 30, 62, 64, 261; criticism of, 26, 62; test of, 29-80

"Rules of thumb" (for scaling equivocation), 41-43, **Appendix A**

Sarcasm, children's understanding of, 210-11

Scale values of messages (*see* Equivocation values)

Scenarios, experimental (*see* Application, Car Ad, Class Presentation, Employee Reference, Gift, Local Musical, Meat Market, Member of Parliament, New Hairdo, New Look, Quiz, Report)

Schizophrenia: and communication: (families, 20; mother's letter, 16-17, 61; patients, 16-17); symptoms, 12

Selection of cases (*see* Research methods)

Sender (dimension of equivocation): applied to reporters' communication, 250-51; correlation with number of words, 124-25, **Appendix B**; correlation with other dimensions, 125, **Appendix B**; definition and measurement, 32-35, 39, 40, 42-43, 48; endpoints for, 40, 42, **Appendix A**; qualitative aspects of, 59, 73-74, 104, 110, 116, 122, 131, 135, 140, 148, 149, 155, 161, 162-63, 205, 229, 239-43, 250-51, 252, 258; significant quantitative effects on, 115, 121, 133, 137, 167, 202, 229; training judges to scale, **Appendix A**

Sentence completeness, in written messages, 124-25

Shakespeare, 13, 33

Siegel, Howard, 13

Situation: of deception, 176; of discourse, 176, 262

Situational antecedents of equivocation, 13, 17-18, 21, 22, 26, **Chapter 3**, 260, 264; tests of, **Chapter 4**, 134, 141, 162; (*see also*, Conflict, avoidance-avoidance)

Speaker uncertainty, children's understanding of, 211-12

Speech act, deception (lies) as, 172, 264; indirect (*see* Indirect speech acts, Indirect replies, Indirect requests)

Spoken Messages, 126-29, 168-69, 262; experiments eliciting, 129-55, 222-231, 236-45; scaling for equivocation, 39, **Appendix A** (endpoints, **Appendix A**; equipment, 127, **Appendix A**; reliability, 50, 52, 133, 137, 143, 147, 153 225, 229, 242; reliability message set, **Appendix A**)

Standard scores (*see* ipsatized scores)

Stimuli for training judges, **Appendix A**

Strategic ambiguity (*see* ambiguous language)

Sum (of equivocation dimensions), correlation with number of words, **Appendix B**; significant quantitative effects in, 109, 115, 121, 137, 143, 153, 160, 167, 202, 229

Systemic level of analysis, 255, 264-65

"Talk for an overhearing audience," 247, 253

Taxonomies, criticism of, 30-31

Telephone, use of (*.see* Spoken messages)

Thomas, Helen, 25-26, 64

Training judges to scale equivocation, 37-44; full details, **Appendix A**

Transcription conventions, 128-29, 157

Truth: and self interest, 59; hurtful, 58-59; "softened," 59

Truthfulness-falsity: as dimension of communication, 175, 177-78, 181, 262; in subjects' messages, 183-189, 190-92, 203-05; measurement of, 180-83, 262 (reliability, 184-88); versus equivocation, 177-79, 184-89, 204

Turner, John, 236-43

Uncoded information, in experiments, 143-49, 150-55, 156-62, 186-88

Unpleasantness, as possible cause of equivocation, 80-85, 96

Validity, internal versus external, 243

Variance, effect on reliability, 48, **Appendix A**

Varied replication, 66, 98, 99

Videotaped messages (*see* face-to-face messages), awareness of camera, 156

Written messages, 76, 88, 262; forced-choice, **Chapter 4**; scaling for equivocation: (end-points, 42, **Appendix A**; reliability, 50, 51, 103, 109, 115, 121; reliability message set, **Appendix A**); spontaneous (subjects' own), **Chapter 5**

Ziegler, Ronald, 25-26, 64

About the Authors

Janet Beavin Bavelas, Ph.D., is Professor of Psychology at the University of Victoria. She has authored or coauthored two previous books (including *Pragmatics of Human Communication* with Watzlawick and Jackson) and about 30 articles or chapters, primarily on interpersonal communication and research methods. She was previously a Research Associate at the Mental Research Institute (Palo Alto, California).

Alex Black, M.A., is currently a doctoral student in psychology at the University of Victoria and will join the faculty of the Department of Speech Communication at the University of Washington. In addition to collaborative work, he has published "The Syntax of Conversational Coherence" (*Discourse Processes*, 1988).

Nicole Chovil, Ph.D., is a Social Sciences and Humanities Research Council of Canada post-doctoral fellow in psychology at the University of California at Santa Barbara. Besides joint publications on equivocation and motor mimicry, she has articles forthcoming on a communicative (versus affective) theory of facial expression.

Jennifer Mullett, M.A., is a doctoral student in pyschology at the University of Victoria and has coauthored articles on equivocation and motor mimicry.

The authors, working in the Psychology Department at the University of Victoria (British Columbia, Canada), do research on verbal and nonverbal communication. They have written extensively on equivocation (or "disqualification") and have also collaborated — with each other or other members of their Victoria Group — on research into motor mimicry, nonverbal mirroring, gestures, and experimenter-subject interaction.